SOX

SOX

From Lane and Fain
to Zisk and Fisk

BY

Bob Vanderberg

CHICAGO REVIEW PRESS

Library of Congress Cataloging in Publication Data

Vanderberg, Bob, 1948-
  Sox, from Lane and Fain to Zisk and Fisk.

  1. Chicago White Sox (Baseball team)—History.
I. Title.
GV875.c58V36   796.357′64′097731   81-10066
ISBN 0-914091-04-2   AACR2
ISBN 0-914091-03-4 (pbk.)

This book was originally scheduled for July, 1981 release, but was
postponed because of the baseball strike.

First Edition
First Printing

All photographs used in this book are reprinted with the permission of the
Chicago White Sox, except where otherwise noted.

Cover Photo: ©Field Enterprises, Inc. 1960

DEDICATION

This book is for friends, old and new, who have sat with me in the stands at Comiskey Park through victory and defeat; for my father, who handed down to his sons his rooting interest in the White Sox; for my wife, Trish, who put up with all the old newspapers, magazines, and yearbooks and with the travel, the tapes, and the interviews, and who typed almost all of the final manuscript; and finally, for my oldest brother, Roger, who, had he lived, would have enjoyed reading this book.

ACKNOWLEDGEMENTS

I am deeply grateful for the excellent cooperation given to me by former White Sox publicity director Don Unferth and by Chuck Shriver and Ken Valdiserri of the present Sox public relations department. Thanks also to Phil Van Huesen and Norm Cohen, journalists and Sox fans, for their suggestions during the preparation of the manuscript. I am thankful, too, for an old Army friend, Mike Fry, who after hearing over and over again of my grand plans to someday write a book on the White Sox, finally snapped, "Well, sit down and do it!"

AUTHOR'S NOTE

Any disparaging remarks made herein about the abilities of former or present major league ballplayers are made in the full knowledge that the author could never hope to have one-thousandth of the talent possessed by even the most maligned player mentioned in this book.

Contents

INTRODUCTION

It's different, being a White Sox fan. Bill Veeck once wrote, "If there is any justice in this world, to be a White Sox fan frees a man from any other form of penance." And, it might be added, pennants. In my lifetime, there has been only one league championship for the Sox. There have been close calls, to be sure. In 1955, the Sox led the American League the first weekend of September. In '57, they were only three games out when the Yankees clinched the pennant. They were two games behind in mid-September 1960. They finished a game back of the Yankees in '64.

Three years later, they were within a half-game of the lead going into the final week but they blew the last five games of the season to the two worst teams in the league—Kansas City and Washington. The Sox would have won the West Division title in 1972—or so the faithful believe—if slugging third baseman Bill Melton hadn't been sidelined with a bad back for the final half of the season.

Even in recent years, there has been cause for hysteria. The '77 Sox were in first place in the middle of August before the roof fell in, as we all knew it would. Invariably, then, the White Sox are a team that disappoints. They build up hope in the fans, only to have that hope dashed by doubleheader defeats in places like Bloomington, Minn., or Baltimore, Md. In watching the Sox play on the road, the inevitability of defeat is a constant. If the Sox lead by a run, it's the same as if the game were tied. If they are tied, it's as though they're already losing. And if they trail by a run, it might as well be by 10. On the road, particularly, the Sox specialize in late-inning losses. Only the names have changed over the years. Whether it be Harry Dorish or Paul LaPalme or Turk Lown or Bob Locker or Rich Gossage or Lerrin LaGrow or Ed Farmer, he's going to give up a line drive into the corner in the bottom of the ninth and the winning run is going to score. Generally, things are better at Comiskey Park, but with all the losing years of the last decade, one can't be too confident about a lead in home games, either.

My introduction to this madness came very early, as I was growing up in the Chicago suburb of Oak Park. With two older brothers to show the way, I became a follower of Nellie Fox and Chico Carrasquel and Minnie Minoso and Billy Pierce and all the rest. Allegiance to the Sox was not then perceived as a form of child abuse; perhaps I was four when my father first abetted my fanaticism by identifying the image I saw on a television screen, standing tall and batting left-handed, as Eddie Robinson. The first "Tenth Inning" guest I can remember Jack Brickhouse talking to was Ferris Fain, the gifted first baseman. I recall the late Bob Elson on the radio, reminding us that Friendly Bob Adams and General Finance were just as close as our telephone. Elson became more of a trusted friend than Brickhouse, for Bob did all the Sox games on the radio. Brickhouse, on TV, split his time between the Sox and the Cubs, who were laughable then as now. Elson, it seemed, seldom made an error, although one night, perhaps confused by the beer commercial he'd just read, he referred to Jim Brideweser, a substitute shortstop, as Jim Bride-WISER.

When I was finally taken in person to a Sox game, in 1954, it was as if my father had sensed that I was ready to learn an important lesson of life. The weather that day was typical for a Sox home game: The skies were overcast and predictions of rain abounded. All the heroes this 6-year-old had adopted as his own were, for the first time, seen in the flesh: Minnie, Nellie, Chico, Billy. There were Jungle Jim Rivera, Johnny Groth, and veteran Phil Cavarretta, who had finally seen the light and had signed with the Sox after all those lost years with the Cubs. Two new friends were made that day, too: reserve infielder Freddie Marsh, who protested so hotly a call at third base that he was thrown out of the game; and Willard Marshall, a washed-up ex-National Leaguer on whom manager Paul Richards called, late in the game, to pinch-hit. Willard responded by lining out to right field. (Impressed, I taped a hand-drawn "27"—Marshall's uniform number —on the back of one of my T-shirts when I got home. It didn't take much to become one of my favorites.)

The game was a microcosm of the typical White Sox season of that era. Chicago grabbed a 5-1 lead over the hated New York Yankees before a Wednesday afternoon crowd of more than 38,000. Pierce, sailing along with the big lead, suffered a split nail on his pitching hand and had to leave the game. Pitcher after pitcher paraded in, attempting to preserve the victory. The Yankees, after a long rain delay, scored three in the eighth to make it 5-4. In the ninth, with two on and two out, Mickey Mantle slammed a Jack Harshman screwball into the centerfield bullpen for three runs and the ballgame—just as my father had forecast only moments before Mantle stepped into the batter's box.

So I learned at an early age that no Sox lead—in a ballgame or in a pennant race—was safe. I also learned to hate the Yankees. Later, more teams would join the Yankees among the despised: the Minnesota Twins, the Baltimore Orioles, the Oakland A's, the Kansas City Royals. And later, more Sox players would become favorites: Luis Aparicio, Ron Northey, Jim Landis, Roy Sievers, Ken Berry, Tommy McCraw, Mike Hershberger, Gary Peters, Juan Pizarro, Joe Horlen, Hoyt Wilhelm, Tommy John, Bill Melton, Carlos May, Richie Allen, Walter Williams, Bart Johnson, Terry Forster, Jorge Orta, and Chet Lemon.

Through it all, I've learned to look at and worry about Sox attendance figures. To worry about who's going to buy the club when the next financial crisis hits. To worry about what would happen if the franchise really did leave town, as so often threatened. (Could I find employment in Denver or New Orleans?) Fans of most baseball teams don't have to worry about such things, but they are concerns a Sox fan lives with. Indeed, they make the relationship between the fan and his chosen team more binding—as if the storms the club must endure make it all the more valued by those of us who spend so many hours watching its performances, no matter how absurd.

And admittedly, absurd performances have been plentiful on the South Side during the last three decades. But so have brilliant ones. Grand-slam home runs served up by Gary Bell and Taylor Phillips and Don Ferrarese have been more than offset by the no-hitters of Bob Keegan and Joe Horlen. The futility of Ted Beard and Eddie McGhee as hitters has been blotted out by the awesome presence of Richie Allen and the line shots of Richie Zisk. The ineptness afield of a Ralph Garr or a Bee Bee Richard is forgotten in the remembered brilliance of an Aparicio or a Landis—though it is remarkable that teams as generally classy as the White Sox teams of the '50s and early '60s performed on the same field as the generally torpid, sorry crews of the late '60s and '70s.

That is what this book is about—the people who did the playing and the managing, the front-office men who did the building (and, in some cases, wrecking), and the broadcasters who told us about them all. It is a journey through time from the early '50s, when the White Sox stopped being the chronic losers they had been since the Black Sox Scandal of 1919 and became constant contenders instead, to the most recent doldrums—20-odd years after that last pennant—of win a few, lose a few more. (Doldrums that, I add hopefully, may finally have ended with the advent of new ownership and its fresh money.)

It is a journey that, beginning with the summer of 1978, took nearly three years of interviewing to complete. Yet, even with all the necessary updating of material, it was a journey that I found quite enjoyable.

Would that the reader find it so.

BV

FRANK LANE:
Billy Pierce for Aaron Who?

The only thing that could ever have interrupted Frank Lane's trade talks happened March 19, 1981, when the former White Sox flesh peddler died in Texas after a long hospitalization. On the day I had spoken to him, it was barely time for civilized men to be taking their second cups of coffee, but Lane was already on the phone, talking deal. However, his headquarters was no longer the general manager's office at Comiskey Park, as it had been a generation earlier. This day, his office was a room on the tenth floor of the Bismarck Hotel, and he was working for the California Angels as a super scout. The White Sox were just another team in the league, a team that, like Kansas City, Texas, and Minnesota, had to be beaten out before Lane's new team could reach the top of the American League's West Division.

"The Yankees want Yount, and they're willing to give up Rivers, but Milwaukee wants more," he told his listener. "Coleman? He'll help you for maybe an inning or two, but I don't know if he could throw hard enough to break a piece of toilet paper. Well, yes, Sutter is probably the best relief pitcher in baseball right now. Saw him yesterday and nobody could touch him. Hernandez? He's very effective one time through the batting order. A good lefthanded reliever . . ."

1

Frank Lane

Lane couldn't get a Willie Hernandez in a deal: The interleague trading deadline had passed three months earlier. But a lefty reliever could be had from the other American League clubs, and that's what this call was about. The man on the other end of the line was Charles O. Finley, owner of the Oakland A's.

"Well, dammit, Charlie, this is what Gene (Autry) has authorized: We'll give you Ken Brett and $400,000 for your lefthander, Lacey. Brett. Yeah, he's pitching against your club tonight. All right. Get back to me."

Nearly thirty years had gone by since Frank Lane burst upon the Chicago sports scene in late 1948 as the newly hired general manager of the moribund White Sox, losers of 101 games in the season just finished. He was brought in by Charles A. Comiskey II, who hoped to bring back the glories that were once so prevalent on the South Side. Comiskey, it is said, handpicked Lane, but maybe it was because everyone he had handpicked before Lane had turned down the job.

"The newspaper people warned me ahead of time," Lane recalled, his conversation with Finley completed. "I was officiating a Purdue at Indiana football game (in the fall of '48), and John Carmichael (of the Chicago Daily News) said to me, 'Don't you know what you're getting into if you take this job? It's a near-bankrupt ballclub. They have no ballplayers.' I said, 'John, listen—there are only so many major league general managers. If it was a perfect job, it wouldn't be open. Maybe nobody else wants it, but I want it.' "

So he took it, even though, as Carmichael had warned, the White Sox had no ballplayers. "Chuck Comiskey told me we had a good nucleus. Well, I asked waivers on all 40 guys on our winter roster and all but two (pitcher Howie Judson and second baseman Cass Michaels) were waived out of the league—and the waiver price at that time was only $10,000. So if we had a good nucleus, it was news to the other clubs."

But Lane, who was to be nicknamed Frantic Frankie by the sportswriters before too many months had elapsed, got the show rolling anyway. It took time, of course. He had to endure a couple of years of managing by Jack Onslow, who had been promised the Sox managerial job before Lane was hired. It was hardly a partnership made in heaven.

3

"I inherited him," Lane acknowledged. "He loved me about as much as I loved him. A very unprepossessing guy. He's dead, and I didn't like him when he was alive, so I don't know why I should love him now that he's dead."

Still, during those first couple of years, Lane did make some headway. His first move was to send veteran catcher Aaron Robinson to Detroit for $10,000 (then as always the franchise needed money) and a kid lefty named Billy Pierce, who was to win 186 games in the next 13 seasons with the White Sox. Lane's next major acquisition was that of a Venezuelan shortstop named Alfonso Carrasquel—"Chico" to everyone who was entranced by his fielding genius. And there were many who were. Lane got him from the Brooklyn Dodger organization, which already had an all-star shortstop in Pee Wee Reese and another sackful of outstanding shortstop prospects waiting in line behind him.

"Luke Appling was 42 years old at the time, and Branch Rickey stopped off to see one of our games (in 1949) and said, 'Judas Priest, Frank, you need a shortstop.' I said, 'Mr. Rickey, that's a very profound statement.' He used to have a list with him. On his list of shortstops in his organization, Bobby Morgan was tops. Opposite Morgan's name he had written $250,000 and three ballplayers.' Down near No. 7 was Chico Carrasquel—'three ballplayers and $50,000.' "

Carrasquel, whom the White Sox had been scouting all along at Ft. Worth, was the man Lane wanted. Rickey, though, was trying to interest Lane in a pair of black players, pitcher Dan Bankhead and outfielder Sam Jethroe, a man blessed with stupendous speed but lacking the one thing a ballplayer needs most: good eyesight. (In fact, Sam was nearly blind.) Lane kept inquiring about Carrasquel. Rickey countered with the name of another Dodger farmhand, Danny O'Connell, also a shortstop.

Lane reminded Rickey that Carrasquel was the man he was interested in. Rickey offered to sell outfielder Irv Noren, who was eventually to have some good years with the Yankees. The haggling went on over a period of weeks in the fall of 1949. One of the bargaining sessions began over dinner in Rickey's suite in the Blackstone Hotel in Chicago and lasted till nearly six in the morning. Finally, Rickey told Lane, 'I'll sell you a shortstop. If you want Carrasquel, and you're prepared to make me a good offer for him, you can have him.' A proviso went along with it, however. The Sox would also have to buy Jethroe if a deal sending Sam to the Boston Braves were to fall through.

But Lane was impatient. A few days later, he flew to New York and called Rickey at his office to ask when the White Sox could release the publicity on the Carrasquel deal. Lane's final offer had been two players (infielder Fred Hancock and pitcher Charlie Eisenmann) and $25,000. Needless to say, Rickey was a bit startled on the other end of the line. "Do we have a deal?" he yelled. Then Lane reminded him that Rickey had said Carrasquel could be Lane's if the Sox made a fair offer. He listened and said, 'Well, Frank Lane, if that's what you have in mind, if you think we have a deal, we have a deal.' "

They had a deal, and the Sox had their shortstop. Chico was the league's most exciting rookie in 1950 and by '51 was outpolling the great Phil Rizzuto of New York in the all-star balloting. Rickey, of course, knew how good Carrasquel would turn out. A month after closing the deal with the White Sox, he offered to buy Carrasquel back at a profit of $50,000 for Chicago. Lane, quite naturally, refused.

The next important acquisition was Nellie Fox, who had hit .255 as a part-time second baseman at Philadelphia in '49. This was another player Lane had had his eyes on for a while. "When I was still president of the American Association in 1948, I stopped off one night in Lincoln, Neb., and I saw their ballclub and they had two little guys I loved as soon as I saw them. A lefthanded pitcher and a second baseman with a huge chaw of tobacco in his left cheek. They were Bobby Shantz and Nellie Fox. I said right then and there that if I ever got to the big leagues, there are two guys I'm gonna get. Well, I never got Shantz, but I did get Fox."

He got him for a veteran catcher named Joe Tipton, a .204-hitting reserve from a place called Copperhill, Tennessee. To make the Tipton-for-Fox transaction look good, all Nellie would have had to do would be to show up at the ballpark on time. But he did much more. By 1951 he had established himself as one of the top second basemen in the big leagues. He played 14 years with the White Sox and was the American League's Most Valuable Player in the pennant year of 1959.

After Pierce, Carrasquel, and Fox came Paul Richards, the man

Lane had wanted as his manager in the first place. Richards, the taciturn Texan from Waxahachie, was 42 when he was given the Sox job in the fall of 1950. "One of the best deals I ever made was when I brought Richards in here to manage," said Lane. "And he was perfect for me, 'cause he'd go out and play golf and I'd stay in the office."

With Richards in the dugout between golf dates, with the new doubleplay combination of Carrasquel and Fox working smoothly for the first time, with Pierce gaining experience, with a good-looking rookie centerfielder in Jim Busby, and with a longball hitter at first base in Eddie Robinson (acquired from Washington the previous Memorial Day), the Sox figured to be somewhat improved in 1951. But before the season was two weeks old, Richards and Lane knew there was still a link missing. Richards, having managed at Seattle in the Pacific Coast League the year before, had seen a dashing Cuban outfielder-third baseman named Saturnino Orestes Arrieta Armas Minoso playing at San Diego. Minoso, called "Minnie," could do everything: hit for power, hit for average, run, and throw. And almost everything the Cleveland rookie did was spectacular. Richards told Lane that Minoso was the man the White Sox had to have. So Frank went out and got him—after 36 hours in the Hotel Commodore in New York and phone charges totalling $260. The Sox gave up outfielders Dave Philley and Gus Zernial (who had set a club record with 29 homers the year before) to the Philadelphia A's, who sent lefty Lou Brissie to the Indians, who sent Minoso to the White Sox. Cleveland originally had wanted Pierce for Minoso straight up, but the Sox couldn't afford to give up their top pitcher, and that set Lane to thinking about the possibilities of a three-team deal. The three parties finally informally agreed on the deal, but hadn't announced it yet when Minoso, who was to be the first black player ever to wear a White Sox uniform, himself almost sabotaged the transaction.

"Minnie had gotten seven hits in a doubleheader at St. Louis," Lane remembered. "He played first base and got three hits in one game, four in the other. And (Cleveland general manager) Hank Greenberg was out somewhere that day playing tennis, so he hadn't heard about it yet. We had the deal all worked out with him and Philadelphia, and I was all set to release the thing to the press. I thought, 'Geez, if Greenberg hears that Minnie got seven hits, he'll never make the deal.' So I

6

called him up at his home in Cleveland and his wife answered. She had no use for baseball and no use for anyone associated with baseball. I said, 'Geez, I've got to get ahold of Hank.' 'Well, Mr. Lane, he's out playing tennis.' 'Well, Hank and I have made a deal and we're releasing the news a day sooner'—I wanted to get it into print. I called about three different times. She kept saying, 'Well, he hasn't come in yet.' 'Well, it's very important because Hank will be mad because they'll be using his name in the deal and I want to OK it with Hank first.'

"So finally, Hank comes in all out of breath and everything and I say, 'Hank, I've gotten hold of your writers, Harry Jones and Gordon Cobbledick, and they're gonna release the deal.' And Hank was anxious to get into the shower, so he gives the OK and we get it into print. Now Hank finds out within an hour that Minnie got seven hits. And oh, was he hot. Later he said, 'Geez, that damn Lane—he got me with my pants down. I was in the shower.' Actually, of course, I got him before he got into the shower."

So that's how Minnie Minoso got to wear a White Sox uniform. He had an immediate effect. First time up for Chicago, he hit a home run off the Yankees' Vic Raschi into the centerfield bullpen at Comiskey Park. The Sox won 20 of the first 24 games Minnie played with them. The new White Sox were on their way. But Lane never stopped building. Players kept coming and going as he tried to find the right combination. Sherm Lollar came from the Browns to do the catching. Lane decided he needed a righthanded power hitter in '52 to go with Eddie Robinson from the left side, so he traded young Busby to Washington for Sam Mele. Also in '52, he picked up Jungle Jim Rivera from the Browns. To provide leadership, Ferris Fain, two-time league batting champ, came from Philadelphia for Robinson. From St. Louis in '53 came another key acquisition, pitcher Virgil Trucks. In 1954, Lane spent $100,000 of Grace Comiskey's money to get George Kell from Boston in an attempt to solve the ever-apparent third-base problem. Fain was subsequently dealt in December 1954 to Detroit for Walt Dropo and Bob Nieman. Clint Courtney came the same day in a deal with Baltimore. And once the '55 season got under way and the Sox were struggling with their bats, Lane picked up veteran Bob Kennedy—until recently the Cubs' general manager—who once had

7

sold peanuts as a kid vendor in Comiskey Park.

"I got him on waivers on Memorial Day from Baltimore where he was hitting .143. Mrs. Comiskey remembered Bob Kennedy from when he played before with the White Sox in the '40s. And she said, 'What are you doing with that old man? He's hitting .140.' I said, 'Mrs. Comiskey, he's a real pro—you wait and see.' A couple of days later we're playing the Yankees at Comiskey Park. Of course, anytime we beat the Yankees one game it was like beating somebody else three. Kennedy's up with a couple of men on and we're a run or two down. And Kennedy popped a foul about 25 feet to the right of where my box was. And Yogi Berra muffed it. The next pitch, Kennedy hit one up into the upper deck for three runs and we won the ballgame. I said, 'Mrs. Comiskey, that's the first dividend.' "

There were more dividends to come, as Kennedy hit .304 with the Sox and won almost a dozen games with his clutch hitting to keep Chicago in the '55 race into September. But not all of Lane's deals— and there were almost 250 of them—were master strokes. He admitted as much when, in 1955, he traded three players to Washington to regain Jim Busby, who had been sacrificed three years earlier for Mele.

"Sam Mele came to me and wound up hitting .259, but the first part of the year, the first couple of months, he was hitting .320. So I said to Richards, 'Well, maybe I'm right for once.' Richards said, 'Well, Frantic, don't start feeling too good over that deal. Tell you what you do. After the game starts, come back down by the dugout runway and just observe what you observe.' And I couldn't understand why he wanted me to watch Sam in the dugout rather than out on the field. So I went back there, and by this time, Sam, who had been around .320, was down to .300 or .295. Sam was trying to light a cigaret and he was so nervous, he kept dropping the thing—he couldn't light the cigaret. Later, Paul said, 'Sam is so afraid he's gonna hit .300 that I guarantee you he won't hit .300.' Well, he hit .259."

Another deal that didn't pan out so well was the one for Fain. When he landed the firebrand first baseman, Lane predicted that it would prove to be the best trade he'd ever made. Whereupon Fain, who had hit .344 and .327 the previous two years with the A's, went out and hit .256 for his new club. "Philadelphia couldn't sign him," said Lane. "He wanted $50,000 and they said no ballplayer's worth $50,000. So I get

Ferris Fain. Now I've got the guy and—well, he was a good-time guy. He was quite a drinker. Fain didn't take very good care of himself, to say the least. He spent more time in the night club than he did on the ballfield.

"I remember before one Sunday doubleheader in Comiskey Park— it was a blistering hot day. I walked into the clubhouse and Ferris was sitting there in front of his locker with his head down. I go over to him, 'Ferris, let me see you.' Geez, you could've chinned yourself on his eyeballs. So I said to Richards, 'Don't play that S.O.B.—look at him over there.' Richards said, 'Yeah, but it serves him right.' 'Yeah,' I said, 'but it's gonna cost us a ballgame.' Well, he played, and it cost us two ballgames."

One of Lane's best customers in the trading department was one Bill Veeck, who before arriving on the Comiskey Park scene in 1959 had been wheeling and dealing in Cleveland with the Indians and then later in St. Louis with the Browns. "Bill is a merry rogue," said Lane, "I like him, but I know how far to trust him. Mrs. Comiskey never liked him. He went into her office one day when she was running the club—God rest her soul, she was a great ol' gal—and he said, 'This is no job for a woman. Why don't you sell this club?' She said, 'You don't have two quarters to rub together—get your ass out of here!' She never reconciled herself to my going along with Bill on the voting at league meetings. I said, 'Mrs. Comiskey, he gives us action. He's putting money in our pockets.' "

The Lane-Veeck action included the Lollar trade, two deals involving Rivera, the St. Louis-to-Chicago express that had reserve shortstop Willie Miranda going back and forth like a yo-yo, and the acquisitions by the Sox of pitchers Bill Kennedy, Tommy Byrne, Gene Bearden, Virgil Trucks, and infielder Freddie Marsh. The two men would make deals, it seemed, just for the sake of making a deal. Some of the blame must be shouldered by Veeck, who insisted on putting in a claim every time a club would ask waivers on a player.

"Veeck used to claim everybody on waivers—even guys he'd already had," Lane laughed. "Once I asked waivers on Freddie Marsh (who had spent all of 1951 with Veeck's Browns, was dealt to Washington that winter and then returned to St. Louis during the '52 season) and Veeck claimed him. So I called Rudie Schaffer (then as later Veeck's financial aide) and asked him, 'Where do you want Marsh to report?' He said, 'Oh God, Frank—didn't you withdraw the waivers?' I said, 'No, I'm gonna teach that damn Veeck a lesson.' 'Well, we don't have the money—I'm getting tired of mortgaging my house, so help me.' Rudie used to have to mortgage the house all the time to meet the payroll with the Browns. 'Well,' I said, 'tell you what. If you let Veeck worry about this a couple of days, we'll cure him of all this, and I'll withdraw.' "

Veeck worried, Lane withdrew waivers, but Veeck was never really cured. He continued to claim anybody whose name happened to appear on a waiver list. Still, Veeck and Lane remained close. They had fun with each other all the time. After Lane's White Sox had taken a pair from Veeck's defending league champs in May, 1949, by scores of 10-0 and 2-0 (before 53,325 at Comiskey Park), Frank had home plate dug up, crated, and shipped to Veeck in Cleveland so the Indians could get a glimpse of it. The fun continued well after Lane left the Sox. As Cleveland general manager after the Sox' title season of '59, Lane got Veeck to give up youngsters John Romano and Norm Cash, plus third baseman Bubba Phillips, for Minoso, who had been sent to Cleveland by the Sox in '58 and who by now was 37 years old—according to the record books. Noting that the Chicago roster already included 40-year-old Early Wynn; Gerry Staley, 39; Rivera, 38; Earl Torgeson and Mike Garcia, both 36; plus Turk Lown, Ted Kluszewski and Lollar, all 35; Lane announced scornfully: "I had to make this deal. I wanted to make sure the White Sox had the oldest club in both leagues."

When Veeck was in St. Louis and Lane was in Chicago, they both made a deal once with Syracuse of the International League. Syracuse tried to interest Lane in Bobo Holloman, a righthanded pitcher. But Lane turned him down, opting instead for another righthander, Bob Keegan, who had won 20 games for the Syracuse club in 1952. At the same time, Veeck grabbed Holloman.

"I gave Syracuse $1500 for Bob Keegan, $13,500 more if we kept him 30 days after the season started. They offered me Holloman first, but I said, 'I don't want that S.O.B.' Now I knew Keegan had a perennial sore arm in the spring, so I had him throwing in the wintertime."

The winter training didn't help and Keegan was on the disabled list

10

early in the '53 season. In the meantime, Holloman was getting a chance to pitch for Veeck's Browns. He won a couple of games in relief, then got pounded around a bit. Finally, he explained that the reason for his ineffectiveness was that he wasn't a relief pitcher—he was a starter. The Browns figured he couldn't do any worse than most of their other starters, anyway, so they gave him a shot. And Bobo promptly fired a no-hit game against the Philadelphia A's. Veeck spilled the beans and newspapers all over carried the full tale of how Lane had turned down Holloman for Keegan, a fellow who hadn't even thrown a pitch in anger for the White Sox.

"I called Bill and said, 'You S.O.B.! You've got me over a barrel. How can I turn down a guy who just threw a no-hitter?' So Veeck, who'd made the same kind of deal I had made, paid the $13,500 to Syracuse and kept Holloman. And that was the last game Holloman won all year." Keegan, on the other hand, went 7-5 when he finally got going that season, then won 16 games the next year and was named to the American League all-star team.

The Lane-Veeck transaction that helped most in the early '50s was the Virgil Trucks deal. With Saul Rogovin and Joe Dobson—the club's big righthanded winners of 1952—going badly, the '53 Sox lacked a solid righthander to go with lefty Pierce. Besides that, the Cubs had just stolen the Chicago newspaper headlines by getting Pittsburgh slugger Ralph Kiner in a deal involving 10 players and a reported $150,000. The whole situation prompted Lane to recall a conversation he had had with Veeck a few months earlier.

"I'd stuck with Bill when he tried to move the Browns to Milwaukee first and then Baltimore. And twice he was voted down (by the league owners), and I went to bat for him both times. The final time, in '53, Bill was almost ready to take the pipe. It was in Tampa, Fla., right after the Governor's Dinner, March 17—that used to be their big St. Patrick's Day celebration down there. I walked around with Bill till 3 or 4 in the morning. He said, 'I'll never forget you. If I can ever help you out . . . ' I said, 'You've got Virgil Trucks. I want first refusal if you ever decide to trade him.' "

Hurting for money, Veeck, by June, was ready to get what he could for Trucks, who though 34 years old was still a quality pitcher who could help a contender. "Well, now, June 4, the Cubs get Kiner,"

11

remembered Lane. "So I said to Roy Egan (a member of the club's board of directors and Mrs. Comiskey's lawyer), 'I've got to get Trucks.' Because we needed him and we were battling the Cubs for ink in the Chicago papers as much as we were battling the Yankees and the other clubs in our league. Roy said, 'What's it gonna cost?' I said, '$50,000 and it's cheap at $50,000.' Because I knew Veeck had gotten an offer of $100,000 and a ballplayer or two from Greenberg (at Cleveland.)"

The Comiskeys OK'd the money and the deal was made. The Sox got Trucks plus veteran third baseman Bob Elliott for the cash and catcher Darrell Johnson and pitcher Lou Kretlow—both of whom had come to the White Sox originally from the Browns, naturally. "Veeck said, 'If I let you have him (Trucks) for $50,000, don't you tell anybody what you paid for him.' Trucks (47-26 in his 2½ years with Chicago) was worth about a million dollars a year to us for three straight years. That's something I'll never forget. When you did Veeck a favor and he made you a promise, he kept it. There weren't many who did."

But while Veeck gave the White Sox lots of activity in the trade market, Chicago's top rival, the Yankees, gave them none, "They always wanted to steal something," Lane snorted. "Dan Daniel, one of their writers, would come in here and say, 'We need a lefthanded pitcher. Whitey Ford's got a bad arm. We need Pierce. You don't need him down here.' I said, 'Screw the Yankees. You want him, you'll pay for him.' That's when I went after them. I wanted Hank Bauer, Gerry Coleman, and Joe Collins. They could've had Pierce and somebody else. George Weiss (Yankee G.M.) called me up and said, 'I'm gonna make you a deal.' I said, 'Who?' He mentioned a guy who was playing first base for their club at Binghamton. I said, 'That doesn't sound like Joe Collins to me.' He mentioned a guy named Frank Verdi who was playing second base at Birmingham. 'Well, that doesn't sound like Gerry Coleman.' Then he mentioned the name of a guy who was playing left field at Binghamton. And I said, 'That doesn't sound like Bauer.' He said, 'That's the closest you'll ever come to making a deal with me.' Which it was. The Yankees would come in here, the great Yankees. If they needed something, you should give it up. Sure, I'll give him up. For three ballplayers. It would've been a good deal, for

12

us and for them. Billy would've won 20 games easy for them."

People like Bauer, Coleman, and Collins weren't the only players Lane was unable to put in White Sox uniforms. The man he wanted the most but could never get—until Lane was in Cleveland and was able to pick him up near the end of the player's career—was Elmer Valo, an outfielder who had been born in a tiny Czechoslovakian town called Ribnik. Valo, who toiled for the Philadelphia Athletics, was a White Sox-type player—a speedy, hustling sort who gave everything he had, and a line-drive hitter with a modicum of power. In short, a player surely made for Comiskey Park.

"But every time we'd be close to a deal with (A's general manager) Art Ehlers," Lane claimed, "we'd be playing the Athletics a ballgame. And that darn Valo would get three or four hits and wreck the deal. This happened two or three different years. I'd call up Ehlers and say, 'Well, let's announce the deal.' We'd agreed on it. I forget who we were gonna give up, but it was somebody who was agreeable to both teams. And he wanted to play for me. He knew I was trying to get him. I'd say to him, 'Well, geez, go 0-for-4 sometime and I'll be able to get you.'

"But if ever there was a guy who'd give you 120 per cent, it was Valo. He'd knock the fences down for you. What a hard-working son of a gun he was and what a good ballplayer he was. But Art Ehlers would say, 'Gee, Frank, you're picking a bad time. I can't trade a guy who just went 4-for-5.' "

Generally, though, when Lane developed a craving for a player on another club, that player would wind up with the White Sox. (Another exception to that rule was the Dodgers' Jackie Robinson, who would've come to Chicago in 1955 but for a last-second waiver claim by Cincinnati.) And then, in many cases, after Frank had had a chance to study the player as a member of the White Sox, another craving would develop—a desire to get rid of the guy. Yet, for all his wheeling and dealing, Lane was never able to give Chicago a pennant—although many of his acquisitions were to form the nucleus of the White Sox championship team of 1959.

"Veeck's been taking all the bows for that pennant-winning team," Lane grinned, "but with one or two exceptions, that was my ballclub." And Lane's new club, Cleveland, was the Sox' closest challenger that pennant year. In fact, the Indians trailed Chicago by just 1½ games when the Sox moved into Municipal Stadium Aug. 28 for a critical four-games series. The Sox won the first game of the series, before 70,383, on a three-run homer by Sherm Lollar in the seventh and then went on to sweep the series. As it happened, Lollar's drive was actually tipped over the fence by the Cleveland leftfielder, none other than Minnie Minoso.

"Minnie couldn't wait for the ball to come down," Lane said, his eyes lighting up at the recollection of that August night. "He jumped up to catch the ball for the third out, and he knocked it over the fence. And I can still see Minnie on his hands and his knees, trying to reach through the wire fence, trying to get at the baseball. As bad as I felt about it, I couldn't keep from laughing.

"Of course I had mixed emotions. I didn't want to be beaten. But if I was gonna be beaten, I'd rather be beaten by the guys I'd left in Chicago: Billy Pierce, Nellie Fox, Sherm Lollar, Jim Rivera . . ."

The closest a Lane-directed Sox team ever came to a pennant was in 1955, when the White Sox went into the final month with a one-game lead only to wind up third, five games in arrears of the champion Yankees. That year also happened to be Lane's final season in Chicago before taking over the G.M. office with the St. Louis Cardinals. The running feud between Frank and Chuck Comiskey, which had been heating up for years, had finally reached the boiling point. And Lane, despite being in only the second year of a contract that ran through 1960, was ready to hunt for another dying ballclub to resurrect.

"I was wet-nursing Chuck Comiskey, and he had no use for me, because the Chicago press treated me real good. Of course I worked my butt off to get the good press, too. When I came here the ballclub was nearly bankrupt. When I left, they had three million dollars in the bank and the club was good enough to win the pennant in '59.

"I had liked Chuck like a son and when I first took the job, Mrs. Comiskey had said, 'I want you to be a father to this guy.' And Chuck was great with me at first. Never second-guessed me or anything else. But after a while he started getting mad because I was running the club. In fact, his father-in-law, Frank Curran, said, 'Does Lane own this club or do you own it?' Chuck had lied to him, said it was in the will that he'd be the next president of the ballclub. It was never in the will. But it got down to where his father-in-law was saying, 'Well, we thought we were marrying the next president of the White Sox.' And it kind of got under Chuck's skin."

The point of no return came on the Sox' last home series of August 1955 before the team departed on what would prove to be a fateful eastern road trip. The Sox were playing a Tuesday night game against the Boston Red Sox, also involved in the pennant race. Boston's Jimmy Piersall, trying to score with two out, was thrown out at the plate by a goodly margin, yet got up and argued violently—as he usually did—with the plate umpire, Larry Napp. Expletives were hurled at and sand was kicked upon the ump, who nonetheless chose to let Piersall stay in the contest. Sox catcher Lollar, once in the dugout and out of sight from everyone save those on the field, voiced his displeasure with Napp's tolerating Piersall's behavior. Napp immediately raced over to the Sox dugout and gave the old heave-ho sign. Word was flashed to the press box—where Lane, Comiskey and a flock of writers were stationed—that the fellow who had been chased was Lollar. So, instead of having Piersall booted out, the Sox were losing Lollar's brains and bat. Worse yet, the only other Chicago catcher was Les Moss, who was still recovering from an injured left thumb. It goes without saying that Lane was furious.

"I'm upstairs, and Jack Mabley, who was the hatchet man with the Daily News at the time, is sitting up there with Comiskey. So Chuck says, 'Hey, Mr. G.M., why don't you do something about the umpiring?' I said, 'You're the vice-president of this ballclub—why don't you do something about it?' Chuck was always great for sitting back and telling you what you should do—but he didn't know shit from apple butter. So before I knew it, from that press box, in two minutes, I was down there in the third-base box where (American League president) Will Harridge was sitting with Cal Hubbard, the supervisor of umpires. So I said, 'Hey, Cal, we're in this league too. Your ump lets Piersall get away with murder and doesn't throw him out. Undoubtedly Lollar said something from the bench, but no one knows—he didn't show anybody up. And he gets thrown out. I'm telling you, I don't like it!'

"And the fans around me yelled, 'That's right, Frankie! You tell 'em! And that's when I realized I'd made a horrible mistake. Here's the league president, one of my real favorites, and I'm yelling my head off. So Mabley's still upstairs and the next day his column comes out: 'Lane's conduct was terrible,' and so on and so forth. Comiskey was feeding him, see. Mabley writes this thing, 'Chuck Comiskey is very irate with Lane and with Lane's language.' They couldn't tell anything about my language. They were upstairs in the press box and I was down in the third-base box seats. And there were 42,000 people in the stands."

Another writer, John Carmichael, took up the chase. He went to Mrs. Comiskey and asked her, "What about this fuss between Chuck and Frank Lane? What are you going to do about it?"

Mrs. Comiskey gave a blunt reply: "Chuck is my son, and I love him. But he couldn't run a peanut stand. Frank Lane is the boss."

Mrs. Comiskey's comments were published, and from Cleveland, where Lane had gone with the ballclub for the start of its final road trip, Frank put in a call back to the home office. "I thought, as loyal as Mrs. Comiskey has been to me, it's a bad thing, because it looks as if I am coming between mother and son. And I told her, 'Sweetheart, I appreciate your allegiance and loyalty, but you've made it necessary for me to leave.' She said, 'Oh, don't give me that crap. You wanted to get away, anyway.' I said, 'No, I didn't, otherwise I wouldn't have signed that new contract.' But that's what precipitated my leaving Chicago. And I'd had two or three offers elsewhere. So I said, 'Well, now's the time to get out.' And that's the reason I went down to take over the St. Louis Cardinals."

He left with his goal, an American League pennant, unaccomplished. But, looking back, he said he never really believed that any of his White Sox teams could win a championship. "If you don't see it out on the field, don't wish for it," is the way he put it. "We didn't quite have it, unless we would've gotten a few more lucky breaks. And Mr. Rickey used to say, 'There's no such thing as luck— luck is the residue of design.' Well, I had the design, but I didn't have the ballplayers. But we played exciting baseball. We got to where we'd drawn nearly a million and a half. If Pierce had been twins, we might've won it. Pierce, that little guy. You didn't need a relief pitcher when he was pitching. If we were a run ahead going into the seventh or eighth inning, the ballgame was over. He had more courage per

16

ounce than any ballplayer I knew."

And Frank Lane, fearless in player transactions, never fretting about how the fans would react to his deals, most likely had more courage per ounce than any general manager Chicago has ever known.

BILL VEECK:
Where have you gone,
Johnny Callison?

I was told by Bill Veeck's secretary to just have a seat in the Bards Room, that Mr. Veeck would be with me shortly. I strolled around the room, reacquainting myself with the familiar pictures of Charles A. Comiskey I, J. Louis Comiskey, George Halas, Mayor Richard J. Daley, and all the rest. After a while, Veeck appeared, greeting me warmly and motioning me to sit with him at his own favorite table.

The table was closest to the Bards Room phone. Veeck has always been naked without a phone. He answered all calls personally— they were not screened. On this morning, our chat was interrupted countless times by calls from well-wishers, friends, newsmen, and an angry fan wanting to know why the Sox hadn't gotten rid of Lamar Johnson yet. But in all cases, Veeck acted as if he were speaking to me as much as to the person on the other end of the line.

"Sure I remember—Al Capone was a great baseball fan," he told a caller after lighting up the first of many Salem Longs. "I remember he would come into the ballpark and people would cheer him." To a reporter from the Miami Herald digging up material for a story on the inseparability of beer and baseball, he talked of his days as a Wrigley Field vendor and told tales of such Hall-of-Fame drinkers as Hack

From left: Mary Frances Veeck, Sox manager Tony LaRussa, and Bill Veeck—before the start of "The Mary Frances Veeck and Friend Show," the Veecks' weekly Sunday morning program on WBBM radio.

19

Wilson and Grover Cleveland Alexander.

A request for Veeck's services as a speaker was the next call. "I'm booked solid through January," Bill told the petitioner. "It's not, you must understand, because I'm good. It's because I'm cheap."

In between phone calls, I managed to get in a few questions of my own for this man who had grown up in the Chicago suburb of Hinsdale, had worked for his father and P.K. Wrigley with the Cubs when they were the scourge of the National League, had set attendance records and won a world championship with the Cleveland Indians in 1948, had owned the lowly St. Louis Browns in the early '50s and had tried unsuccessfully to move them to either Milwaukee or Baltimore, and who—after failing to purchase either the Philadelphia A's in 1954 (and move them to Los Angeles) or the Detroit Tigers in 1956— finally returned home in 1959 to buy controlling interest of the White Sox from Dorothy Rigney, older sister of Chuck Comiskey.

By that time, he had already angered the stuffed shirts among the Lords of Baseball by using a midget for a pinch-hitter, by bringing tightrope walkers and baseball clowns like Max Patkin and Jackie Price into the park, by staging cow-milking contests on the field, by allowing a group of grandstand managers armed with cue cards to dictate strategy, and by publicly scorning the Establishment types who disagreed with Veeck's shocking theory that people come out to the ballpark not only to see a baseball game but to have a good time as well.

I had heard from Ed Short that Veeck was ready to pull another stunt as soon as the Sox gathered for spring training in Tampa in '59. Bill was intent on signing the ageless Leroy "Satchell" Paige, who by official baseball records was 53 years old at the time but was probably older even than that. Veeck, who had brought "Satch" to the big leagues with Cleveland in 1948, had seen Paige just a couple of years earlier while running the Miami minor league club for a couple of old friends.

"We played an exhibition in the Orange Bowl, and Leroy pitched," Veeck remembered. "It was 180 feet to the rightfield fence and 690 to the one in left. And there was not a single ball hit off Paige to the rightfield side of second base in nine innings. Not one. And we hit about five over the rightfield fence."

So Veeck figured Paige might be of some help to Sox manager Al Lopez. "But Al said, 'If you bring him in, I'm leaving.' So that was that. Paige wasn't hard to handle. He never missed a ballgame. He might arrive late or in an unorthodox way, but he was always there. He was sometimes forgetful of planes and trains, but he'd find some way to get there. He was a remarkable character. I thought he was very good for a ballclub. But Al didn't agree."

The two men didn't agree on the Sox' chances of winning the '59 pennant, either. Veeck, seeing the team squeak out one tight victory after another, sought to obtain another of his longtime favorites, Roy Sievers, from the Washington Senators to provide a little punch. Lopez kept telling Bill not to worry, that this was the kind of team he liked to manage. Veeck, failing to secure Sievers, then began proclaiming to one and all that his ballclub simply didn't have enough offensive firepower to win a pennant. But the Sox, clinging to the lead through August and September, went on to prove him wrong and clinched the pennant Sept. 22 in Cleveland, home of Veeck's only other big league championship club.

"There's always two ways to approach something like that," said Bill. "You could say, 'We're gonna win the pennant.' And you don't. Then everyone's disappointed. If you start by saying, 'We should win this thing,' you haven't achieved anything, really. All you've done is added a burden to playing. So I would rather be wrong that way. As a matter of fact, I was the same way in Cleveland in '48. I kept telling everyone there was no chance. Then, when you don't win, there's no disappointment. There's disappointment, but it's not as acute as if you have been selected to win. I don't mind being wrong. I was delighted to be wrong in '48 and in '59."

The '59 pennant delighted him even more because it meant a shot at the World Series and its loot. The Sox and Dodgers, helped by the three straight 92,000-plus crowds that jammed the L.A. Coliseum, split a then-record Series pot. But Veeck's team was beaten in six games, never coming close to repeating the opening-game 11-0 rout of the Dodgers at Comiskey Park.

"Two guys beat us, really: Maury Wills and Larry Sherry," Veeck opined. "We thought we would have by far the best shortstopping with Luis Aparicio, but it turned out that Wills had a remarkably fine

21

series in the field. And Sherry, of course, never pitched as well before that and never pitched as well after that. (Sherry won two games and had a 0.71 ERA in the Series.) Which is the same syndrome as Bucky Dent in the World Series recently past ('78). You always have that, for some reason. One reason, I suppose, is that element of the unexpected. You pitch through a good batting order and you let up unconsciously. Or you anticipate that if it's a Lefty Grove or a Rich Gossage coming in from the bullpen, that he'll be phenomenal. But you don't anticipate that a Larry Sherry is going to close the door on you.

"The other things that I remember don't have to do with the games. We had the tickets selected by lot. We had a group of outstanding citizens do the selecting so there wouldn't be any accusations of favoritism. Which pleased a lot of people and got a lot of other people annoyed. Because customers of customers of customers didn't get tickets and the real fans did. In Los Angeles, they had no problems because they had so many seats. I gave the seats in our box to Chuck Comiskey and Hank Greenberg (Sox vice-presidents) and Mary Frances (Veeck's wife) and I sat out in left field.

"You remember lots of little things, like the Star Spangled Banner which Nat 'King' Cole sang. Only he forgot the lyrics. We sat up here before the game with Nat and his agent, and we had the lyrics printed up on cards for him. I'd known him a long time. He said, 'Now, c'mon—no problem.' 'Well,' I said, 'take them along—once in a while you might forget them.' He said, 'No no. No way.' So he forgot them. And he went right on fine with different lyrics. And he made up better ones than the ones we have. I thought so, anyway.

"Another thing I remember is how we got rid of 20,000 roses. We'd had them ordered for the ladies for every game. Including the seventh game, which was never played. So at the end of the sixth game, they were bringing them in for the next day. Well, there was no point in keeping them and letting them die here, so we loaded up a station wagon and went down State Street, asking people, 'Would you like three-four dozen roses to take home?' We got rid of all of them, but you'd be amazed at the difficulty of getting people to believe that you were just giving them to them. It was interesting."

That offseason was interesting, too. Veeck shopped around at the winter meetings for hitting, hitting, and more hitting. He coveted Cincinnati outfielders Gus Bell and Jerry Lynch, Cleveland's Minnie Minoso and Vic Power, and Phillies third baseman Gene Freese— not to mention his old buddy Sievers. He couldn't come back with all those guys, but he did nab a couple. He got Minoso back in a White Sox uniform (after a two-year absence) but the price wasn't small: He sent young first baseman Norm Cash, 25-year-old catcher John Romano (who'd led the A.L. in pinch-hitting in '59), and third baseman Bubba Phillips to the Indians for Minoso, a catcher named Dick Brown, and two lefthanded pitchers—Don Ferrarese and Jake Striker. (Only Minnie lasted the entire '60 season.)

Next, he picked up Freese, who'd hit 23 homers for the Phillies in '59 but whose glove was highly suspect. This time the cost was 20-year-old outfielder Johnny Callison, generally agreed to be the best-looking prospect the Sox had come up with since Luis Aparicio. So far, Cash, Callison, and Romano—each a future all-star—had been shipped away by Veeck. But still he wasn't through. During spring training of 1960, with the ballclub on an exhibition tour of Puerto Rico ("It was like Veeck waited for us to get away as far as possible before he made the deal," said Jack Kuenster, then covering the team for the Daily News), Bill finally landed Sievers. The price was another young catcher, Earl Battey; another youthful first baseman, Don Mincher; plus $150,000.

So the Sox suddenly had Minoso, who hit .311 with 20 homers and 105 RBI in '60; Sievers, who hit .295 with 28 homers and 93 RBI; and Freese, who hit .273 with 17 homers and 79 RBI. But future standouts like Callison, Cash, Battey, and Romano were gone. And the Sox wound up third in '60 and a distant fourth in '61—the year Veeck left baseball for health reasons. Many South Side fans have yet to forgive Veeck for mortgaging their future. Veeck, however, will defend his deals to the death.

"What happened was that the people we had depended on the year before fell off," he said. "Looie and Nelson (Fox) didn't have their finest years, the centerfielder—Jim Landis—had a bad year, and Sherm (Lollar) had a bad year. And that after Al had assured me he was not gonna catch either Battey or Romano. So I figured, 'Let's see what we can get for them rather than leave it on the bench.' That's

23

why I included them in those deals. I could've made them another way, but in any event, we were going to go for broke. I wasn't interested in what was gonna happen five years down the road. I wanted to win back-to-back.

"We had bulwarked the club pretty well, I thought. It was a good ballclub. We hit the ball around a little bit. (The Sox' .270 team average led the league.) The only ones who kept us competitive were the new players—Minoso, Freese, and Sievers. But the line down the middle—the positions where you felt you could count on: center field, shortstop, second base, and catcher—is where we were betrayed."

I mentioned that Bob Shaw, who'd gone 18-6 in '59, didn't repeat his excellence in 1960, either. "Well, that didn't really surprise me." Veeck said. "I didn't think he was that good a pitcher. But he got away with it in '59. It was just one of those years. I thought, 'Well, if we got another good year out of him, it would be luck.' "

But even with the off-years from Shaw, Landis, Lollar, and the others, the team was still good enough to stay in contention until the final weeks. And it was exciting enough to attract a city record 1,644,460 fans into the ballpark at 35th and Shields. Veeck's nightly fireworks displays, plus his new $350,000 exploding scoreboard, were almost as much an attraction as his pennant-contending ballclub. But the team was older and slower in '61 (Veeck did come up with a good young pitcher, though, when he acquired Juan Pizarro along with vet Cal McLish from the Reds for Freese during the winter), and not even the fireworks displays or the exploding scoreboard could prevent the Sox' slide to fourth place and a dip of 500,000 in total attendance. It was during that season that Veeck, on advice from doctors at the Mayo Clinic, sold the club and left baseball to, as he himself worded it, put his affairs in order.

But it turned out that Bill Veeck was not quite ready to leave this world. And 14 years later, his skin much more wrinkled and his attire consisting more of turtleneck sweaters than open-collared sportshirts, Veeck came hobbling back to Chicago and to the White Sox. Sox owner John Allyn was near bankruptcy (the team had drawn only 770,800 in '75) and he had two alternatives: Let the American League take over the franchise until it could set up a deal with buyers in Seattle, or sell to Veeck and his group, which would keep the team in

Chicago. Allyn had bought the team from his brother, Art, five years earlier to prevent the team from moving to Milwaukee, so he wasn't about to let the Sox become the Seattle Kings or whatever.

So he sold to Veeck, who needed 46 other partners to come up with the necessary $10 million for the purchase. But Sox fans didn't seem to care if these were indications that the club might later prove to be under-financed. The important thing was that the White Sox were still in Chicago and that good ol' Bill Veeck was back. Bill quickly named an old friend, Paul Richards, to manage the team instead of Chuck Tanner. Richards had been named to manage the Sox for Frank Lane 25 years earlier. Nostalgia was going to be the big thing from now on. Among the team's new coaches would be Minnie Minoso and Jim Busby, the two players who had been most responsible for the "Go! Go!" chant that had first swept through the old South Side ballpark in 1951. Veeck changed the name of the stadium back to Comiskey Park—it had been renamed White Sox Park during the Art Allyn regime of the '60's—and spent a couple of million refurbishing the place. Veeck also gave the club new uniforms, patterned after duds worn by the White Sox during the early '30s.

But for all the changes, there wasn't much progress shown on the field. Even with all the new blood—Veeck-acquired players included first baseman Jim Spencer, second baseman Jack Brohamer, pitchers Ken Brett and Clay Carroll, plus the good-hitting, poor-fielding and highly paid leftfielder, Ralph Garr—the Sox lost 97 games and finished a distant last in the West Division. The hitting was such that former leadoff man Pat Kelly was being employed by Richards as a cleanup hitter, of all things.

So it was that Veeck decided to put together a team that could score a few runs. Pitching was forgotten: A poor decision left young right-hander Pete Vuckovich unprotected in the draft to stock the league's two new teams, Seattle and Toronto (Vuckovich was quickly grabbed by Toronto), and Rich Gossage and Terry Forster (who under baseball's new rules would be free to play out their option in '77 and sell themselves to the highest bidder) were shipped to Pittsburgh for slugging outfielder Richie Zisk. Then Veeck sent another player he was having trouble signing, shortstop Bucky Dent, to the Yankees for lefthanded longball hitter Oscar Gamble and a couple of minor league pitchers, Lamarr Hoyt and Bob Polinsky.

Then he took a chance on Eric Soderholm, the Minnesota third baseman who had played out his option after sitting out the entire 1976 season because of a mangled knee. Veeck signed him when all other clubs took a pass on him. The same applied to pitcher Steve Stone, another bargain-basement free agent. Stone, who had been with the Sox four seasons before, no longer seemed sound of arm, having been able to pitch only 75 innings for the Cubs in '76. But Veeck, himself possessing but one sound leg and uncertain hearing, provided opportunities for Stone and Soderholm, adding that, "Sooner or later, the lame, the halt, and the blind all seek refuge with us."

That's pretty much how the fans and sportswriters envisioned the '77 Sox before the season opened. New manager Bob Lemon, another old Veeck pal, wouldn't have much to work with. It would be a rag-tag team, consisting of unhealthy players like Stone and Soderholm, oldsters like Garr and Spencer, youngsters like Chet Lemon and Alan Bannister, plus the potentially loud bats of Zisk and Gamble—"rented" for the year by Veeck, who reasoned that they were in the final years on their contracts and most likely would opt for free agency at season's end. The outlook was far from bright—some writers even picked the Sox to finish last in the West behind Seattle— and interest lagged further with the knowledge that the Sox would be opening the season in the home park of the Toronto Blue Jays, the other new team.

"How's that for a natural rivalry?" Veeck said to author Roger Kahn. "The White Sox, a charter American League club, at Toronto? But we have a chance to win, if we can get there. If necessary, I intend to lease dog sleds."

The team got there, all right, but, despite a first-inning homer by Zisk, the White Sox, in the midst of an April snowfall, lost the game and looked awful while doing so. But amazingly, things began improving almost immediately. More than 34,000 showed up for the home opener and the White Sox beat Boston 5-2. The team stayed above .500 as Zisk, Soderholm, Lemon, and Bannister smacked the ball around with regularity and new bullpen ace Lerrin LaGrow snuffed out one enemy rally after another.

The key month was July, when Garr suddenly went on a hitting rampage after getting off to a relatively slow start and sparked Chicago to 22 victories in 28 games. The Sox opened the month by sweeping a four-game weekend series from first-place Minnesota as Zisk blasted a couple gigantic homers and big crowds sang "Na Na Hey Hey Goodbye!" to the bruised and beaten Twins. By mid-month, the Sox—now being called the "South Side Hitmen"—had grabbed the West Division lead and the crowds were getting bigger: 41,597 turned out on a Friday night to see the Sox whip the East Division-leading Red Sox 9-7. The White Sox were hitting .284 as a team and had knocked 106 home runs, and the all-star game hadn't even been played yet.

The month ended on a high note. The Sox drew 131,276 for a four-game weekend set against second-place Kansas City and won three out of four. The noise level was deafening, especially during a four-run seventh-inning rally that won the Friday night game and after Chet Lemon's second two-run homer of the game tied the Sunday doubleheader opener in the bottom of the 10th. The noise wouldn't subside until the home-run hitter had emerged from the dugout, waving his cap to the crowd. It was a marvelous weekend, one that ended with the Sox owning a 5½-game lead over the Royals.

"I can't believe it, I can't believe it, I can't believe it," said Zisk, shaking his head in the clubhouse after the Friday night thriller, won by an 11-8 score. "I've never seen anything like this before. Not the crowd, not the game. That crowd is unbelievable. That game is unbelievable. We're unbelievable.

"But I'll tell you, that's the way it's been all along and that's the way it's going to be. That crowd charges us up and as long as they keep going like that, we'll keep going."

The fans kept going, but the Sox did not. They quickly lost three out of four to the visiting Texas Rangers—in one of the games they blew a 7-0 seventh-inning lead—and then dropped three in a row at Kansas City. The pitching, somewhat shaky all along, was finally giving out. Slumps by Zisk and Bannister contributed to a decline in run production during the month of August, meaning that the team's defensive shortcomings were no longer being covered up by the once-awesome offense.

Still, after a Monday night Comiskey Park throng of 45,433 watched the Sox score three runs in the eighth to beat the Yankees 5-3 on Aug. 22, Chicago trailed the Royals by just a game. (Minnesota likewise was a game back, Texas a game and a half.) But then Kansas City went on a tear, winning 32 of their last 41 games while the Sox were losing 20 of their final 41. All hopes of a division title faded, but the players were going to finish with some impressive statistics. Soderholm would wind up with 25 homers, a .280 average, and the Comeback Player of the Year award; Zisk with 30 homers, 101 RBI, and a .290 average; Gamble with 31 homers and a .297 average; Spencer and Lamar Johnson with 18 homers each; Lemon with 19 homers; Jorge Orta with 84 RBI; Garr with his usual .300 average; Stone, he of the questionable arm, with 15 victories; LaGrow with 25 saves and a 2.45 ERA; and Bannister, Dent's replacement at shortstop, with a misleading .275 average—he'd been around or above .300 almost the entire season. (Unfortunately, he also committed a whopping 40 errors.)

Veeck, too, was having a good year. So good, in fact, that he had a goal of not only breaking the White Sox season attendance record— set 17 years before during his first stopover at Comiskey Park—but also the all-time Chicago record of 1,674,993, set by the Cubs in that wonderful year of 1969. Veeck wanted the record badly—as much as he'd wanted that record of 2,260,627 in Cleveland back in 1948. And, according to Frank Lane, he was willing to do whatever it took to get it.

"Fact of the matter is, 200,000 of the 2.6 million in Cleveland were phonies," Lane told me. "Bill would run up the goddamn bleacher turnstile. He was getting ready to do it here too—the last three days of the '77 season. If he had had three good days, he would've done it here.

"But the first day, when he'd anticipated about 25,000, he only had 8-9,000 on a rainy night. And Bill talked openly about it. He said, 'Gee, I guess I can't do that—it would be too noticeable.' He couldn't turn around and give out a figure of 25,000 when there were only 8,000 people in the stands."

So Veeck had to settle for a final attendance figure of 1,657,135, which at least was a record for the White Sox. It was an increase of almost 750,000 over the '76 figure and 235,000 more than even the '59 pennant-winning team had drawn. The attendance record is one of the reasons why Veeck savors the '77 season more in his memory than the '59 campaign.

"Seventy-seven more so than '59, because of the response of the fans," said Veeck, who also cherished '77 more because that Sox team was one he had built, while the '59 Sox team was one he had inherited. "I have never seen anywhere the kind of enthusiasm that was engendered in this ballpark in '77."

I asked him if it had all been a surprise to him.

"We played better in some respects than I had hoped and not as well in others as I had hoped," he replied. "Obviously, I thought I was getting something in Zisk and Gamble. So I can't say it was a complete surprise. They picked up the other fellows. Now Soderholm was a very pleasant surprise, because it was a gamble whether his leg would be as good as it was. Orta was really somewhat of a disappointment. He had a good year but not as good as I had hoped, surrounded as he was by more good hitters.

"So I was pleased by what happened in '77, but I can't say amazed— except by the fans."

To reward those fans, then, he immediately sought replacements for Zisk and Gamble, who were granted free agency after refusing Veeck's best offers—which probably should have been made much earlier than they were. First, Veeck gave a guaranteed, four-year, $600,000 contract to lefty-swinging Ron Blomberg, the former Yankee who had been hampered by knee injuries and been to bat twice in a season and a half. Knocking on wood, Veeck announced that Blomberg would take Gamble's spot in the lineup.

Then, he sent pitchers Chris Knapp and Dave Frost and catcher Brian Downing to the Angels for a speedy young outfielder named Thad Bosley, a 18-year-old pitcher named Richard Dotson, plus much-talented and much-traveled slugger Bobby Lee Bonds. Bobby had hit 37 homers, driven in 115 runs and stolen 41 bases in '77 and, promised Veeck, would more than replace Zisk as a righthanded hitter. In addition, Bonds would catch flyballs, items that Richie sometimes had had difficulty getting to.

Finally, in spring training, Veeck figured his team was still missing a good lefthanded relief pitcher. So off to Oakland went pitcher Steve Renko and first-string catcher Jim Essian for a Venezuelan lefty called Pablo Torrealba. The catching would be handled by rookie Bill Nahorodny and Wayne Nordhagen.

Things started out well enough. Before a record opening-day crowd of 50,754, Blomberg hit a one-out, game-tying homer in the ninth and the Sox won it the same inning on Nordhagen's double. Torrealba pitched well in relief the next game and the Sox beat Boston again. But from then on, it was disaster. Blomberg had problems with his knee and wound up going to bat just 156 times all season. He was cut from the roster the following spring. Torrealba, after three months of ineffective pitching, came down with a kidney ailment that rendered him totally useless. And the Sox were in last place and Bonds had hit all of four home runs when he was shipped to the Texas Rangers in mid-May for Claudell Washington.

To make matters worse, Washington didn't report to the Sox for nearly two weeks. And when he finally did, he had a rather unusual excuse: "I overslept." Claudell, blessed with great ability but not with great desire or intelligence, never really did quite wake up. And when he departed in June, 1980 in a deal with the Mets, Claudell's memory was preserved by an outfield banner which read: "Washington slept here."

So 1978 was not the year Veeck had hoped it would be, although the White Sox did please Bill by drawing 1,491,100 despite finishing fifth with a 71-90 record and going through two managers—Bob Lemon and ex-Sox outfielder Larry Doby, another old friend of Veeck's from the glory days of Cleveland. But there was a hopeful glint in Veeck's eye as I ended my conversation with him on this November morning. He had hired former Cub star Don Kessinger as his new manager only a week earlier, and Veeck seemed convinced that Kessinger—who had been acquired from the Cardinals for the '77 stretch drive at the cost of a promising pitching prospect, Silvio Martinez—would be the perfect choice to lead a new, young Sox team to maturity and, shortly thereafter, to contention.

Veeck based his optimism on youngsters like third baseman Kevin Bell, first-round draft choice Harold Baines (Veeck's personal "discovery"), catcher Mike Colbern, and shortstop Harry Chappas, the stubborn dwarf; on the return to full health of Chet Lemon, Nord-hagen, and Bannister; and on the promise of a corps of young pitchers.

"I try not to kid myself," he said. "You know, I don't mind romancing someone else, but to fool yourself is pretty devastating and dangerous. But we have a group of young pitchers, and I can never remember having seen as many good-looking young pitchers in one place since St. Louis when they had Rochester, Columbus, and Houston in the days of Hank Gornicki, John Grodzicki, Red Munger, Preacher Roe, Ernie White, and Fred Martin—and I left out Howie Pollet and Harry Brecheen.

"Since then, I've never seen a group like this. This is a whole group together. How it will work out, I don't know. They're really all so young." He ticked off the names of lefties Steve Trout, Ross Baumgarten, and Richard Wortham and righthander Fred Howard. "I haven't mentioned some of the babies—that's Paul Richards' term—like (Britt) Burns, who's 19. And (Richard) Dotson, 19 years old. Some pretty good arms.

"So things are looking up. We're optimistic. And I think, with good reason."

I went back to the Bards Room just a little more than two years later. Veeck seemed a bit more jovial and appeared in better health than he had during our last visit. He had finally given up smoking and where he had formerly quaffed beer, he now sipped coffee.

But the last two years had not gone well for Veeck's White Sox. Kevin Bell had failed at third and had been released, Harry Chappas had long since been forgotten, Mike Colbern had been found wanting and was no longer considered a prospect, and Alan Bannister had been traded to Cleveland. Veeck, who had been changing managers almost as often as rock stars change sex partners, had dumped Kessinger in August of '79 and had replaced him with Tony LaRussa. Tony, a bright young man who in addition to managing also found time to pass the Florida bar examination, thereby qualified as baseball's only genuine clubhouse lawyer.

The Sox as a team were 73-87 in '79 and 70-90 in 1980. The only bright spot had been the continuing development of the pitching staff: Britt Burns, Steve Trout, Ross Baumgarten, and Richard Dotson

31

appeared to be becoming every bit as good as Veeck had hoped. But there was no appreciable gain in the standings. Veeck's old "Give 'em a winner in three years" theory of operation just wasn't working anymore. So in two weeks, Bill and his group would be selling the White Sox to a partnership headed by Skokie real estate magnate Jerry Reinsdorf and television executive Eddie Einhorn—five months after it had been announced that the team would be sold to Ohio millionaire Edward DeBartolo.

(DeBartolo, with a personal fortune of some $500 million, was the first choice of Veeck and his group, but American League owners twice voted down the Ohioan's application—on the rather hypocritical grounds that DeBartolo owned racetracks and would have been an absentee owner. Of course, several other owners also were absentee owners and numbered racetracks among their holdings. The real reason behind the defeat of DeBartolo was that he was simply too rich. He would be another George Steinbrenner or Ted Turner, willing to pay huge salaries for free agents, thus forcing up the payscale. The owners were simply protecting themselves against each other.)

Veeck was getting out because he could no longer compete financially—something he had long ago realized. Two weeks after Veeck's purchase of the White Sox in December 1975 was when it had hit home. That was when federal arbitrator Peter Seitz overturned baseball's reserve clause and declared Los Angeles Dodger Andy Messersmith and Baltimore Oriole pitcher Dave McNally free agents, able to sell their services to whoever was willing to come up with the best offers. The reserve clause, which had bound a player for life to the team that originally signed him, was tossed out the window. Henceforth, players gaining free-agent status would become objects of bidding wars, with bidding getting so out of hand that the dear departed Claudell Washington—even with all his faults as a ballplayer—is now earning more than $700,000 a year.

"You knew our corporate structure was going to be deadly two weeks after you bought the club," Veeck told me, a bit gloomily. "But then the die is cast. There's nothing you can do. But it was unfortunate. More unfortunate, because we were sure that the Messersmith decision was not worrisome. Baseball's attorneys didn't anticipate what the arbitrator decided."

32

So Veeck's organization, which had bought stock rather than assets and had been set up as a corporation, would soon find itself in a difficult financial position—one from which they couldn't escape by changing the structure around.

"Internal Revenue won't let you," Veeck said. "Unless, of course, it was with different people."

But that wasn't especially desirable. After all, Veeck's investors had come to his rescue and that of the White Sox. He wasn't about to cast them adrift. So, in 1979, he began proposing sale of the franchise to a group that could come in and set itself up differently and more advantageously. And it didn't make that much difference to Veeck— whose group finally sold the team for $20 million, doubling its original investment—whether DeBartolo bought the club or Reindorf's group bought it. It was going to be a better setup either way.

"They're both partnerships," he explained. "DeBartolo's partnership would have been him and his daughter (Denise York). Reinsdorf will have a group of partners—but nonetheless a partnership. Now that means that the depreciation of the assets—the players—can flow through and be used by the partners. It depreciates as a tax writeoff against personal income tax. Which really amounts to saving 50 per cent of your cost of players—salaries, acquisitions, etc. Because the government pays half of it. And the people who own ballclubs are at least in the 50 per cent bracket.

"We couldn't do that. When we signed a player, we were dealing in 100-cent dollars, because we didn't have any tax writeoff. When Steinbrenner signs one, he and his partners have the depreciation flowing through so they take it off as income tax savings and the government pays half. So if I pay $100,000 for a player, that's real money. Steinbrenner and his partners are paying $50,000 for the same one. That's the way it's structured. Partnerships can take depreciation. If you're corporate, you can't. That is, the corporation can, but only against profits."

The great irony of all this is that Veeck was being forced out of the game, in the end, by the overturning of the reserve clause, something for which he had been campaigning ever since he had taken night-school law courses at Northwestern University some 40 years ago. "We studied it for the better part of a semester," Veeck recalled, "and

33

we concluded that the reserve clause was indefensible at law and certainly no one could argue that it was defensible morally. And I suggested in a letter in 1941 to Judge Landis (then the commissioner of baseball and a dear friend of William Veeck, Sr.) that we change it before we were required to change it. And that ultimately we'd be required to change it, with great disadvantage to the club owners."

Veeck finally got a reply from Leslie O'Connor, Landis' bailiff and later general manager of the White Sox. "He wrote, 'Dear Bill: Some very bright fellow once said that a little knowledge is a dangerous thing. And you just made him out to be a wizard.' Which was a quick and terse putdown."

So nothing was done about the reserve clause, which was upheld— barely—in court in 1970 after being challenged by Curt Flood, who had refused a trade from the Cardinals to the down-trodden Phila- delphia Phillies. Veeck testified on behalf of Flood, an action which, of course, served to annoy the Lords of Baseball. "I was trying to help baseball, contrary to what the owners then felt. I was decried as a villain for having the temerity to say that all is not perfect.

"But in reality, I was providing a solution that Marvin Miller (director of the Players' Association) would've taken that day. And that was an equity contract, for seven years, with scheduled raises or free agency—just like a motion picture star's contract. You'd have to give them a raise or they'd become free. The thing that worried me was, the judge would rule against the reserve clause and suddenly all players would be declared free agents, and you would have chaos. The wealthier clubs could dominate and make it much more difficult over the long haul to have competition. So I suggested it be done in an orderly manner, with the new contract replacing the old one gradually so that you didn't dislocate a particular market."

But the decision went in favor of baseball, with the presiding judge warning, however, that baseball's owners and its players' association negotiate the matter and come up with some modified form of the reserve clause, that maybe another person somewhere down the line might rule against the reserve clause. Which is exactly what happened, in 1975. Only then, with the players now holding the upper hand, were the owners forced to negotiate a new Basic Agreement with a whole new set of rules. Because of them, Veeck, who had called for such a renegotiation so many years before, would eventually be forced to leave baseball—his second coming to Chicago hardly to be remembered as an artistic success.

"But the important thing," he told me, smiling, "is that it hasn't been static or dull around here. Something's always happening—good or bad."

I asked him which of his actions in the last two years he'd been proudest of. "I've survived," he grinned. "A dinosaur in a world in which there no longer are trees from which I can eat. So survival is important, particularly when you consider that we've been playing with a short deck. Which, of course, is the reason that I've been advocating, for a couple of years, the sale of this franchise. But in the interim there has been a steady improvement in personnel—particularly the younger personnel."

He pointed to an improved scouting staff, a record for signing draft choices (the Sox inked 14 of the 17 players they selected in the June 1980 draft of high school and college players—their best showing since the draft began in the '60s), and to five players named to the 1980 all-star team in the Florida Instructional League: centerfielder Cecil Espy, 6-6, 230-pound first baseman Wesley Kent, shortstop Mike Morris, second baseman Tim Hulett, and catcher Ricky Seilheimer.

All these, plus his doubling the value of the Sox franchise in five short years, are things he's quite proud of. "But we look with some sadness upon the fact we've been something of a farm team for the rest of the league the last couple of years, in that we couldn't afford to keep some players anymore. Like Steve Stone. He'd all but given up pitching and then we conned him into coming back and he did pretty well for himself. (Stone played out his option with the White Sox, signed a multi-year contract with Baltimore and last season won the Cy Young Award.) I regretted it, but I knew we couldn't afford it. We had the last right of refusal. Not by agreement, but because he's a very decent man. He said, 'Here's what I can get.' I said, 'We just can't afford it.' If we could've, we would've. Same thing with (Jorge) Orta. (Orta signed a long-term contract with Cleveland after playing out his option with the Sox in '79.)

Nor is Veeck proud of some deals he made, like the one for Torrealba. (He got Essian back, of course, but at a cost of $1 million for

35

four years.) And the inclusion of righthander Silvio Martinez in the deal to get Kessinger from the Cardinals. "It didn't make sense to give up a pitcher like Martinez (a 15-game winner in '79). But if you have an outside chance, like we had in '77, in fairness to your players and fans, you've got to take it. Even though it's against your better judgement. We didn't want to give them Martinez. When we got Martinez from Pittsburgh (along with Zisk), we knew what kind of pitcher he was gonna be."

He IS proud, though, to have once again made Comiskey Park a fun place to see a ballgame. Even so, I said, a lot of the hard-core Sox fans have been staying away because they feel the place has been taken over by brawling, drunken creeps who didn't know a ball from a strike. "We have had some problems here," he admitted. "Oh sure, it bothers me. But look at Detroit, where they had to rope off about 10,000 seats. And in Philadelphia, what did you see at the World Series? Mounted police and attack dogs.

"So it isn't something that happens only at Comiskey Park. Something's happened to our society. I don't think necessarily there are more violent people per thousand. But there are more thousands.

"But no group of people is above this sort of thing. You know what goes on at soccer games in South America. And even in the Far East— the inscrutable Far East, where their expressions never change and where they are always so polite. Well, we went to Japan to do their all-star game for ABC a few years ago—actually, we did two of them so we could show the best game. So we did the one in Tokyo and then we were supposed to go to Nagasaki the next day, except they couldn't play at Nagasaki because they had burned the ballpark down. The inscrutable, unemotional Far Easterners. They'd burned the whole joint down. An umpire's call had upset them a little bit. I shouldn't say they burned the whole park—they burned the leftfield stands down."

A sort of Japanese Disco Demolition, I ventured. He cringed, thinking back to that July evening in 1979 when hordes of young rock fans, celebrating the destruction by fireworks of thousands and thousands of disco records, poured onto the Comiskey Park playing field, causing the second game of a twi-nighter to be forfeited and thousands of Sox fans to swear they would never again go near Comiskey Park until that goofy Veeck left town.

"Disco Demolition," Bill said, "was a disaster. And the strange part about it, it was a disaster because I had done insufficient investigation. It had never occurred to me that anything like that could have happened."

What surprised Veeck, in addition to the unscheduled near-riot, was the crowd, announced at 47,795. The promotion, tied in with disk jockey Steve Dahl and his war against disco music, enabled anyone bringing along a disco 45 to get in for 98 cents. Veeck hadn't figured there would be this many disco-haters in Chicagoland, or that Dahl had built such an enormous, not to mention rude and obnoxious, group of followers.

"The most he had drawn anywhere before that was 4,500. He drew that night, in total, at least 100,000 people. Because there were more people outside the park than there were inside. It took six squads to close the gates so no more people could get in, although we hadn't sold the place out. And cars were backed up on the Dan Ryan all the way to north of Fullerton. (That represents a backup of nearly eight miles.) This was after the first game was over—they were still backed up.

"And inside, they had all those signs, and that was the worst thing, the most offensive thing. Oh, it was so embarrassing. But it is remarkable what a promotion it was. The promotion was too good. It was a disaster only because if we had had any idea what was going to happen, we could've controlled it. But it had never occurred to anybody. They kept coming and coming and coming."

Veeck himself hobbled out onto the field, armed with the public address mike, pleading with the celebrants to clear the field. But his efforts went for naught. "I couldn't get anybody to leave, which was a pretty humbling experience. I stood on that field for 45 minutes. I couldn't get anybody off. But I didn't want to cause a real riot by bringing in the police. You know, I felt, let them run until they run themselves out. Actually, we could've played the second game, but the umpires were frightened. But that was a disaster. I suppose you're entitled to one every four years."

There were other nonpromotional-type disasters, of course, like the drainage problems in the outfield. Those problems were made all the worse by the torrential downpours of August '79 which, coupled with a wave of music enthusiasts drawn to a Comiskey Park rock concert,

37

turned the turf into one gigantic quagmire. Games had to be called off, even with temperatures in the 80s and the sun shining brightly. It was one of Veeck's worst hours, and the fact that the ballclub was going so poorly did little to help matters.

It was then that the search for a buyer began in earnest, a search that eventually produced DeBartolo in August of 1980 to provide Veeck with one final anti-Lords of Baseball story he can tell with bittersweet humor to all those who believe, as he does, that the powers-that-be among major league club owners are not people upon which to heap honor and praise. When DeBartolo was voted down the second time by American League owners—much to the dismay of Veeck, who saw nothing wrong with his would-be successor other than the fact he had $500 million to help build the White Sox into a solid contender—Yankee boss George Steinbrenner claimed that the 11-3 vote against DeBartolo was really a vote against Bill Veeck.

"That was a very interesting thing," Bill smiled. "But Steinbrenner, of course, is, as you know, a liar. He convicted himself right in the meeting, when he got up to speak in behalf of DeBartolo. And then he says, if you'll recall, after voting against DeBartolo, 'Well, I just decided to vote with the majority.' Ha! But also, if the vote were against me, listen to this: In September, when I was given that 'Night' at the ballpark, the league sent me a new television set. And on it there was a placard, listing all the things I had done for the league and how sorry they were to have me go, and how I've been good for baseball, and so on and so forth. Now, in a month, I'd become a complete villain. Isn't that strange? In one place or the other, they were all lying, weren't they?"

The TV reminded him of another going-away present the league had sent him, several years earlier. "Arthur Goldberg was the lawyer for Flood in the reserve clause case, and he was worried that (Commissioner Bowie) Kuhn and the owners would fight strenuously about whether I was qualified as an expert on baseball. 'Well,' I said, 'I don't think you have to worry about that. I'll bring along some written proof.'

"In '61, when I left because of what they told me at Mayo Clinic, the league wrote this nice letter—like they send to widows. You know, when the husband dies, 'adopted by the board of directors, etc . . .'

Well this was adopted by the league and signed by all the members: 'Oh, how we'll miss you and how much you've meant to the league . . .' The same kind of garbage that was on the placard on the new TV. They figured I would die so they thought, 'We might as well send something.' It was suitably embossed.

"So when I went to testify in the Flood case, I said, 'Don't you think it'd be easier to put this into testimony, because these are the very same people who now question my expertise on baseball.' They were not very pleased, as you can imagine."

But now Veeck's in-fighting with the stuffed shirts of the American League would be ending. The only thing that concerned him now, as far as baseball went, was the future of the White Sox.

"I can't help but feel that the ballclub is going to play so much better and I will take pleasure and pride in that," said Veeck. "Because the team that will go to spring training is the one we put together. And one doesn't have to be there to enjoy it.

"We'll watch carefully—though not quite as carefully—whatever happens."

Bill Veeck got a lot of undeserved credit when the White Sox won the 1959 pennant with a cast of characters put together by Frank Lane and John Rigney and Chuck Comiskey. A new owner will get a lot of credit if and when this current group of White Sox players wins a pennant.

That seems like poetic justice, yes. But somehow, Bill Veeck will always be, in my mind, intertwined with the White Sox. And when Harold Baines hits a two-run homer in the bottom of the ninth against the Yankees to win the American League playoffs some season in the not-too-distant future, Bill Veeck's scoreboard will blow its top.

And somewhere, Bill Veeck will be wearing a satisfied smile.

ED SHORT:
"Let's just say I cheer
for the American League."

When the White Sox traded relief specialist Bob Locker to the Seattle Pilots for pitcher Gary "Cow" Bell early in the 1969 season, I figured that general manager Ed Short—who had made so many fine deals since succeeding Hank Greenberg in 1961—had finally arrived at a point where he was no longer playing with a full deck.

Running the White Sox will do that to a person, I thought. Especially when your team had been so close to winning the pennant two years before and then had plummeted all the way to ninth place the next season. In 1968, '69, and '70, when the Sox were averaging almost 100 losses a year, I sometimes feared I was on the verge of a mental collapse. And I wasn't even connected with the club. Imagine what a wreck Short must have been. After all, he was the fellow ultimately responsible for the entire mess.

When I met with Short in his Skokie apartment, though, he denied having been ready for the funny farm the day he sent Locker to the Pacific Northwest for the portly Bell. "We needed a starting pitcher at the time," Ed recalled. He was right. With Gary Peters having his problems, the only dependable Chicago starters were Tommy John and Joe Horlen—a fact which gave rise to a new, early-season South

Ed Short

Side chant: "Tommy and Joe and pray for snow."

"We figured Gary Bell would help our starting rotation," Short said. "It didn't turn out that well, but at the time, we needed another starter badly."

To say that the deal didn't turn out too well is like saying being an infantryman in Vietnam could have been hazardous to your health. The deal was a disaster. Bell's earned run average with the White Sox was close to 10.00. After he'd been dropped from the starting rotation and banished to the bullpen, we used to wait for the Sox starting pitcher to get into his inevitable jam and then, from our leftfield upper-deck perch, we'd begin chanting, "Milk the Cow, milk the cow . . . " And, if we were lucky enough to get manager Don Gutteridge to wave in Gary from the bullpen, we'd start ringing cowbells in adulation.

The Bell deal was bad enough, but when Short later picked up Fat Jack Hamilton to join Bell in the bullpen (the two even roomed together, giving them what had to be the highest total earned run average of any roommate combination in major league history), I knew Ed's days at the helm of the Sox were numbered. True, he seemed to make progress before the '70 season opened by getting rid of Bell and Fat Jack and a number of other major league imposters, like Woodie Held, Jerry Arrigo, Don Pavletich, and Dandy Don Secrist. But, alas, in their place came people like Virle Rounsaville, Tommie Sisk, John "Pineapple" Matias, and Jerry Janeski. The end came in early September of 1970, when vice president Stu Holcomb announced that both Short and Gutteridge had been relieved of their duties and would be replaced by Roland Hemond and Chuck Tanner from the California Angels' organization. Short, who had come to the Sox from radio station WJJD in 1950 and had served as traveling secretary, publicity man, and finally general manager, had been cast out of the family.

"I wasn't very happy—let's put it that way," he said. "We had some new owners in there, as you'll recall. John Allyn took over from his brother, Art, and John's favorite was Holcomb. Holcomb did me no favors. He had gotten involved with the soccer team (the Mustangs, also Allyn-owned) and they had signed him to a five-year contract. Then when the soccer team folded, they sent him over to the ball-

42

club."

And Holcomb, in turn, sent Short out the door. But Ed can still look back on a career of good deals—transactions which, in the main, helped keep the Sox in contention through the '60s. That should not have been surprising, because he had learned at the feet of such professors as Frank Lane, John Rigney, and Bill Veeck. "When I was the P.R. man, I learned a lot about the value of ballplayers. You watched the way these fellows operated, Lane in particular. You got a better insight as to how you went about making a deal. And all the time I was there, I never made a deal without the concurrence of the manager. Because he had to play the players.

"Now this wasn't always true in the case of Veeck. At one time he wanted to bring in Satchell Paige. And I know if he had brought in Satchell Paige that Al Lopez would've packed his suitcase and gone home. In fact, I had to talk Bill out of it in the lobby of the Tampa Terrace Hotel in spring training of 1959. I knew Al would have left. Satch had his own set of rules and Lopez wouldn't have put up with it."

Lopez ("the finest manager I ever saw," Short said) worked closely with Short in rebuilding the club after Veeck had rid the team of younger players like Johnny Callison, Norm Cash, Earl Battey, John Romano, and Don Mincher. "I made about three deals within a period of three days at the 1961 winter meetings," he remembered. "I traded Roy Sievers to Philadelphia, then Billy Pierce to the Giants, and also Minnie Minoso to the Cardinals. I announced the Cardinal deal first because I didn't want them to think we really needed a first baseman— we got Joe Cunningham in that deal—because if they had known Sievers was gone, the price might have gone up on Cunningham.

"So we announced that deal first and held off the Sievers announcement (Sievers to the Phillies for third baseman Charlie Smith and pitcher Johnny Buzhardt). And the Pierce deal (Pierce and Don Larsen for pitchers Eddie Fisher and Dominic Zanni and a couple of minor leaguers) was announced when the meetings were shifted from Tampa to Miami."

Trading away two South Side institutions like Pierce and Minoso was tantamount to treason, so Short was expecting the hate mail he received. "No matter when you make a deal, you're gonna catch some flak," said Short, who two winters later traded away another Comiskey Park legend, Nellie Fox, and got a real zero (minor league pitcher Jim Golden) in return from Houston. "But a deal doesn't prove itself or disprove itself sometimes for a year or two years after you make it. But we were rebuilding the club after the '61 season. It succeeded. We had some pretty successful seasons after that." And so did Fisher, Buzhardt, and Cunningham.

So Short continued his policy of disposing of legends the next winter when he sent Luis Aparicio and Al Smith to Baltimore for rookie third baseman Pete Ward, shortstop Ron Hansen, outfielder Dave Nicholson, and grand old relief pitcher Hoyt Wilhelm. It was one of his finest trades. "We were making our press tour at the time through the midwestern cities," Short recalled. "And every time I got a spare moment, I was on the phone to Lee MacPhail of Baltimore."

He spent plenty of time on the phone in January, 1965, with Kansas City's Charlie Finley and Cleveland's Gabe Paul. Finally, a three-team deal was announced—the deal Short calls the best one he ever consummated. The Sox sent to the A's outfielders Mike Hershberger and Jim Landis and young pitcher Fred Talbot. To the Sox came slugging outfielder Rocky Colavito. Thirty seconds later, Colavito and catcher Camilo Carreon were passed on to Cleveland for catcher John Romano, a young lefty by the name of Tommy John, plus a rookie centerfielder named Tommie Agee. Romano, though past his prime, tied for the team lead in home runs with 18; John won 14 games and is still going strong; and Agee—after being farmed out in '65— hit 22 home runs and was the American League Rookie of the Year the next season.

Short was the man responsible for picking up pinch-hitter deluxe Smoky Burgess in September 1964 and for bringing knuckleballer Wilbur Wood to Chicago. He managed to accomplish the latter by sending sore-armed Juan Pizarro to the Pirates, who gave the Sox Wood off of their Columbus roster. Another transaction Short pulled off was the reacquisition of Aparicio, who returned to Comiskey Park for the 1968 season along with Matias and outfielder Russ Snyder —who hit a grand-slam homer at Yankee Stadium one June evening and was traded the next day to Cleveland for Leon Wagner, because, Short explained, the Sox needed a lefthanded longball hitter.

To get Aparicio back, Short gave the Orioles infielder Don Buford plus pitchers Bruce Howard and Roger Nelson. The key was Buford, who was an excellent base stealer but hadn't approached his .283 average of 1965 and who had shown an inability to play either second or third base as well as the Sox would have liked.

"Baltimore moved him to the outfield," said Short, who must have wondered why his own managers, Lopez and Eddie Stanky, hadn't thought of that. "He had trouble making the pivot at second base. I remember one year he was playing down in Puerto Rico and we had Tony Cuccinello go down there for a couple of weeks and work with him on making the pivot. But part of the problem was due to a physical disability. He had had the cartilage removed from his knee, and it gave him a lot of trouble when he had to make the pivot. It was from an old football injury from when he played at Southern Cal. A lot of people don't know that."

A lot of people don't know how hard Short tried to put Johnny Callison back in a White Sox uniform. It had been Short, as Sox publicity man in 1958, who had been in on the ground floor of the production of a promotional movie on Callison's rise through the organization to the big leagues at age 19. "One of our sponsors— Pepsi Cola bottlers—came to me and they wanted to make a film with the White Sox, because they were going to be supplying the soft drinks at the ballpark. And we decided to do it around Callison. After we got the film made, Callison didn't stay around too long. He went to Philadelphia for Gene Freese. I tried for years to get Callison back. In the Sievers deal, I tried to get him in that one and they wouldn't deal him. After that, I tried every year, it seems."

He tried just as hard to land Bill "Moose" Skowron, who he finally picked up from Washington in '64 for Cunningham. "That was a disappointment—the length of time it took to get Skowron. If we had been able to get Skowron when we first went after him, he'd have spent a lot of time with the White Sox. I first went after him right after I took over in '61. Not only was he a good ballplayer, he was a local fellow and he would've brought in some fans—which he later did. I made so many different offers to the Yankees for him, but they just weren't dealing him. And when they did deal him, they made sure they dealt him out of the league (to the Dodgers after the '62 season) so he couldn't come back and haunt them. (An offer of Fox and pitcher Frank Baumann at the '63 winter meetings failed to tempt the Dodgers, who then traded Skowron to Washington.)

"I also made a number of unsuccessful attempts to get Carl Yastrzemski before he had that great year in '67. But he was a favorite of Mr. Yawkey's and they just wouldn't trade him. I thought we were close once, after the '65 season. I offered them Skowron and Buzhardt for Yastrzemski. Of course Skowron could've played first base for them and would've beaten a tattoo on that wall."

Late in the '67 season, Short picked up two guys, Ken Boyer and Rocky Colavito, who he figured would beat a tattoo on opposing pitchers. Boyer joined the team in late July and was an immediate help, but the former Cardinal great was injured in mid-August during a critical series with the Twins in Bloomington and was of little help thereafter. The Sox, who had led the league since mid-June, lost the lead by losing all of three games of that series, which ended with manager Eddie Stanky refusing Vice President Hubert Humphrey— the Twins' No. 1 fan—entrance to the Sox clubhouse.

"I still think we might've won it in '67 if Boyer hadn't pulled a hamstring in that series," said Short. "He couldn't play at all that series (he was struck down on Friday night, the first game of the set) and wasn't ever 100 per cent after that."

Still, Chicago had an excellent chance to win the pennant. With five games remaining, the Sox were just percentage points out of the lead and had the schedule on their side. There were two games at Kansas City against the 10th-place A's and three at home against the ninth-place Senators. Figuring they would win maybe four of five, the Sox went out and lost all five. The key was a doubleheader loss at Kansas City on Wednesday, Sept. 27—always to be remembered as Black Wednesday—to a couple of kid righthanders named Catfish Hunter and Chuck Dobson. The losing pitchers were Chicago's best: Gary Peters and Joe Horlen.

"I still say to this day that if Joe Cronin, president of the American League, had agreed to play those two games in Kansas City on single nights . . ." Short began, his voice trailing off. "See, we were scheduled to play there Tuesday and Wednesday and we got rained out Tuesday night. And Thursday was an open date so we could've stayed there and played. But he insisted we play two on Wednesday. He was afraid it'd rain again Wednesday and we'd have to play two on Thursday—which would've been all right with us. It would've been another day's rest for our pitchers."

The twin debacle started the slide of the Chicago White Sox, who would never again be the consistent contender they had been for 17 years. Short tried mightily to improve the club in the offseason, getting Aparicio from Baltimore and sending Agee and Al Weis to the Mets for another starting pitcher—Jack Fisher—plus a badly needed .300 hitter, Tommy Davis. But the Sox lost their first 10 games and never recovered, and with Davis' batting average at .194 on July 12 and the team's record at 34-45, Short dumped Stanky as manager and announced that Lopez would come out of retirement to take over. That initiated a parade of managers which would not cease until Tanner was hired two years thereafter.

"The one thing that hurt us the most," Short sighed, "was all the managerial changes we had to make. Eddie Stanky was let out and Lopez was brought back. And Al was doing a fine job until he had an emergency appendectomy. And he was operated on and he had to be in the hospital. And then we had to put Les Moss in as manager pro-tem. And Les just didn't seem to have the enthusiasm from the players that Lopez had. And then of course the next year Lopez came back but his stomach just couldn't take it anymore and he had to leave and Don Gutteridge had to take over. But Don had been too close to the players. He had been a coach for years and he had practically grown up with a lot of them and was on more of a kidding basis with them than an authoritative basis."

And so followed the disasters of '69 and '70 and Short's sudden dismissal. Eight years later, the hurt, it was obvious, remained. As I got up to leave, I asked him if he was still a White Sox fan.

Ed Short thought about the 20 years he had given the Sox, the happy times under Frank Lane, John Rigney, and Bill Veeck, and the good trades he had made when the Sox were annual contenders. Then he thought of Stu Holcomb and John Allyn and the day he was given his walking papers. He looked at me finally and said:

"Let's just say I cheer for the American League . . . "

ROLAND HEMOND:
A Gift from the Angels

Frank Lane, quite frankly, didn't think much of Roland Hemond, who sits in the general manager's office at Comiskey Park where Lane himself sat 30 years ago.

"Roland Hemond's just a go-fer for Veeck," Lane told me when I visited with him in 1978. "He has no more authority to make deals for the White Sox than I do."

Maybe Lane was right at that time, but before Bill Veeck returned to Chicago in 1975, Roland Hemond made himself some awfully good trades for the White Sox. He began his dealing one month after coming to the Sox from the California Angel organization in September 1970 along with new manager Chuck Tanner. And he began with a holdup of the Kansas City Royals, who gave him Pat Kelly, who could hit and run, for Gail Hopkins—who could hit but couldn't do much else—and John Matias, who couldn't do anything.

Later, at the winter meetings in Los Angeles, he robbed the Angels, who should have known better. Sure, he traded away Ken Berry, one of my all-time favorites. But in return he got Tom Bradley, a fine young pitcher, along with Crazy Jay Johnstone and huge catcher Tom Egan, who would join such immortals as Dave Nicholson and Buddy

48

Roland Hemond

"Boom Boom" Bradford on the list of those who have hit baseballs over the roof at Comiskey Park. Remarkably, in the same deal, Hemond talked the Angels into taking off his hands a poor-fielding, poor-hitting infielder named Sir Sydney O'Brien and a pitcher, Billy Wynne, who did nothing but lose. He also managed to get two players—Mike Andrews and Luis Alvarado—from Boston for shortstop Luis Aparicio, who though coming off the best year—average-wise—of his career was 36 years old.

"We felt we had to use in deals the two players who had had their best years: Aparicio and Berry," Roland told me. "They were the only players who could bring you some value. And then, we were adding youth to the club. The deals worked. We added 23 victories to the club the first year (the Sox went 79-83 after that dreadful 56-106 record of 1970)."

So other clubs should have been forewarned when Hemond arrived at the December '71 winter meetings looking to talk deal again. But the Los Angeles Dodgers and New York Yankees were taken in, anyway. The Dodgers traded slugger Richie Allen to Chicago for lefty Tommy John and infielder Steve Huntz. Allen became a Chicago folk hero. Then Hemond sent infielder Rich McKinney to the Yankees for Stan Bahnsen. McKinney had won the second base job in '71 from Andrews because of his timely hitting but not because of his glove. The Yankees announced he would play third. Hemond, who had watched McKinney try to play third, too, stifled a laugh. McKinney hit .215 for the Yanks in 37 games and made a zillion errors. He wound up playing most of the year in the minors. Bahnsen, meanwhile, won 21 games in Chicago. It was hard to decide which was the bigger steal.

"When we first came here in 1970," Hemond said, "I called Bing Devine and expressed an interest in getting Dick Allen (then with the Cardinals). "However, I guess we didn't have what he'd be looking for in return."

Apparently, the Cardinals didn't think much of the Sox second baseman, Bobby Knoop. Or the Sox catchers, Ed Herrmann and Duane Josephson. Because after Hemond hung up the phone, Devine sent Allen to the Dodgers for second baseman Ted Sizemore and a young catcher, Bob Stinson. But Hemond was ready to try again the

50

next offseason.

"We just found out at the convention that Allen would be available," he recalled. "He had had a good year with the Dodgers (23 homers, 90 RBI, .295) and the last five or six weeks of the season, he had carried that club. So at the time, going to the convention, I didn't think he'd be available. Actually, we had gone to the convention looking for a centerfielder (Johnstone had been found wanting), and we thought Tommy John could bring us a centerfielder. And one we had in mind, actually, was Rick Monday, who was with Oakland. But the Cubs had, I think, made the deal with the A's for Kenny Holtzman before they went to the convention. It was announced the first day.

"So we shifted gears. You don't set your mind on just one deal. You have to be flexible. We did find then that Allen was available and the Dodgers were looking for pitching and we were able to work out the deal. I thought it was a good trade despite Tommy John's continued success. It's still one of the best trades the club has ever made because Allen just revitalized the franchise completely. He carried our club in '72 just sensationally, and we finished 20 games over .500—and that despite losing Bill Melton at midseason with a back injury."

Hemond, though, still couldn't bear to look out toward center field and see Rick Reichardt—who had taken the job from Johnstone—playing there. So he went to the December 1972 convention with one thought in mind: to get a bonafide centerfielder. He returned with Ken Henderson, who was just such a player.

"The Giants had indicated that they weren't going to trade Henderson," Roland said. "I visited with Horace Stoneham in September of '72 when we played at Oakland. And he indicated that he didn't feel they'd be trading Henderson. I talked to Charlie Fox and Jerry Donovan (San Francisco's manager and general manager), and they didn't feel they'd trade him. Then I went down to a general manager's meeting in Phoenix and they still weren't gonna trade him. I came back here and checked again, because our sights were set on Ken Henderson. Chuck had seen him in the Coast League when Ken was 19 years old.

"At the winter convention, then, Jim Enright—who was covering the meetings for Chicago Today—told me the Giants seemed quite disappointed that the Angels had traded Andy Messersmith to the

51

Dodgers in the Frank Robinson deal. They thought they had Messersmith for Ken Henderson. So that's when I found out he was available. See, I had been trying to trade Stan Bahnsen for Henderson. They kept telling me they would not trade Henderson, but then I detected, in talking to Jerry Donovan, that they wouldn't trade him for Bahnsen. He finally said it would probably take a young pitcher like Tom Bradley.

"So Bradley must've been second on their list behind Messersmith. But I said we couldn't give up Bradley. He'd pitched two years in the major leagues—he'd struck out over 200 batters both years and had won 15 games both years, and it looked like he was going to be a 20-game winner the following year. So I said we'd probably need a pitcher, too, in return. That's when they included Steve Stone, and then we felt that we were making a deal we should make."

The '73 Sox went into the season looking like a good bet to dethrone the A's, who had slipped past the Sox in '72 for the West Division title and then went on to win the World Series. The Sox led the division by five games on May 25 when Henderson, who was hitting .311, slid clumsily into home plate against the Cleveland Indians and suffered damage to knee ligaments. The injury, Sox officials announced, would sideline Ken for "a week to 10 days." Knowledgable fans chuckled, knowing he'd be out at least a month. When he returned in July, he played some left field on a still-gimpy knee but was used mostly as a designated hitter. But he couldn't run, so any groundball with men on base was a sure doubleplay.

Hemond remembered the night of the injury. Henderson was at third, with a runner at first and the slow-footed Ed Herrmann at bat. Herrmann hit what appeared to be a sure single to right, but Indian first baseman Chris Chambliss backhanded the ball nicely. Then, he threw to the plate to nail Henderson. "Actually," said Hemond, "I thought Chambliss could've thrown the ball to second to start an easy doubleplay—Herrmann, after all, was the batter. And I think that's what upset Henderson, threw him off. It was a surprise play at the plate, and he went into an awkward slide, a late slide, and he twisted his knee. Then we had some other injuries, and Allen broke his leg and was lost for the season. It was really disappointing."

The disappointment continued into 1974 and '75. "I think Dick

Allen lost some of his enthusiasm because of what had happened in '73, because it was a big disappointment to him. He had wanted to be with a winner and he had come so close in '72. Then, too, some of the other players weren't performing up to their capabilities. Bill Melton had undergone a back operation and he wasn't swinging the bat with the same abandon. Ken Henderson's injury took something away from him, also. (He hit only .251 in '75 after a big year in '74.) So there was a decline in performance. I don't blame the fans for getting down on us. We were no longer providing the same excitement."

Hemond, though, kept trying to provide excitement with his deals. His 1974 acquisition of Cub great Ron Santo—in exchange for Stone, Ken Frailing, Steve Swisher, and a minor league pitcher, Jim Kremmel—caused lots of it, even though it never did pan out. And it was Hemond who did pull off another deal that will go down as one of the all-time steals in Sox history when he sent Bahnsen and minor league lefty Skip Pitlock to Oakland June 15, 1975 for reliever Dave Hamilton and a 20-year-old third baseman by the name of Chester Earl Lemon, who was then playing for Oakland's Tucson farm club.

"I think overall, in terms of longevity, the Lemon deal will prove to be the best deal," Hemond agreed. "If he stays healthy, he should have a long and fine career. And actually, Hamilton gave us a very fine second half of the season when we first acquired him. That's when he pitched his best ball for us.

"One deal that no one seemed to look at as a deal—and I under-stand why, because it was a waiver purchase—was the acquisition of Jim Kaat. Yet that was a much more complicated waiver transaction than anybody realized. This was in August of '73, when we'd had all the injuries and we'd pretty much fallen out of the race. We were about 13 games back. I had to go to our league's summer meeting in Milwaukee. The deal was complicated because Jim Kaat had been in the majors for 10 years and the last five with Minnesota, so he was under the 10-5 rule, which was basically a new rule. And there had never been a player that waivers had been requested on under the 10-5 rule. (The rule states that a player who has been in the majors for 10 years and the last five with the same club can veto a trade if he doesn't approve.)

"So we put in a claim on Jim, and two clubs that were ahead of us in

53

the standings—Kansas City and the Yankees—also put claims in on him. Now I was trying to find out whether or not Kaat would still be awarded to us as the lower club, which is the normal case on waivers, if the team doesn't withdraw the waivers. But if a player's a 10-5 man, what is the determination? There had never been a case like it yet. Does he say, 'I'm not going to go to that club—I'm going to the other team.' Or does he have to remain with his team if he doesn't accept the lower club's claim? That's what I was trying to determine. What the ruling turned out was that if Kaat hadn't accepted assignment to us, he would've had to remain with Minnesota.

"But at the time, I got a lot of phone calls. Being 13 games behind in August, I had to do quite a selling job to explain why we picked up a 35-year-old pitcher. And I was very proud of Jim. He joined us, pitched a shutout his first start against Detroit, finished the year 4-1 with us, then won 21 games the next year and 20 the next. Then we traded Jim to Philadelphia for Alan Bannister, Dick Ruthven, and Roy Thomas. Then we traded Ruthven with Ken Henderson to Atlanta for Ralph Garr and Larvell Blanks. Then we traded Blanks to Cleveland for Jack Brohamer. So for the $25,000 waiver price, we got 45 victories, and three players."

I mentioned how odd it was that Kaat, at age 42, was still pitching, while one of Roland's former pitchers, Bart Johnson, was through at age 29. "I really thought Bart Johnson was going to be a Cy Young award winner. I thought he was on his way to accomplishing that in 1971, when he had that great year in relief. He threw the ball past Frank Robinson, Harmon Killebrew, Boog Powell—all of them. And then we had a play in Oakland where Mike Epstein and Bart got into a fight and Epstein really twisted Bart all to pieces. That winter, he was shooting baskets and his knee gave out—and the next year, he wasn't able to push off the rubber. A lot of people misunderstood Bart. But he had torn some knee cartilage.

"I remember in spring training of '74, he threatened to quit and go sell tickets for the Chicago Fire football team. Then he came back and we sent him to our club in Des Moines. I saw him pitch against Oklahoma City, and he got knocked out in about the sixth inning—Tommie Smith hit an opposite-field home run, a high flyball to left. And I got excited about it. I said, 'Oh, he's got it back,' Second

54

game, Jim Kern pitched for Oklahoma City—a real fireballer. And Bart's velocity was right with Kern's. And I came back and told Chuck Tanner, 'Bart's almost got it back.' We sent Fred Shaffer to look at him the next time out and he said, 'Bart's ready.'

'He came up the first Sunday in July at Detroit and pitched a two-hitter. Norm Cash hit an opposite-field homer for their only run. He wound up 10-4, and he was like a machine out there. He'd put that hard slider right there on the corner. He looked great. Then he hurt his back the next spring and missed the whole season. That was unfortunate. That was sad. The next year ('76) we didn't have a good club, yet I felt he pitched decently.

"He was misunderstood and he had a lot of tough breaks. If it hadn't been for the injuries, he would've been a big, big winner."

When Johnson went on the shelf in '72, the Sox had Terry Forster, the smoke-balling lefty, ready to take his place. And, thanks to Hemond's connections with Mexican baseball officials (which also enabled the Sox to get first crack at Jorge Orta and Francisco Barrios), there was help for Forster, too: a tiny but hard-throwing righthander named Cecilio "Cy" Acosta, who replaced Johnson on the roster early in June when Bart was placed on the disabled list. A Sunday double-header with the Yankees was already in progress when Acosta finally arrived at Comiskey Park.

"Acosta got off the plane in the morning after flying all night from Tucson," Hemond remembered. "He couldn't speak any English, couldn't get into the ballpark. Finally somebody brought him upstairs and said, 'This must be your missing pitcher.' That day he came into the second game in the ninth inning before 51,000 people. He got out of the inning and Allen hit the three-run pinch homer off Sparky Lyle to make him the winning pitcher.

"He didn't pitch again until the next Sunday. He pitched the ninth inning again and struck out Dave May, George Scott, and Johnny Briggs. Then Carlos May hit a triple to win it. And there were 36,000 people there THAT day. So in his first two games, he won two ball-games and pitched before 87,000 people. And everyone was saying, 'Where'd he come from?' "

It wasn't long before they were saying, "Where did he go?" Acosta had an excellent year in '73, when the Sox started using Forster as a starter. Acosta was 10-6 (with an ERA of 2.23) with 18 saves that season, but developed arm trouble and drifted out of the big leagues by 1975. I always thought it was because little Cy was overworked. Hemond seemed to agree.

"He pitched winter ball in Mexico," he said. "The guy was pitching every night. I was down there and I talked to his manager and said, 'Hey, take it easy on him—you'll ruin him.' He said, 'All right, I won't use him as much.' That same night, that manager was fired. Next night, I'm driving through Mexico, listening to the radio, and Acosta comes into the game in the seventh inning for his new manager. I started worrying right away. It was just too much strain."

Hemond went through a period of mental strain late in 1975, after John Allyn sold the club to Bill Veeck's syndicate. "People were coming up to me at the winter meetings at Hollywood, Fla., asking 'I heard you're getting Alan Bannister.' I told them, 'I can't say anything. I don't know where we're going to play. The team may be moved to Seattle. I don't even know if I'm going to have a job.' "

Veeck, however, kept Hemond on the job, thanks in part—oddly enough—to a tip from Frank Lane. "I told Bill, 'You better not let Roland get away,' " Lane told me. " 'You've been away for 14 years. Roland knows where the bodies are.' " And Hemond joined his new boss to set up a "trading post" in the hotel lobby the final day of the meetings and the pair combined to complete four separate trades just before the interleague trading deadline.

"We made four deals in the final hour and 15 minutes of the convention," Roland smiled, remembering the acquisitions of Ralph Garr, Jack Brohamer, Clay Carroll, and Buddy Bradford. "That was exhilarating—real joy. Conventioneers were cheering. It was great. Like show biz. And people who frowned on it at the time now tell me, 'Hey, that was great.' "

Not that Hemond always made the deals he wanted to make. "I was hoping to get Andy Messersmith when I first came here, but I wasn't able to swing it," he said. "Then Doug Griffin, the second baseman. I was hoping very much to bring him here. Chuck had managed him at Hawaii. He suffered some injuries. He had a back injury and he was beaned by Nolan Ryan, so the true Doug Griffin never came out. But I know the fans would have loved him here. Excellent fielder, could steal a base. A good, tough, young ballplayer.

"I tried to get some assurance from Dick Walsh, general manager of the Angels, even when I came here to be interviewed by Stu Holcomb, that he wouldn't trade Griffin without giving us a chance. He ended up trading him to the Red Sox in the Tony Conigliaro deal—and I don't blame him. At the time, he couldn't wait for us and I don't think we had the right ingredients to deal for him, anyway. But that was quite a disappointment.

"Then we tried to get him right after he'd gone to Boston—instead of Mike Andrews in the Aparicio deal. But they had just traded for Griffin and they had expounded about his ability and they'd played up the fact that they were so happy to get him—and they'd just given up Conigliaro, who'd been a big favorite in Boston. So they weren't going to trade him. But he would've been a real asset to us and maybe he wouldn't have had the injuries with us that he had in Boston."

But Roland Hemond's biggest disappointment in Chicago hasn't been his failure to acquire Doug Griffin. It's been the failure to be a part of a championship organization here. He's had thrills, to be sure. Like the first three games of the '71 season, when his newly rebuilt White Sox swept a doubleheader at Oakland and then came home to beat the defending West Division champion Minnesota Twins in the home opener in front of 44,250. And the final weekend of July, 1977, when Richie Zisk, Oscar Gamble, Eric Soderholm, Chet Lemon, and the rest of the South Side Hitmen beat Kansas City's Royals three out of four at Comiskey Park before crowds of 45,919 and 33,945 and 50,412 to extend their lead in the West to 5½ games. And there was the entire '72 season, when Richie Allen provided so many magic moments.

"Allen, it's true, in 1972 gave me just as many thrills as any player ever did in one single year," Hemond said. "And I was with the Braves during the '50s with Aaron and Mathews and the like as assistant farm director. Naturally, those years brought great thrills and this is what you keep striving to attain again. You try to explain to people the tremendous exhilaration and thrill that you get out of winning the world championship. First winning the pennant in '57 with Aaron's home run off Billy Muffett to clinch it. And then to beat the Yankees in seven games and to do it in Yankee Stadium. The heroics and the fanfare. And the parade in Milwaukee.

"This is what you hope to be a part of here again in Chicago."

He is not, to be certain, the only person in this city harboring such hopes. And now that Veeck is gone and Hemond can be his own man again, perhaps he will be able to help bring those hopes to fulfillment.

PAUL RICHARDS:
The Wizard of Waxahachie

There is no question that the White Sox ceased to be chronic losers the moment Frank Lane signed Paul Richards to manage them for the 1951 season. Lane and Chuck Comiskey were showing the former big league catcher around Comiskey Park the day of the signing when Richards spotted a placard on the wall outside the Sox clubhouse. The sign, in old English lettering, read: "Be a good loser."

That was enough to anger the new manager, brought in by Lane from Seattle of the Pacific Coast League. He ripped the sign off the wall and threw it into the nearest trash can. "The housecleaning starts right here," he muttered. "If you're a good loser, you keep on losing."

And Richards would have none of that. The new Sox manager, who had first gained prominence as an ambidextrous pitcher for a brilliant high school baseball team in his hometown of Waxahachie, Tex., and later built successful minor league managing records at places like Atlanta and Buffalo, quickly turned the White Sox into winners. The Sox, after losing 94 games in 1950, led the league for 34 days the next season, a 14-game winning streak enabling them to take over the top spot May 31 and hold on till the all-star break.

Then, in a July 12 twilight-night doubleheader, the Sox lost twice to

Paul Richards in the dugout during the 1976 season.

Boston—the second game going 17 innings, with losing pitcher Saul Rogovin going the distance. The twin defeat, even though followed up the next night by a 19-inning victory over the Red Sox, ended the Sox' stay in first place. Chicago, 36-14 at one point, ran out of gas and wound up fourth, 17 games behind the first-place Yankees.

Still, strides had been made, and the White Sox had begun a 17-year period of successive first-division finishes. Richards, more than anyone else, had been responsible for the sudden progress, though he seemed hesitant to accept the credit when I called him at his home in Waxahachie.

"We just learned pretty quickly that our players needed a little bit better knowledge of baseball," he said, remembering his first Sox training camp in Pasadena, Cal. "Once they gained that knowledge, they just automatically became better. It was a matter of knowledge and showing them what they were doing wrong—and that once they would correct those things, it would help us win ballgames."

He got them to win 20 ballgames out of 27 during the exhibition season, but the talent available to him wasn't the greatest around. There was Nellie Fox, a young second baseman who had hit only .247 and had experienced difficulty making the doubleplay the year before. There was no standout catcher—only oldtimer Phil Masi and Gus Niarhos, a 160-pounder who hit .103 for the Red Sox one year and blasted one home run in his entire nine-year major league career. There was no outstanding pitching, although young Billy Pierce had shown promise in '50 and 34-year old Joe Dobson—acquired from Boston in a winter trade—figured to add an experienced arm to the staff.

On the plus side, there was outfielder Al Zarilla, also picked up from Boston in that winter deal. Zarilla, who had hit .325 in '50, was counted on to supply punch in support of long-ball hitters Eddie Robinson and Gus Zernial. And there was the league's top rookie of the season before, shortstop Chico Carrasquel. But there were question marks in center field—where rookie Jim Busby, competing with Dave Philley, was destined to become a Richards favorite—and at third base, where veterans Floyd Baker and Hank Majeski were battling for the starting job.

Richards was concerned, too, about another problem: a lack of speed. Zernial, Zarilla, Robinson, et al., were not exactly rabbits.

61

Carrasquel and Fox could run some, and Busby was a 9.8 sprinter. But overall the club still couldn't play the running game that Richards knew he'd have to play to compete successfully in a big ballpark like Comiskey. So it was that Richards kept telling Lane to continue his pursuit of a swift Cuban named Orestes "Minnie" Minoso, who was opening the season on Cleveland's bench but who the year before had hit .339 with 40 doubles and 10 triples for San Diego in the Pacific Coast League—in full view of an admiring Paul Richards.

"I'd seen him in the Coast League the year before," Paul recalled. He also recalled how Minoso had played third base, right field, and left field—none of them too well. "Frank Lane said, 'He can't play anything.' I said, 'Don't worry about him playing anything—I'll find a place for him. We'll just let him hit and run.' "

So Lane kept plugging away. He'd already offered Cleveland one of his lefthanded pitchers, Bill Wight, in exchange for Minoso and pitcher Steve Gromek. That had been at the winter meetings, and the Indians turned that one down, asking instead for Pierce. There the negotiations stalled, Lane having no burning desire to part with his best lefthander. Now, Lane would renew the quest.

Meanwhile, the Sox had opened the regular season by clobbering the St. Louis Browns, 17-3. Richards' opening day lineup read: Carrasquel, ss; Baker, 3b; Zarilla, rf; Zernial, lf; Robinson, 1b; Masi, c; Busby, cf; Fox, 2b; Pierce, p. The same group, with Randy Gumpert pitching instead of Pierce, knocked off Detroit 5-0 in the home opener, punctuated by Busby's theft of second and third on successive pitches and an ensuing perfect suicide squeeze bunt by Gumpert.

Then the team stalled some, holding at 8-8 on the last day of April. But then Lane announced his three-team deal with Cleveland and Philadelphia. Richards finally had his man. Minoso came to Chicago, as did outfielder Paul Lehner from the A's. The deal cost the Sox Zernial—who'd hit a team-record 29 homers the season before—and Philley, who'd driven home 80 runs in '50. But neither of them had the speed and potential brilliance of Minnie.

Immediately, Richards put him in the starting lineup at third base for a Tuesday afternoon game against the visiting Yankees. With one out in the bottom of the first, Lehner singled. Up stepped Minnie,

Chicago's first black ballplayer, to face New York ace Vic Raschi. Raschi's first pitch was ripped over the bullpen fence in center, 415 feet from home plate. The White Sox, and their fans, had an instant hero.

"After the game," Richards remembered, "the sportswriters gathered in the clubhouse and stormed him for an interview. He couldn't speak hardly any English at all then, and Luis Aloma, the relief pitcher, was his interpreter. They asked a lot of questions and Aloma relayed them to Minnie. Finally one of the guys asked, 'Don't you think it's gonna be hard to play major league baseball if you can't speak any English?

"So Aloma relayed the question and Minnie answered in English: 'Ball, bat, glove—she no speak English.' "

With the hard-charging Minoso leading the way with his hitting and base-stealing, the suddenly brash White Sox whipped off 20 victories in 24 games. Minoso and Busby, whenever they reached base, were threats to steal—causing Sox fans to begin a chant of "Go! Go!" that rocked the ballpark and along with it the opposing pitcher's nerves. Soon the chant went up whenever any of the White Sox got on base. They stole 99 bases that year, an unheard-of figure in those days. They were now the "Go-Go Sox," and Richards had the kind of running team he had always wanted.

There were other reasons for the Sox' surge to the top. Like Rogovin, whom Richards had managed at Buffalo and who had been acquired from Detroit in mid-May for lefty Bob Cain. Rogovin would finish the year as the league's earned-run average champion. The day after they grabbed Rogovin, Richards and Lane picked up third baseman Bob Dillinger from Pittsburgh on waivers. Dillinger, a lifetime .306 hitter, had led the American League in stolen bases in '47, '48, and '49 and thus fit in nicely with Richards' running game.

But although the Sox kept running all year, their amazing early-season hitting fell off and the pitching staff had not yet reached the point it would eventually reach in subsequent seasons under Richards and pitching coach Ray Berres. Still, the team was only 3½ games behind first-place New York and Boston when it arrived at Yankee Stadium for the opener of a four-game weekend series July 27. Trailing 3-1 in the ninth inning of the Friday night opener, before 50,125 people and under threatening skies, the White Sox finally got going.

Eddie Robinson led with a single and Joe DeMaestri went in to run for him. Eddie Stewart walked, and then Floyd Baker batted for Busby and singled to right, driving in a run. That made it 3-2. Then came a 26-minute delay caused not only by showers but by arguments resulting when the umpires tossed New York's Gil McDougald out of the game for what they felt were stalling tactics. The rains had started and McDougald, no dummy, was trying his best to drag things out. Yankee manager Casey Stengel told the umps he was playing the game under protest, but helped delay matters himself by waving in one of the five pitchers he ended up using that inning (starter Tom Morgan, Joe Ostrowski, Frank Shea, Jack Kramer, and Eddie Lopat).

When play finally resumed, Dillinger batted for rookie catcher Bud Sheely and tried to bunt the runners over to second and third, but failed, Stewart being forced out at third. Now there were runners at first and second with one out. Don Lenhardt was sent up to hit for Carrasquel and the big outfielder walked to load the bases. Another pinch-hitter, Bert Haas, then batted for Pierce and singled in the tying and go-ahead runs. Then, after a walk to Fox filled the bases again, the rains came. But Richards wasn't too concerned. At first, anyway.

"The umpires said they'd hold it for three or four hours and try to get it in," he recalled. "And then they waited exactly 30 minutes and called it."

So the score reverted back to what it had been after eight full innings—3-1—and the Yankees had themselves a tainted victory. The Yankee clubhouse, according to newspaper accounts, was "the scene of wild celebration." Sox players, on the other hand, were furious. Richards was livid.

"I charged into the umpires' dressing room," he remembered. Then he paused, chuckling to himself. "Actually, the first place I went was into Stengel's office—I got it mixed up with the umpires' room. But I finally made it to the umpires' room and gave 'em hell. But they didn't do anything. By the time we left the stadium, the moon was out and the skies were clear. If they'd waited another 30 minutes, we'd have been able to finish the game."

But they didn't and the Sox were now 4½ out instead of 2½ out. All Richards could do was vent his frustration to the sportswriters. "The umpires told me the game would be finished if it took all night," he informed them. "Then they changed their minds. They must all have had dates."

Rain washed out Saturday's game, giving Richards and the Sox more time to brood about what might have been. Unfortunately for the Chicagoans, though, the rains stopped Sunday. The Yankees, with Joe DiMaggio slamming two homers off Lou Kretlow, won the first game of the doubleheader 8-3 and then sent the throng of 70,972 home happy by winning Game Two 2-0 as ex-Sox Bob Kuzava two-hitted Chicago and Rogovin. Now the gap was 6½ games and the White Sox were down for the count.

Richards' second year in Chicago didn't start out as well as the first one had and in early May of '52, Lane tried to stir things up by sending Busby, the fleet centerfielder who had hit .283 and stolen 26 bases in '51, to Washington for longball hitter Sam Mele. "Over my violent protests," Richards told me. "I was violently against that deal. I didn't think we were getting enough back and I knew you needed a strong centerfielder in Chicago.

"The only thing that saved our lives later was that we were able to get Jim Rivera from the Browns in late July. Or otherwise we'd have been in really bad shape."

As it was, Rivera played center well enough to enable the Sox to climb to third in '52. Then Lane annoyed Richards even more by trading Paul's fellow Texan, Robinson, to the A's for the league's two-time defending batting champ, Ferris Fain—who turned into a .256 hitter in Chicago.

"That was another deal where we gave up too much," sighed Richards. " 'Cause we gave 'em Joe DeMaestri and another young centerfielder (Ed McGhee) plus Robinson for Fain, and Fain came over and he was a washout for us. That was another deal Lane shoved down my throat.

"After some of those deals, it developed that Mrs. Comiskey said Frank couldn't make any more deals without my permission."

If Lane sometimes angered Richards with his trades, Richards sometimes pained Frank with his innovative managerial methods. One of Paul's favorite moves was putting pitchers at third or first base so a reliever could be brought in to pitch to a certain hitter—after which

65

the original pitcher would return to the mound to finish the game. It worked sometimes, like in Boston in '51 when Harry Dorish moved to third while Pierce was called in to retire Ted Williams. Dorish then moved back to pitch the remainder of the inning and gain the victory.

But it didn't always go so well. "One time we're playing in Cleveland," Lane told me. "It was in May and colder than blue hell. We got a run in the top of the 13th and Richards brought in Jack Harshman (a lefty) to pitch to Larry Doby (a lefthanded hitter). And he moved Sandy Consuegra, who had been pitching, to third base. And Sandy's trying to play third base with a jacket on. But the umpire made him take the jacket off."

Harshman walked Doby and Richards went out, yanked Harshman, and brought Consuegra back to pitch to righthanded hitting Wally Westlake. "Sandy had already struck this guy out two or three times in the game. But the umpire wouldn't let Sandy warm up again. And this guy proceeds to hit one into the upper deck with a man on, and we lose. That was the last of that kind of maneuvering.

"The year before that, in '53, we're playing in New York and Billy Pierce is pitching. Richards put Billy over at first base in the eighth inning—we're ahead 5-2—and he brought in Dorish to face a couple righthanded hitters, McDougald and Bauer. Now McDougald hits a ball down the third-base line and our third baseman throws the ball to the home-plate side of first base, and Billy had to come out to get the throw—right in the baseline. Well, McDougald avoided him. But if that had been Bauer, Bauer would've cut his leg off. Bauer was known for that.

"Well, we won the game, and later Richards said, "Well, what did ya think of that?' I said, 'You really want to know? Let's wait until we get into your office.' We get there, and he says, 'That must've had 'em laughin' in Waxahachie. That must've had 'em rollin' in the aisles in Buffalo.' I said, 'We came damn near to losing a million-dollar pitcher.' 'What do ya mean?' I said, 'If that had been Bauer running instead of McDougald, Bauer would've cut his leg off.'

"He looked at me and said, 'Well, I knew that'd be too deep for you.' "

Despite their occasional bickering, however, Lane and Richards proved a successful team. Richards got the Sox up to 89 victories in

1953 and the team was 91-54 on Sept. 14, 1954 when he announced he was leaving Chicago immediately to accept a dual role as field manager and general manager of the Baltimore Orioles. Paul's decision was not necessarily made because he believed the Go-Go Sox to be slowing down. "At that time, we were still building and the Yankees were in the midst of their dynasty and Cleveland had a real good club. We were not really quite good enough. But I didn't think the Sox were goin' downhill. They were goin' good. I just wanted a three-year contract."

That security was not granted, but apparently not because Mrs. Grace Comiskey, the club president, no longer wanted Richards around. Rather, it seems, vice-president Chuck Comiskey no longer wanted Richards around. "Lane sent Chuck Comiskey over to see Mrs. Comiskey, to see if she'd OK it (the three-year contract for Richards)," Paul told me. "He comes back later in the day and says, 'No, she wouldn't.' "

So Richards set his eyes on Baltimore, heading East to build up the league's seventh-place team. On his way, he discovered some interesting news. "We found out that Chuck hadn't even gone to see Mrs. Comiskey," said Richards. "So that's one of the reasons she had her falling out with Chuck."

It's also one of the reason why the Lane-Comiskey feud became hotter, too. But for Richards, all that was in the past. He would go on to build a winner in Baltimore, just as he had in Chicago. He would leave the Orioles late in the 1961 season to return to his native Texas to get the new Houston franchise off the ground. He would later answer friends' calls to aid in the development of the Atlanta Braves. Within two years, the Braves—under the managerial reins of Richards' longtime assistant, Luman Harris—would reach the National League playoffs.

And then, in 1976, he answered the call of another friend, Bill Veeck, who had returned to baseball as president of the White Sox. Richards, then 67 years old, agreed to manage Veeck's team, which didn't have much save young pitchers like Rich Gossage, Bart Johnson, Terry Forster, Pete Vuckovich, and Francisco Barrios. Yet Richards' young team ran off a 10-game winning streak in May—25 years after his first Sox team had run off that 14-game streak—and

67

was five games above .500 by the second weekend in June. Then, on a Friday night in Cleveland, Forster gave up a two-out, two-run pinch homer to Indians' player-manager Frank Robinson in the last of the 11th to turn a 4-3 victory into a 5-4 defeat. From that point on, the Sox were 37-75, finishing last in the West Division with a 64-97 record.

Some years later, Richards told Bob Verdi of the *Chicago Tribune*, "If there was a league in this nation that that ('76) team could have won in, it has not been brought to my attention. And that includes the Little League." Apparently Paul hadn't been fooled by that early-season success. "Ralph Garr was in left field, so that meant that every flyball hit that way was an adventure movie.

"Francisco Barrios, at that time, was just a big kid from Mexico. Had one fella who always dressed pretty and wore an earring. Coggins. Rich Coggins was his name. Never quite could play, but he sure did have some nice clothes."

Richards' sense of humor helped make the '76 season easier to take. At all-star break, when writers asked him if he was looking forward to the second half, he opened his calendar to October, where he had the last day of the season circled with a black magic marker. "That's the day I'm looking forward to," he told them matter-of-factly.

Once, after an Oakland rookie named Paul Mitchell shut out the Sox on the West Coast, Bay Area reporters asked Richards if he had been impressed by the youngster's performance. Paul, mindful that the Sox were well on their way to being blanked 21 times that season, replied, "I'd have to see him pitch against someone else. Shuttin' us out is no big deal."

And it was no big deal when Richards went to Veeck at season's end and told him he wanted out of the manager's job. Bill simply hired Bob Lemon to manage and made Richards director of player development. It was a task Richards took seriously, helping to expedite the maturation of such young pitchers as Britt Burns, Steve Trout, Richard Dotson, Ross Baumgarten, and others. He was also the person most responsible for the signing of minor-league prospects like centerfielder Cecil Espy, big first baseman Wesley Kent, catcher Ricky Seilheimer, and second baseman Tim Hulett—names that could be big ones on the South Side before too many years go by.

So thirty years on 35th Street began with Richards in '51 and ended with his departure in the wake of Veeck's sale of the White Sox to Jerry Reinsdorf and Eddie Einhorn in January '81. But he left with words of hope:

"With proper financial support and with the nucleus that they have right now," he said to me, "there's no reason why the White Sox can't be a contender within a couple years."

If, and when, that happens, White Sox fans had better be thankful for Paul Richards.

MARTY MARION:
A pinch-hitter for Nellie Fox

Marty Marion led the way into the lounge of the Stadium Club in St. Louis, overlooking the playing field of Busch Memorial Stadium. "So what is this for, a book or something?" he asked, as he found my wife and me a table.

"Yeah, a book on the White Sox," I replied.

He looked at me with a grin. "Hey, don't waste your time on that. Why don't you write a book on the Cardinals?"

First and foremost, Marty Marion is a Cardinal. He's a lot of other things, too. He is a millionaire. He is president of Embassy Investments, a land-holding company that has all sorts of property and farms in central Illinois. He is one of the owners of the Stadium Club itself. He is on the board of directors of the second-largest savings and loan association in St. Louis.

But above all he is a Cardinal.

He spent 11 years as their all-star shortstop, starting in 1940. He led them to a third-place finish in 1951 as a 33-year-old rookie manager. He played in four World Series for them and represented them in five all-star games. So it's easy to see why Marty still thinks Cardinal when you talk baseball with him.

Marty Marion making a point during spring training, 1956, in Tampa.

But Marion managed the White Sox between the Richards years and the Lopez years and got the team closer to a pennant than Richards ever did. The ready smile becomes a slight frown when he recalls that near-magic year of 1955, his first full season on the Sox job after taking over for Richards in September of '54. "We had a nice team. Too bad we couldn't have won it. We'd have won that thing if it hadn't been for Donovan—if ol' Tricky Dick hadn't gotten appendicitis on me."

Donovan was stricken on July 30, when the Sox were in first place and when his record stood at 13-4, his earned run average at 2.70. He missed three weeks. He came back, all right, but his post-operative record was 2-5, his post-operative ERA 5.07. Even with a different Donovan, the Sox led the league going into September, but sloppy play on a two-week eastern road trip cost them the championship.

"Donovan, I guess, was the big story of that year," said Marion. "We'd picked him up from Atlanta (then a Milwaukee Brave farm club). He'd been up with the Boston Braves and with Detroit and hadn't gotten much of a chance and they'd sent him back down. So I remember our first series in Kansas City, in April, and Dick was getting knocked around pretty bad. And I came out to take him out and he wouldn't give me the ball. See, he remembered those other times. He was so afraid he wasn't gonna get another chance. I said, 'Now Dick, don't worry. I guarantee you you'll get another start in five more days.' So he finally gave me the ball."

Sure enough, Marion started him against Boston five days later and Donovan came through with a four-hit, 7-0 victory in Comiskey Park for his first big league triumph. Donovan's success in Marion's first year as Sox manager, though, was offset by the dull season turned in by Minnie Minoso, who was hitting only .254 with two homers and 28 RBI at the all-star break in mid-July. A 23-game hitting streak in August got him up to a .288 finish with 70 RBI, but it was not a typical Minoso year.

"Minnie was always talking RBIs—you know, you hit third or fourth, you think RBIs," said Marion. "I don't know what happened but, you know, you change lineups to try to get something happening. Anyway, I had him lead off. And we started winning. And he'd come into my office every day, complaining that he didn't like to lead off—

72

he wanted those RBIs. But I kept him in there quite a while because we were winning with him leading off. And we'd argue about it every day."

Marion had begun paging through a 1955 yearbook I had brought along. "Billy Pierce—the first year I pitched him only about once a week," he remembered, recalling how the prize lefty was slowly coming back from arm trouble the year before. "And he'd get his complete rest and he was tough." So tough was Pierce that he led the league in earned run average and won 15 games. One of the victories came in the second game of a late August doubleheader against the Yankees in Comiskey Park. The Yankees had won the first game and, though trailing 3-2 in this one, had put runners on first and second with two out against Pierce in the seventh.

Hank Bauer was due up. Out strolled Marion. He took the ball from Pierce and called in reliever Dixie Howell. Pierce received a thunderous ovation as he departed, but those same 50,990 customers booed Marion lustily as he walked back toward the Sox dugout. "Billy was the fair-haired boy in Chicago then," Marty remembered, "and I recall John Carmichael telling me later, 'Boy, you've sure got a lot of guts taking him out in a situation like that.' But here's what happened: Bauer hit a shot to left, right at Minnie, to end the inning. And that saved my life."

Earlier that same week, Marion had caused the Comiskey faithful to question his sanity when, with two out in the bottom of the ninth and the Sox behind Baltimore 2-1 with the tying run at third base, Marion called back Nellie Fox and sent up seldom-used utility infielder Bobby Adams to pinch-hit. The Oriole pitcher was Bill Wight, a lefty. Adams, a righthanded hitter, had the percentage going with him, Marty figured. But Adams was also hitting .095. Fox was an established .300 hitter. The crowd let Marion know how it felt. It let him know even more boisterously moments later when Adams struck out to end the game.

"But when I was managing," said Marion, "I could care less what your record was. I played to win a baseball game. I didn't care if you were hitting .350. If I didn't think you could hit that particular pitcher, I would take you out. Like with Lou Brock here in St. Louis. Brock is trying to get 3,000 hits (which he finally did accomplish, chalking up

No. 3,000 against his first big league team, the Cubs). But it's a very difficult situation. It's difficult to try to make records for individuals and also be a good manager and win ballgames—which is what you're paid for."

He turned the page of the '55 yearbook. "Chico Carrasquel. I could never get him to hustle. Chico was always complaining about being hurt. He was hurt, I guess, sometimes. But he wasn't a fiery-type ballplayer. He was lazy. He was never the shortstop for me that they say he was for Richards. Chico wasn't a bad guy but he just didn't put out like I thought he should. He was a methodical ballplayer." (Marty sent Chico and Jim Busby to Cleveland for Larry Doby that winter.)

Marion's eyes focused on Jim Rivera's page. "Ol' Jungle Jim. He had just fair ability—never a great ballplayer—but he got a lot out of it. But I gave him a lot of tough times. I was on him a lot. He'd kinda loaf around on me. I had to jack him up all the time."

Sherman Lollar was next. "Sherm was my assistant manager. You'd walk out to the mound and you'd look in Sherm's eyes and you knew whether the pitcher had anything or not. I made a lot of my decisions on Sherm's comments—and his looks." On the next page was Walt Dropo, looking fearsome with his big bat. "Good ol' Moose," Marty grinned. "You always figured he could do more than he did. He wasn't the greatest fielder in the world, wasn't the greatest runner in the world. But he had power. And really, in his own heart, I suppose, he gave you all he had."

Leafing through the rest of the book, Marion would pause occasionally. He turned to George Kell, who led the '55 club in hitting (.312) and runs-batted-in (81). There was Bob Nieman, and Jim Brideweser. "Jim game me a hard time. He wanted to play. I told him, 'You play for two weeks and you get so tired you can't even lift the bat up.' But he did a good job for me. . . . Connie Johnson was so wild you could never depend on him. He could throw hard—very hard. Probably a 90 m.p.h. fastball . . . Dixie Howell was our best relief pitcher in '55."

The discussion of Howell, who as a rookie at age 35 won eight games in relief and saved 13 others after joining the Sox in June, brought back memories of another oldster whom Marion picked up for relief work a year later—righthander Ellis Kinder, born 42 years earlier in an Arkansas town called Atkins. "Yeah, he was 42 years old, but he had a good arm," said Marty, a smile beginning to form. "And he kinda liked his booze a little bit. I'll tell you one thing: When I'd call down to the bullpen to find out how he was feeling, I said, 'If he's sleeping on the bench down there, and it looks like he's got a hang-over, send him in.' He was always good when he'd been drinking.' "

And even though Marion was four years Kinder's junior, the manager had no problem handling the veteran pitcher. "You don't really tell him what to do," Marion said. "All you do is bring him in and take him out. He knew that although you had certain rules on the club, like no carousing, you knew damn well he wasn't gonna pay any attention to 'em. But as long as he pitched for me, I didn't bother him."

That pretty much was the Marion method of handling veterans. "When you have a curfew, the only guys you want to be strict with are the young guys. You don't want the young boys to get away with anything and start getting bad habits. Older guys you don't really worry about too much as long as they're producing. Now if they've been out carousing all night and they're tired and it shows in their play, then they're hurting the ballclub. That's when I'd shackle 'em. We caught a few of 'em. We fined a few guys."

Marty was all set to fine four of his players after a beer bash in Baltimore early in '55, but the four turned out to be five. Marion walked into the clubhouse the day after the bash and said, simply, "Those four guys who were out after curfew last night, I want you in my office right now." Four players arrived after a few minutes. "That'll cost each of you $200," Marion began. Suddenly the office door opened and a fifth player, Clint Courtney, sheepishly stepped inside. Clint apparently hadn't seen who had entered Marion's office. "That'll be $200 for you, too, Courtney," Marty announced. "I can't help it if you're so dumb that you can't count to four."

So Marion surprised many of his critics, who had figured Marty would be the same nice guy as a manager he had been as a player. His own players, many of whom had known him as their first-base coach under Richards in '54, were a bit shocked, too. So were the umpires. "They thought I'd gotten too tough," he grinned. "I was an easy-going ballplayer, you know. Never argued with the umpires or anything. When I was managing, I'd argue with the umpires and they thought that was terrible.

"But you change your personality when you become a manager. You certainly don't want anybody to run over you. So you do things you wouldn't ordinarily do. You lose your temper quicker as a manager than you do as a player. My whole personality changed when I was a manager—for the worse."

That's one of the reasons he left his managerial career behind at age 38—another reason, of course, was the pink slip he would get from Chuck Comiskey and John Rigney, who believed Marion hadn't gotten the most out of his players. Marty was gone after the 1956 season, a season climaxed by a dramatic four-game weekend sweep of the Yankees in late June. The series drew 125,433 to Comiskey Park and the fans saw great pitching by Donovan, Pierce, and Jim Wilson; clutch hitting by Sammy Esposito and Dave Philley; and three king-sized home runs off the bat of Larry Doby. "My biggest thrill in the American League," Marion called it. There would be no more. His two Sox teams finished third both years, going 91-63 in '55 and 85-69 in '56.

"I enjoyed managing, don't get me wrong," he told me. "I enjoyed it very much. But the job of managing . . . your whole outlook on what you're doing personally depends on what 25 guys are doing. That's what I didn't like. I also hated the travel. I'd been in baseball since 1936 and I'd traveled an awful lot. I'd love coming back home here to St. Louis. The reason I got fired in Chicago was whenever we had an off-day, I was always running back here to be with my family. The White Sox didn't like that. And I don't blame them now, looking back. I wasn't there in the office with them, talking baseball. I guess if I had been the owner, I'd feel like they did. But I was always home-sick. I had four daughters and I always wanted to be with them. And I was making good money here, and I didn't really need the baseball job."

At the time, he already had that land along the Illinois River in central Illinois, and that investment was bringing in some good returns. He was also working with a printing firm in St. Louis and receiving a healthy salary there. So it was goodbye to baseball for Marty Marion, at least for the time being. "Of course, now I have the club here," he said. "I'm one of the Stadium Club's 10 owners. But I'm the only one of the 10 who works at it, and they pay me very well to oversee it. But this isn't really a job. It's kind of a fun thing. We have over 4,000 members. I get to see all the ballgames. It's really kept me close to baseball.

"I also do a radio show in St. Louis on KMOX. Been doing it for 15 years. And I've got nine grandchildren. So I'm pretty busy."

And, it seemed, pretty happy.

AL LOPEZ:
The Senor from Tampa

It was early July of 1964, and the White Sox were in their customary spot in the American League standings: second place, three or four games behind the Yankees. It was a Friday night, and my brother and I decided it was safe to drive in and see the Sox play. Safe, we figured, because the Yankees, mercifully, had already left town—having swept four games (1-0 in 11 innings, 2-0, 2-1 in 17 innings and 6-5) from our hitless heroes.

Dick Donovan, the former Sox righthander, was the scheduled pitcher for the visiting Cleveland Indians, which meant that lefty first baseman-outfielder Tommy McCraw—one of the few Sox who had remembered what a bat was for—would be in the lineup for sure. Tommy, in his first full season in the majors, had his average up to .294 according to the weekly averages in the Daily News that afternoon. He was, we all agreed, a kid headed for stardom.

But when the lineups were posted up on the scoreboard, McCraw's number, 14, did not appear. He wasn't injured, we knew. And there had been an off-day the day before, so he couldn't have been tired. Whatever the reason, Joe Cunningham, hitting a robust .248, was going to be that night's first baseman. McCraw would not be playing

Al Lopez charges from the dugout after game-ending doubleplay the night of Sept. 22, 1959—the night the White Sox clinched their first pennant in 40 years. [ASSOCIATED PRESS PHOTO]

79

left field that evening, either. The leftfielder was going to be veteran
Gene Stephens, whose average lagged far behind even Cunningham's
and who was nothing more than someone you put into the game in the
late innings for defense. We wondered, then, if Al Lopez's senses had
left him.

Typically, the game itself droned on and on, three up and three
down in endless monotony. Donovan himself scored the go-ahead run
in the 11th to make it 2-1, but the Sox put two runners on with two
out in the bottom of the inning. J.C. Martin was due up, so we figured
we'd finally see Tommy McCraw. We were right, sort of. Lopez
stunned the crowd by allowing the .190-hitting Martin to bat for himself. My brother and I exchanged bewildered looks. J.C., we knew,
had no more chance of getting a hit in that situation than our father
did. The fans responded with catcalls, aimed more at Lopez than at
Martin. Then, to appease the crowd, it seemed, Lopez sent out
McCraw to the on-deck circle. "You dummy!" a man to my left
shouted, making sure Lopez could hear him. "He's not gonna get a
chance to bat!"

The fan, of course, was right. Martin tapped one of the weakest
rollers I've ever seen back to the mound for the final out of the game.
McCraw turned abruptly and strolled back to the dugout, Lopez
having managed to keep him out of the game. We left in an ugly
mood. As we passed by the players' parking area on the third-base
side of the park, I yelled at the cop on guard, "Which car is Lopez's?"
The cop must have seen the final inning. He responded, "The one with
the bomb under the hood."

That all came back to me as I drove toward Lopez's home on Tampa
Bay. I remembered the feelings I used to have about the most
successful manager the White Sox have ever had. The writers always
wrote about what a genius the friendly Senor was, how brilliant he
must be to have another weak-hitting White Sox team battling for a
pennant again. At the time, I had my doubts. I wondered if Lopez
wasn't just a wee bit overrated, if the Sox shouldn't be winning more
than just the one pennant they would win during Al's term in Chicago.
But by now, having seen what happened to the franchise once he had
departed, I had long since come to the conclusion that, for once, the
writers had been correct.

Lopez was relaxing at poolside, having just taken his daily morning dip. As I approached, I realized that I had never read or heard how the Sox had first acquired his services. I made that my initial question.

"Well," he answered, "I was disappointed in Cleveland."

"Who wouldn't be?" I pointed out, before remembering that here was a man who, in six years as manager of the Indians, had never won fewer than 88 games, had never finished lower than second, and whose team had won a record 111 games in 1954—only to lose the World Series to the New York Giants in four straight games. Why, indeed, the disappointment?

"It started in '55. With two weeks to go, we came home tied for first place and we had a night game with Detroit. We went out to the ballpark and there were 6,000 people in the stands. I thought to myself, 'My God, this doesn't look good. If the fans start getting down on your club, you're gonna be in trouble.' What had actually hurt us was the World Series that we lost. We'd had a great year, won 111 games. When you do that, you haven't had a slump all year. So we go into the World Series, hit a slump, and that was it right there."

Things didn't get any better in '56 as far as Cleveland attendance went, so Lopez, seeing the dark clouds ahead, informed Cleveland president Hank Greenberg that he had had enough—that he was getting out, effective at season's end. The baseball grapevine being what it was, the White Sox quickly learned of Lopez's decision and Chuch Comiskey and John Rigney put one of their operatives to work.

"After I resigned," Lopez recalled, "Hollis Thurston, a White Sox scout, called me from Los Angeles. I remember it was on a Saturday night—the season was over the next day. I hadn't heard from him in quite a while. He and I had been roommates in Brooklyn, real close friends. I was in the hotel lobby, ready to go out to eat, and the desk said, 'Al, you've got a long-distance call.' And it was Thurston. He said, 'Al, I understand you're not going back to Cleveland.' 'No, Hollis, I've already told Hank I'm gonna quit.' 'Would you be interested in managing the White Sox?' 'Hollis, I don't have anything in mind. But what are they gonna do with Marty Marion? I think Marty's got another year to go on his contract.' 'Well, they asked me to call you.' 'Well, you tell them I'd be glad to sit down and talk with them.

"After the season was over, I was home maybe a week to 10 days when I got a call from John Rigney and Chuck Comiskey, asking if I'd want to come up to Chicago to talk to them and to meet Mrs. Comiskey. I said yeah, I would. They told me to catch a plane and come in under an assumed name, so none of the writers would find out. I said, 'John, I don't like to do this—you've got a manager under contract already.' He said, 'Al, whether you come here or not, Marty Marion is through here. We're gonna make a change.' So I flew up to Chicago, they picked me up at the airport, took me over to see Mrs. Comiskey, we talked, I signed, they took me back to the airport, and I flew back down here—all in the same day."

Lopez, though, was still wondering where Marion had gone wrong. "Marty was a good manager and it looked like he had authority. I remember he came into Cleveland one time and wanted to talk to Hank and me about a ballplayer we had, an outfielder named Dave Pope. They were real hot for him for a while. He offered cash and a ballplayer for him. Here's a manager of a club offering something like $100,000 and a ballplayer for one of your players. You figure, 'Hey, Marty's got a lot of say-so.' "

But now it was Lopez who would have the say-so. At spring training in 1957 in Tampa—in the ballpark named for him—he tried to make a third baseman out of outfielder Bubba Phillips and a first baseman out of Jim Rivera—although the Rivera experiment eventually would be shelved and Jungle Jim would return to the outfield. Lopez had been watching the Sox steadily slow down from their Go-Go days of the early '50s and he realized that the club had to start taking more advantage of their huge home park. By putting Phillips and Rivera in the infield, Lopez was adding more speed to the lineup and opening up a spot in the outfield for swift rookie Jim Landis, who in two years would become a main cog in the '59 championship team.

"I enjoyed Landis very much because he improved so much," Lopez said. "I played him even when he was hitting .180 because, for one thing, he had great speed—he was a great outfielder. He wasn't gonna hurt you in the outfield. He could steal a base for you. He had a lot of attributes that were good for a ballclub. The thing he did—he was very choosy at the plate. Like at first, he couldn't make up his mind on pitches, whether or not to pull the trigger. But in a way, it wasn't bad, because he'd draw a lot of bases on balls. And he'd score runs. Another thing I liked about him was, even in batting practice, when he swung at the ball he always made contact. You like to see contact with the ball—and Landis had that."

So Lopez's first Sox team—which led by as many as six games in early June before Sherm Lollar's broken wrist contributed to a fade to second place, eight games back of the Yankees—had Landis, Phillips, Rivera, Nellie Fox, Luis Aparicio, Minnie Minoso, et al., but it also had veteran centerfielder Larry Doby (later a White Sox manager), whom Lopez had traded away from Cleveland two seasons earlier and with whom Al was now stuck in Chicago. As soon as the season was over, Lopez began looking for a place to dump Doby. The dump site turned out to be Baltimore, and with that deal—and deals that followed—Lopez showed that he may have had more say in player transactions than Rigney and Comiskey.

"I always felt that we worked together," Al countered. "But I guess they had confidence in my judgement. They always asked my opinion on deals. Like when the Minoso deal was made, Frank Lane was with Cleveland (as general manager) and we had just made the deal with Baltimore—the Doby deal. (The Sox sent Doby and Jack Harshman to the Orioles with two minor leaguers for pitcher Ray Moore, infielder Billy Goodman, and outfielder Tito Francona.) Frank comes up to our suite at the winter meetings in Colorado Springs, and we'd been up there about six hours trying to work out this deal with Paul Richards and the Baltimore club. And we were sitting around relaxing, having a drink. And we were gonna go outside and get some fresh air, maybe get a bite to eat, and then come back up.

"Lane walks in and says, 'Congratulations, I heard you made a deal.' 'Yeah, we just made a deal with Baltimore.' 'Well,' he says, 'those are just mediocre ballplayers. If you really want to make a deal, let's make a deal for a name ballplayer.' So John Rigney said, 'What do you have in mind, Frank?' 'Well, I'm talking about the Minoso-type—I'm not talking about any second-rate ballplayers.' He was always like that.

"Rigney looked at me, Comiskey did too. Comiskey said, 'What do you have in mind for Minoso?' Lane said, 'Well, would you trade him?' We all looked at each other and Comiskey said, 'Yeah, if it was the right deal, we might be willing to trade Minnie if you like him that much. Who would you give us for Minnie?' Lane said, 'Well, offhand, I'd give you Early Wynn.' We said we couldn't trade Minnie for Early Wynn. Wynn had maybe two-three good years left and Minnie might have five or six. 'Well,' he says, 'wait a minute—I'll put Al Smith in there too.' So Comiskey says, 'Well, Frank, give us a few minutes here. You mind if we go into this other room for a bit to talk it over?'

"So all three of us go in and we sit down and Rigney asks me, 'Well, what do you think, Al.' I said, 'Geez, it's a helluva deal for us, if he'll make it. 'Cause Smitty isn't as good a hitter as Minnie but he's a good ballplayer. We need pitching badly, and Early will win us 15-16 ballgames maybe for a year or two.' (He won 22 in '59 to help win the Sox a pennant.) We needed pitching—our pitching was getting old. So he said, 'Well, let's go make it.' I said, 'Fine, let's go do it.' So we worked together on that deal."

Another one was the trade that brought another key to the '59 pennant—young righthander Bob Shaw. The Sox got Shaw and 33-year-old Ray Boone from the Tigers for pitcher Bill Fischer and Tito Francona on the June 15 trading deadline in '58, but Lopez himself wasn't sure if he really wanted to part with Fischer. "John McHale (Detroit G.M.) called us back after we made the deal and said, 'Al, I know you really like Fischer—you rated him really high. If you'd like, we can do the deal over. Let Boone for Francona stand, but you can have Fischer back and we'll take Shaw back.' I told him I'd call him back after I talked it over with Rigney and Comiskey.

"And I liked Fischer. He was a good bullpen pitcher for us, a real nice guy, a good guy to have on a club. But we decided we needed the good young arm—Shaw was only 25, a big, strong kid and he could throw real good. So I called McHale back and told him we were gonna let the deal stand as made."

The '58 Sox had gotten off to a horrible start (for the White Sox, years ending in 8 have been years that belonged in straitjackets), but they played the best ball in the league over the last three months. So Lopez was his usual overly optimistic self the next spring. And, as usual, the experts made light of that optimism. But Al didn't mind.

"I always said, 'The Yankees can be had.' And I believed it. I've seen great clubs go into a season and things go bad for them and they can get beat. I did it to give the players confidence that I believed the Yankees could be had. And at the same time, you have to consider the public, too. They're paying the money. They don't want to hear the manager saying, 'Aw, the Yankees are too tough.' I think that's the wrong attitude. You're giving up before the season starts. Hell, I wouldn't concede anything to anybody. Let them go out and beat me."

Nobody did in '59, the year Lopez designed his offense around Aparicio's speed. Aparicio had never stolen more than 29 bases in any of his first three years in the majors. Now it was time to turn Looie loose. And the hit-and-run play? Who needed it? "I never was a great believer in the hit-and-run," Al said. "I thought it was more of a defensive play. In all my years in baseball, I can recall only three or four hitters—Billy Herman, a couple others—who were good hit-and-run men. So now you're trying to make everyone else good hit-and-run men. But it's tough enough to hit a good pitch solid, let alone having to swing at the pitcher's pitch—you know, over your head, on the ground, or wherever. And then you miss it, and the guy gets thrown out at second.

"Personally, the way I played it in Chicago, I put Aparicio and Landis and guys like that on their own, and let them steal. Get a jump and steal. And if the first pitch was a strike and they didn't steal, it was just a strike. Sometimes, with Aparicio on, we'd have to put the take sign on for Fox. Nellie was an aggressive hitter, liked to hit everything. We'd have to put the take sign on to give Aparicio a chance to steal. But for the other guys, we wouldn't put the take sign on. Looie was stealing and if the guy swung and got a base hit, Looie would go to third. Or, if he hit a groundball, we'd at least be out of the double-play. But he'd actually be stealing—it wasn't a hit-and-run. I didn't want to send a guy who couldn't get the good jump for stealing because if the batter missed the ball, the guy would be thrown out at second.

"But Aparicio was only thrown out 13 times the year he stole 56 (in '59). So the percentage, with no outs, is to let him steal. Now you have him at second with no outs, and now Nellie can hit, pull the ball, bunt, get him over to third. And a sacrifice fly or something like that and you've got the run."

The run was the all-important item. "That was my theory," said Lopez. "We'll get a run in one way or another. Let them make the mistake. Just don't you make the mistake."

The theory was compromised that winter when Lopez went along with owner Bill Veeck's blueprint for a second straight pennant. The plans called for more power—in newly acquired Minoso, Roy Sievers, and Gene Freese—and less defense: Minoso was erratic as ever in the outfield, Sievers was a designated hitter born 20 years too soon, and Freese, with his wild heaves from third base, was a threat to patrons seated back of first. "We talked the thing over and Bill said, 'Al, if you won with that ('59) club, all we have to do is get a couple pretty good hitters and you can win again.' That was his theory. And I thought we could, if we could get a couple hitters without hurting the rest of the club. But we hurt the rest of the club. And the club just didn't jell the way it should have. There wasn't that closeness."

The 1960 team made a race of it but finished third. Veeck unloaded Freese (Said Bill, "Al told me that he simply wasn't going to play him, so I might as well get rid of the guy") and got a hard-throwing young lefty, Juan Pizarro, in return. But the '61 team was almost a carbon copy of the '60 team, except it was another year older. The team wallowed in 10th place in the early going, trailing even expansion clubs Los Angeles and Washington.

"We were in last place and we were playing at Baltimore," said Lopez. "I figured we were in trouble. If we lose three in a row we'll really be in bad shape. So I called a meeting. I had kind of a talk with the fellows. I went around asking, 'Is everyone all right? Everyone healthy?' 'Yeah.' 'Well, it's early. Let's get going. This is a much better club.' I wanted to pump them up, make them believe they were better than what they were showing—which they were. And then we went out and got shellacked real bad.

"So I was burned up. I came back into the clubhouse and I went through there and said, 'Fellas, I want to apologize. I thought I knew something about baseball. I thought this was a good club. But I can tell you the way you played today that this is not a good club. This is a horseshit club.' And I just kept on walking. Nobody said a word. Ater that, we won 19 out of 20 and got back into contention."

But the team was graying around the temples and had to be rebuilt. Lopez, now that Veeck had moved on during the '61 season, was back in control of his own destiny, ably supported by new general manager Ed Short. Deals sent Minoso, Sievers, and Billy Pierce to the National League, bringing Cunningham, John Buzhardt, Eddie Fisher, and others in return. The next winter, Aparicio was sacrificed along with Smith in a trade with Baltimore that yielded reliever Hoyt Wilhelm, shortstop Ron Hansen, one-time bonus baby outfielder Dave Nicholson, and a rookie third baseman named Pete Ward.

"Ward was just 23, and we had to rebuild third base," Lopez remembered. "Charley Metro (then a Sox scout) had tremendous reports on Ward, and I liked him too. Hansen was only 25, and though he didn't have Aparicio's speed, he wasn't an out at the plate. He could hit the ball and he wasn't gonna hurt you at shortstop. And a fine guy on a club. Nicholson was one of my biggest disappointments—we thought he was a guy who had a chance to be a real superstar—but Wilhelm did a tremendous job for Chicago all the years he was there. We gave up Aparicio, who was still gonna play a lot of years, and Al Smith, who we figured was near the end and might play another year or two. In return we got four positions. We got four players in that deal and that deal kept us in the first division."

And it put the Sox back into their usual role of runner-up. Lopez's teams won 94, 98, and 95 games in successive seasons ('63-'65) but had nothing more to show for it than three second-place finishes. But second place was a lot better than ninth, where the Sox were in July 1968 when Lopez—who had retired after the '65 season—came back from Tampa to manage once again. He didn't last too long, an appendectomy forcing him to leave the club for six weeks that summer. But he did come back for the start of the '69 season, this time staying for 17 games (eight won, nine lost for a final Sox record of 852-672) before more stomach problems told him to give up managing for good. And he didn't leave until he had made room in the lineup for a 20-year-old outfielder who would soon become a favorite of the fans: Carlos May, who later that season, at Marine Reserve camp in California, lost a thumb in a mortar accident. He was hitting .281 with 18 homers at the time of the mishap.

"I liked his bat, and we needed a bat," said Lopez, who used May as a leadoff man in '69. "But he wasn't a very good outfielder. He was on the lazy side. He could've been a real good hitter. It's too bad he blew his thumb off. But he was a good hitter—he always got a piece of the ball. The first time I saw him was when I was laying off in '68. I saw him at Lynchburg. I said, 'That boy, I think he can hit anywhere.' The way he was swinging the bat, you could tell the way he stood up there that he had confidence that he could hit. Now in the outfield, I don't think he cared if he caught the ball or not. But he could hit."

Lopez's wife had returned from her morning shopping. Al had given me about an hour and a half, more than I had asked for. But before I left, I told him that Bob Elson had a question he wanted me to ask for him: Why hadn't he started Billy Pierce in one of the World Series games in 1959?

Al grinned and said, "They're still asking that back there, eh? Well, Billy was starting to slip a little bit. He never complained but I think his arm was bothering him a little. Just before we clinched the pennant that year, Billy had pitched against the Yankees in Yankee Stadium and had beaten them 4-3. He'd pitched a good game. Then he pitched again and hadn't looked good. Now our last series was in Detroit. I stayed in Chicago because the Dodgers were coming in to play the Cubs, so I put Tony Cuccinello in charge of the club. And I said, 'I want you to pitch Billy in Detroit, get him ready for the Series.' Because it was gonna be Wynn, Shaw, and Pierce in the Series. I told Tony, 'Let him go seven innings and give me a report on how he looks.' Tony came back and said, 'Al, he wasn't throwing good at all.' So that's one of the reasons we switched to Donovan in the third game (which the Sox lost 3-1 to fall behind two games to one).

"Then Wynn pitched the fourth game, Gil Hodges hit the home run off Staley and we lost 5-4. Then Shaw started the fifth game and I relieved with Pierce and Donovan (and the Sox won 1-0). So I figured for the sixth game, what the hell, I might as well come back with our strongest pitcher, Wynn." (Wynn was pounded and the Sox lost 9-3.)

"The same thing happened in Cleveland. Bob Feller was a great favorite. I was gonna pitch him in the World Series in '54. We went into the Polo Grounds and I opened with (Bob) Lemon and Wynn. And we lost two tough ballgames. I figured if we'd win one of those two games, I was gonna pitch Feller in the third game—at Cleveland.

Instead, we get beat two ballgames and I have to come back with my third-best pitcher, (Mike) Garcia. And a lot of people criticized me for not pitching Feller.

"But I don't mind that. What the hell, Billy Pierce was a great pitcher in Chicago and was a great favorite and a great kid. Feller the same way in Cleveland. But when you get in a short series like that, you've got to give 'em your best. Go with the best you've got. A lot of people were talking about a matter of personalities, or that so-and-so's in the doghouse. To me, that's the most asinine statement anybody could make. If there was anybody I didn't like on my club, he wouldn't be on my club. I'd try to get him off the club, because I wouldn't want to pick on a guy. Everybody I had on my club, those were my players and I was tickled to death to have them on my club."

And Chicago White Sox fans were tickled to death to have Al Lopez managing their team.

EDDIE STANKY:
He locked the door on Hubert Humphrey

Figuring that I would be near Eddie Stanky's Mobile, Ala., home on my trip south, I phoned the former manager of the White Sox and asked if the two of us would be able to get together for a brief visit. His answer startled me.

"My doctors tell me I can't talk to writers here in my own backyard," said Stanky, who had undergone heart surgery some months earlier. "I get too excited when I talk about things in the past. So they tell me, 'No interviews.'

"But if it's all right with you, here's what I can do: I'll fly to Chicago at your expense. We can sit down and cut a tape and I think it'll be really fine for your book. I'll be able to visit with some old friends while I'm there, too. If you want to do that, you let me know."

After pulling myself up from the floor, I allowed that I would talk to the publisher about such a venture, and then I said goodbye. I was truly disappointed. If there was a single most fascinating individual to wear a White Sox uniform the last three decades—one person with whom I would most want to sit down and talk—this was the man. Eddie Stanky, nicknamed "The Brat" when he played second base for the Cubs, the Giants, the Braves, and the Dodgers in the '40s and early

Eddie Stanky (left) poses with an old friend, Leo Durocher, before the
1967 Cubs-Sox Boys' Benefit game at Comiskey Park.

'50s. The hustling pest of whom it had been said, "He can't run, he can't hit, and he can't throw—all he can do is beat you."

Eddie Stanky, who when once asked if Hoyt Wilhelm's knuckleball was more lively at night or at daytime, gave his inquisitor a pixieish grin, pursed his lips, and then answered, "There, and in Denver." Eddie Stanky, who after losing a third straight game to the Twins at Minnesota to fall out of first place in August 1967, refused the Twins' No. 1 fan—Vice-President Hubert Humphrey—entrance to the Sox clubhouse. And Eddie Stanky, who later explained that controversial move by declaring: "Humphrey tries to come into my clubhouse. Big deal. What do I need Humphrey for? He can't hit."

But sportswriters, not Vice-Presidents, were Stanky's chief enemies. He fought with out-of-town writers and carried on a love-hate relationship with Chicago writers. When the hometown reporters wrote critically of him or his team, he would complain about how his "own flesh and blood" had betrayed him. One writer, eventual Pulitzer Prize winner Tom Fitzpatrick, more than betrayed him. In 1966, after hearing Stanky's complaints about "new breed" ballplayers and managers and his long tirades against everything from immorality in contemporary society to the evils of communism, Fitzpatrick daily began poking fun at Eddie (alias, Dandy Little Manager, Little Napoleon, Captain Ahab, and Captain Queeg) and the fact that Stanky had 27 pictures of himself hanging on his office walls. He even went so far as to suggest that perhaps Stanky, burdened as he was by a slumping ballclub, was finally starting to crack up.

That did it. Stanky got owner Art Allyn to petition the Daily News to remove "Fitz" from the White Sox beat. Allyn's efforts succeeded. Soon, Stanky's team began succeeding as well. The Sox, nine games under .500 at the halfway point of the '66 season, wound up the year 83-79 to make Stanky's first campaign as Chicago manager a success —though not a rousing one. In fact, the Sox had wound up with 12 fewer victories than the Sox team managed by Al Lopez the year before. That didn't exactly enable Eddie to wipe Lopez's memory from the minds of Sox fans.

The truth is, Stanky was not the club's first choice to replace Al. Nor, in fact, was he the second choice. Nor the third or fourth. Lopez recommended Mayo Smith, then the Yankees' top scout and formerly a manager in the National League. But Smith held out for a two-year contract, and because Ed Short was only willing to give him a one-year deal, Mayo told Short to look elsewhere. Then the job was offered to Cleveland third-base coach George Strickland, Lopez's shortstop on his outstanding Indian teams of the early '50s. Strickland took a glance at the Sox roster, decided only a genius such as Lopez could have gotten the team as high as second place, and indicated that he would remain in Cleveland. The Sox then turned to one-time Kansas City manager Harry Craft, who also said no. Short, with the winter meetings under way and his team still without a manager, then cornered Grady Hatton, who had played for the White Sox in 1954 and had just managed Houston's top farm club—Oklahoma City—to a championship. Grady listened politely but he, too, said no. A week later, the Texan had the job he wanted all along: manager of the Houston Astros.

So here was the situation: Short was running all over hotel lobbies trying to make deals and trying, at the same time, to find somebody to manage the White Sox. The managerial search was the most critical— a new manager might have enabled him to close the deals he was attempting to hammer out: Danny Cater and John Buzhardt to the Yankees for Roger Maris, or Juan Pizarro and Al Weis to Cleveland for Leon Wagner.

But nothing was accomplished. Short returned to Chicago with neither a new slugger nor a new manager. Finally, a few days later, he and Lopez met in Tampa with Stanky—who had been working in the Mets' farm department—and offered the Sox job to the little guy from Mobile. Stanky jumped at the opportunity and immediately pronounced the White Sox a solid contender. But injuries to Ron Hansen, Pete Ward, Pizarro, and others—plus the sudden decline of catcher John Romano—killed any hopes Stanky might have had. Besides, it would take a while for Eddie to put his own brand on the Sox—to make them "my kind of team."

First, he had to teach the Sox how to run the bases his way, which among other things meant knowing how to break up doubleplays. "I still use things he taught me," said Tommy McCraw, a Cleveland coach who was Stanky's first baseman and his best all-around baserunner. "He taught us to slide to the side of second base that the ball is hit to. That's the best way to break up a doubleplay. The other guy's gotta come across to get the throw. He's gotta come to you. And you really get to pop him good and put something on his mind. We used to intimidate some pretty good ballplayers that way."

Stanky intimidated some of his own players, although he may not have known it. Once, McCraw remembered, Stanky was giving one of his many pregame chalk talks—Eddie was one of the few managers who went in for this sort of thing—and was going over a play that had been executed rather poorly the game before. "He was really chewing some behind that day," McCraw grinned. "Everybody's real quiet, you know, heads down. And he was ranting and raving and carrying on, and all of a sudden he just popped that blackboard—and it busted. And everybody shook.

"But he was a ballplayer's manager, if you played hard and you weren't afraid. If you were afraid of getting hurt, or afraid of physical contact or afraid of being aggressive, then you couldn't play for Eddie, in my opinion. You had to love to slide, to break up doubleplays, to have contact with other ballplayers. That was his style. That's the way he played."

And if someone didn't play that way for Stanky, he would soon be gone. One such individual was Danny Cater, who had hit well for Lopez in '65 but didn't respond to Stanky's leadership the next season. It is around Cater that the following story is woven, illustrating how some of Stanky's players judged his ability as a manager.

"Stanky would do things to get guys to run through walls and do anything to win ballgames," one of Eddie's former regulars told me. "But then he'd do things to deflate them just as fast as he had pumped them up. When you're playing 162 games in the big leagues, you have to maintain an even keel. You can't have a lot of ups and downs, because the game is as much mental as it is physical.

"Here's an example. We're in Kansas City, playing good ball and really rolling. Danny Cater has been traded to Kansas City earlier in the season for Wayne Causey. Denny Higgins and Danny Cater are the best of friends. If you write this and use my name, I'm gonna come and find you. But it probably should be written. Stanky had this thing about knockdown pitches: When he requests that you hit somebody, it's $500 if you don't. And it's in the head.

94

"Higgins came in and hit Cater in the head while the game was still up for grabs. Got Kansas City so fired up they beat us a doubleheader, But see, when he hit Cater in the head, that affected us because a lot of the guys liked Cater. But Stanky hated Cater. And really, Cater hadn't done anything for us except hit close to .300 and fill in just about everywhere. Nothing flashy, but the kind of guy you like to have around because he can play everywhere. But Stanky didn't like him because he wasn't enthusiastic enough. But that was Danny's personality. So Higgins hits him and they're the best of friends and a lot of our guys felt bad about it. That knocked the wind right out of us."

Still, Eddie got enough out of his players to have them in first place most of the '67 season. And he kept the fans chuckling with bright quotes all through those wonderful days of June, July and August as his team won one 2-1 game after another. To the Chicago writers who claimed that "watching the White Sox play is about as exciting as watching paint dry," he retorted: "If my team is so dull and the other teams are so talented and so exciting, how come we've been in first place most of the season?" And then, in one memorable "press conference" on the eve of a late-August, five-game home series against the Boston Red Sox—who trailed by mere percentage points—he provided the writers with enough material for an entire season.

"My team is making a laughingstock out of the American League," he began. "It embarrasses the rest of the league to pick up the paper and see the White Sox in first place. I see where the managers of the other contenders (Boston, Detroit, and Minnesota) say that the turning point in their season was when they beat us a series there or beat us two out of three here. They get a big kick out of beating the White Sox because it embarrasses them when they lose to us—when our 44-year-old lion (Wilhelm) and our 37-year-old (Don McMahon) come in and get out their .319 hitters.

"Those other teams should be embarrassed. There's Boston. The City of Culture. That's a laugh. Everybody's making a big to-do about how well Boston's doing this year. Well, big deal. Boston's only had the best young players in the league the last five years. Where the hell have they been hiding?

"And Detroit, the City of Motors. They should be embarrassed, too. They should be 10 games in front. They have the best infield in the league and an 18-game winner (Earl Wilson) and a 14-game winner (Denny McLain). Then there's Minnesota, the Cheese State. They only have Killebrew who's hit 34 homers, and (Rod) Carew and (Dean Chance. Minnesota's not the Cheese State? Well, it should be. There's a lot of cheese in Minnesota."

The talk turned to the big series that was to open with a twi-nighter the next evening. "I understand that 12 writers are coming here from the City of Culture. Coming in for the kill. Well, I know one thing: Not all of them are going to get into MY office. One of them called today and asked how I could think of starting (rookie Cisco) Carlos in this big, big, 'crooshal'—with two o's—series. Hell, somebody has to pitch. What was Carlos' record at Indianapolis? Ask the public relations man. I don't care if he was 0-20 at Indianapolis. He's pitching tomorrow night.

"The City of Culture has been crying about the injury to Conigliaro all week. (Tony Conigliaro had been beaned and was out for the year.) Big deal. The world is coming to an end. We've had players injured all season, but we aren't crying about it. We just put someone else in uniform.

"My pitching rotation for the series? It's Peters and Carlos tomorrow night, Horlen will pitch Saturday, then everybody goes on Sunday. That'll make a helluva headline, won't it? 'Stanky Doesn't Even Know Pitching Plans For Big Series.'

"I don't care if we go 5-0 or 0-5 against the City of Culture this weekend. All I know is that my team is first in the league in guts and that we're gonna be in the World Series."

Well, the Sox didn't win the Boston series, let alone the pennant. Peters was bombed out early in the first game of the twi-nighter and wound up a 7-1 loser. But then Carlos, the rookie just up from Indianapolis, pitched no-hit ball into the seventh inning of the second game and the Sox won 2-1 on Ken Berry's single in the ninth. A tough loss Saturday was followed up by an even tougher 4-3 loss in the first game of Sunday's doubleheader, when Berry, carrying the tying run, was thrown out at the plate for the final out. But Peters, coming back on one day's rest, blanked the Red Sox long enough for Rocky Colavito to come up in the last of the 11th with the bases loaded and get hit by a pitched ball to force home the only run of the nightcap.

Stanky's club kept fighting through the final month, a month high-lighted by Joe Horlen's no-hitter against Detroit, a three-game sweep of Hubert Humphrey's Twins in Chicago, and a 10-inning, 4-0 victory over Cleveland (Don Buford's grand-slammer won it), immediately followed by a 17-inning, 1-0 triumph over the same club. But the month—and the season—ended in disaster: the twin setback on Black Wednesday in Kansas City and the three straight season-closing losses at home to the Washington Senators. It was after the first loss in that Washington series—a 1-0 defeat, what else?—that Stanky finally came to the sad realization that his team could no longer win the pennant he had wanted so badly for it to win.

"Now Detroit and Minnesota and Boston can feel relieved," he said in his office. "The laughingstock team of the league isn't in this race now."

"The elephants have been fearful of the mouse all year. I have been laughing at the rest of the league for more than 150 games now. And I've enjoyed every minute of it. Damn, I wanted it to go down to the last day. I couldn't have cared less if we'd lost then, because we would have had them crawling until the last moment."

The room grew quiet. Finally, a writer asked Stanky who he thought would now go on to win the pennant. Would it be Boston? Or Minnesota? Or Detroit?

"I don't give a damn who wins it now," he said, his eyes a bit moist. "Because my club didn't."

It would never be the same again for Stanky and the White Sox. Winter trades brought Luis Aparicio and Tommy Davis but took away guys like Hansen, Buford, Tommie Agee, and J.C. Martin— people who, unlike Aparicio and Davis, had never played on a pennant-winner and who had an overwhelming hunger to do so. The team, on paper, appeared improved. But some of the '67 club's "in-tangibles," as Stanky himself liked to call them, were gone with Hansen and Buford and the others.

So maybe we shouldn't have been so shocked when the '68 Sox opened the season by losing their first 10 games. Soon Davis and others began grumbling about Stanky's rules on dress and other weighty matters. Stanky's chalk talks, what with the ballclub losing so often, became far more annoying to the players than when they had been winning. Inevitably, the story of the Eddie Stanky White Sox ended in mid-July, with the team 11 games under .500. Stanky was called into Ed Short's office and was told he was through, that he was to be replaced by the man he had replaced—Al Lopez. Shaken, he left the park without even saying goodbye to his ballplayers.

I was at the ballpark that night with friends to see the White Sox play the Yankees. We all agreed that Eddie had been given a raw deal—that, if Tommy Davis had hit more than the .194 he was hitting that day, Stanky's job might well have been saved. As if to underscore this, one of our number screamed at Davis from our leftfield, upper-deck perch: "The season's half over, Davis, and what have you DONE?" Davis could only stare at the grass beneath him.

It was a sad evening. We had lost a hero. After all, how many of us could have told the Vice-President of the United States where to get off?

CHUCK TANNER:
Richie Allen and rose-colored glasses

The morning skies were overcast, the temperature was in the low 40s, and it was barely 9 o'clock as I approached the Clark Street press entrance at Wrigley Field. Yet already scores of people were lined up outside the gates, waiting to get inside. Cub fans, I decided, were an odd breed.

I was there to talk to Chuck Tanner, the former manager of the White Sox who was now managing the then-defending world champion Pittsburgh Pirates. I walked up the old wooden steps to the visiting team's clubhouse and knocked on the already-ajar door to Tanner's office. He looked up from the newspaper he was reading and rose to greet me like an old friend. "Hi Bob," he smiled warmly. "Glad you could come."

Six years earlier, visiting Comiskey Park to do a story on Sox outfielder Ken Henderson, I ran into Tanner in the runway to the home team dugout. Chuck had just been given a five-year contract extension, and I introduced myself and congratulated him. He thanked me profusely, putting his arm around my shoulder as if we were pals from way back. That, I had been told, was his way. I could tell now that it was still his way.

Chuck Tanner

He was reading a Sun-Times story hailing the abilities of Steve Dillard, a weak-hitting utility infielder who had happened to deliver the pinch double that had enabled the Cubs to defeat the Pirates the day before. "Steve Dillard," Tanner chuckled derisively. "I'd like to see him do it again . . ."

He put the paper aside, stuffed some Red Man chewing tobacco in his mouth, pulled over a waste basket for expectoration purposes, and started talking about the September night, a decade earlier, when he had first addressed the lowly Chicago White Sox as their newly appointed manager. It was in Kansas City, and fortunately, the game would be rained out. Fortunately, because the Sox were already 40 games under .500 and were on their way to a 56-106 finish, worst since the horrid '48 club had staggered home 51-101.

"I remember exactly what I said," Tanner told me. "I had a meeting with them and told them, 'I'm here to observe you and analyze you. I'm not gonna give any signals. If you want to hit and run, go ahead and hit and run. If you want to bunt, bunt. I'm just gonna watch you, how you play the game. You can do anything you want. The only thing we'll do is change pitchers.'

"And that's what we did. They even had their starting rotation all set for the rest of the year, so I didn't even change that. And they won three and lost 13. I was charged with that record because I was listed as the manager. But to me, I wasn't really managing. All I did was let them play."

He didn't start managing until the following spring and, by then, many of the players he had observed and analyzed the September before were long gone. Tanner and Roland Hemond, both of whom had been brought to Chicago from the California Angels' organization by Sox vice-president Stu Holcomb, had gone out that winter and acquired Angel products like Tom Bradley, Jay Johnstone, Tom Egan, Steve Kealey, and Rick Reichardt—all of whom had played for Tanner in the minors. They also sent shortstop Luis Aparicio to Boston for a badly needed second baseman, Mike Andrews, and a shortstop to replace Aparicio, Luis Alvarado. Another important addition was outfielder Pat Kelly, obtained from Kansas City.

"We wanted to get more good players," Tanner explained. "We had a couple excellent players (Aparicio and Ken Berry, who went to the

Angels in one of those winter deals) and a lot of below-average players. So we were able to get two-for-one. We gave up an excellent player for two good players to get that depth that would give us a chance to be more respectable."

Surrounded by the new players, Tanner set out in spring training in Sarasota to instill a new attitude in the still-shellshocked remnants of the 1970 disaster squad. "We just went to work," Tanner recalled. "We put in a new system and worked on baseball the way I wanted it played. Not only the big league club but all through the farm system. Everybody had to do everything the same way. We tried to teach them what we thought was the right way to do the job. We taught them how to slide and how to run the bases. Rundowns, pickoff plays, cutoffs, and relays.

"And we tried to win as many games as we could in spring training to give them confidence. We won the Grapefruit League title and I played those games like it was the regular season."

In fact, in one game against Baltimore's defending world champs, Chuck made several pitching changes in the ninth inning after having used almost a half-dozen pinch-hitters the inning before. "They all said, 'Why's he doing that?' Well, I wanted to win. And I think our players started realizing we had a chance to win some ballgames."

That became obvious Opening Day at Oakland. A's owner Charlie Finley, forced to open the season against the lowly White Sox (against whom his team had been 16-2 in 1970), scheduled a doubleheader for a Wednesday instead of single games Tuesday and Wednesday. That way, he figured, he would get better attendance. And what better way to start off the new season than with two easy victories in one day?

He got the good attendance—by Oakland standards, anyway: 23,000-plus. But he didn't get the sweep. The A's were the ones who got swept. The White Sox, decked out in flashy new uniforms of light blue with red trim, won the first game 6-5 on Rich McKinney's two-run pinch single and then clobbered Oakland pitching for a 10-4 win in the second game.

The new White Sox started a lineup which included a rookie short-stop named Bee Bee Richard—less than a year out of Southern University in Baton Rouge, La.—and newcomers Reichardt, Johnstone, and Andrews. The new blood blended nicely with the holdovers:

rightfielder Walter Williams, third baseman Bill Melton, catcher Ed Herrmann, and first baseman Carlos May, whom Tanner had moved in from left field. Richard collected four hits for the day, Johnstone and Andrews hit homers, Melton hit a grand slam (beginning his drive to the A.L. home run title), and May hit perhaps the first out-of-the-park triple ever seen: joyous over hammering an apparent three-run homer in the first inning of the nightcap, Carlos leaped when he got to home plate, but when he came down he missed the base. The A's noticed the omission and May was called out, but the other two runs stood up. Tanner's new White Sox were off and running.

A crowd of 44,250 showed up for the home opener against defending A.L. West champ Minnesota two days later, and McKinney singled off Ron Perranoski to win the game 3-2 in the bottom of the ninth. But then came seven straight losses, and people started thinking, "Same old White Sox." But Tanner could not and would not let himself believe that—nor would he allow his players to.

"Attitude is everything," said Tanner, after ridding his mouth of a load of tobacco juice. "When things were going bad, I conducted myself in the same manner as if we were winning. I walked tall, 'cause you have to walk tall. And I talked and acted positive, and I think that after a while it carried over to the ballplayers."

It did take a while, however. The team was competitive but, because Richard seemed to boot every other grounder hit to him and because Johnstone and some of the other outfielders went after flyballs as if they had never before seen a baseball in flight, the Sox' record was well below .500 by mid-June. In one particularly galling stretch that month, they lost six out of seven—all six losses by one run. After one of them, Tanner, as the team bus left Tiger Stadium enroute to the Detroit airport, rose from his seat and addressed the troops:

"I was going to wait until we got to Minnesota until I told you this, but I can't wait anymore. I'm more proud of this ballclub than any other club I've managed. This team is going to win a pennant next year or the year after and you are the guys who are going to win it. I'm proud of this team—so proud."

Tanner's players responded. From that point on, the Sox went 57-47 and wound up third in the West Division at 79-83—an improvement of 23 games over 1970. But even Tanner will admit it took more

103

than his little busride sermonette to turn close losses into victories. It took some improved outfield defense in the persons of Kelly and Mike Hershberger, who were summoned from the club's Tucson farm that same month. Before their arrival, new radio announcer Harry Caray more than once had moaned, "Boy oh boy, if Mike Hershberger and Pat Kelly can't make THIS outfield, they must be just HORR-ible."

Hershberger, especially, made an immediate difference. "That was a turning point," Tanner remembered. "When he joined us, we started to win some games because he was a good defensive outfielder with a strong arm (just as he had been when he first came up to the majors with the Sox in the early '60s). That was the start of it, I'd say— when Mike Hershberger joined us. He pulled a hamstring in spring training or otherwise he'd have made our ballclub then. So we sent him down and he was getting better and I told Roland, 'Get Mike Hershberger up here because it'll stabilize us.' Because we had young guys in the outfield. Immediately he settled us down and we started to win."

It helped, too, that Tanner and his new pitching coach, Johnny Sain, had decided to make a starter out of ace reliever Wilbur Wood. Wood, sometimes pitching with just two days' rest, pitched 334 innings, winning 22 games and posting an earned run average of just 1.91. He struck out 210 batters and walked only 62 and threw seven shutouts. In addition to Wood, Bradley won 15 games in his first full year in the majors, 21-year-old Bart Johnson became Mr. Smoke in the bullpen, and 19-year-old lefty fireballer Terry Forster gave evidence that he, too, was going to become a brilliant relief pitcher.

So the '71 season ended on an upbeat, especially when Melton tied Norm Cash and Reggie Jackson for the league home run lead on the next-to-last day of the season and then won the title on the final day by belting his 33rd homer off Milwaukee's Bill Parsons. Still, Tanner felt the club needed one more all-star caliber player in order to become a contender. That player turned out to be Richie Allen, who cost the Sox lefty Tommy John and utility infielder Steve Huntz, who had spent most of the '71 season masquerading as a shortstop for the Tucson Toros. Then, to replace John, the Sox sent McKinney to the Yankees for starting pitcher Stan Bahnsen.

Bahnsen went on to win 21 games, but Allen was the whole show in

'72. He hit .308 and won the league home run title with 37 and led in RBI with 113. He seldom took batting practice, he seldom showed up at the ballpark on time and he seldom made public appearances. But seldom did he fail to send electricity through the Comiskey Park stands when he approached home plate, bat in hand. You just KNEW Allen was going to do something absolutely terrible to that poor little baseball the pitcher was getting ready to fire plateward.

"He had one of the greatest individual years anybody ever had in their life," said Tanner, whose high school in New Castle, Pa., was in the same conference with the Allen family's school in Wampum and whose friendship with the Allens had helped convince Richie to continue his career in Chicago instead of retiring from the game at age 30. Even today, Tanner pooh-poohs the popular notion that Allen was a bad actor, a troublemaker, a lousy guy to have on a ballclub.

"All I know," he began, looking me straight in the eye, "is that he's one of the best players who ever played. Nobody ever played harder than him and all that other bullshit is just that: bullshit. If a guy hits .180, nobody ever says a word about him. I managed a lot of ballplayers and he's been as fine a player on a team as any player I ever managed. They talk about he's this and he's that . . . well, that's what they talk about and that's what they write about and say. But I don't believe that. I just judge a person on how he is with me. That other stuff's a bunch of baloney. He's the greatest player to put on a White Sox uniform, in my opinion. Everytime he went out onto the field it was like there was a big spotlight shining right on him."

It was Allen who was in the middle of Tanner's most memorable moment from that '72 campaign, when the White Sox actually held first place in the A.L. West until early September, when the Oakland A's overtook them and won the first of four straight division titles. It was the first weekend in June, and 51,094 showed up for a Bat Day twin bill with the Yankees. After winning the first game, the Sox trailed 4-2 with two out and a man on in the ninth inning of the second game—which Allen had spent on the bench, sitting out for the first time that season.

"Mike Andrews was up and I let him hit for himself, and he walked," said Chuck. "Then I pinch-hit Allen against Sparky Lyle and the second pitch he hit up into the upper deck and we won the doubleheader. That was the most exciting finish of the year. I'll never forget that one."

Nor will he forget another game, this one in Boston in '73, with the Sox again in contention. "I got to the ballpark early, just like today, and Danny Murtaugh, who was scouting for the Pirates, was telling me, 'How can you guys be fighting for a pennant? You don't have any speed, the defense is poor.' I said, 'Don't tell the ballplayers that. They don't know that. They think we're gonna win it. Besides, I've got something up my sleeve for you today.' He says, 'What's that?' "

Tanner showed him the lineup card he had made out. He had written Allen in at leadoff, with Melton batting second. Murtaugh shook his head and wandered out of the office. "Wilbur Wood was pitching that day and we were down a run going into the ninth and there were two out. And Allen came up and hit a home run and then Melton hit a home run and we won by one run."

The next day, Tanner tore up his brainstorm lineup and went back to his regular batting order. "I scrapped it," he smiled. "I told Murtaugh, 'Lightning can't strike twice.' "

That game was one of the few times in '72 and '73 that Allen and Melton delivered the longball in tandem. In '72 Melton—like so many Sox third basemen before him (e.g., Pete Ward and George Kell) developed back problems and missed the final three months. Hemond purchased Ed Spiezio to fill in for Melton, and the Joliet native did an adequate job. But he was no Melton, and everyone still wonders whether or not the Sox could've won in '72 had Melton not been hurt.

"Oh, it's hard to say—you don't know," Tanner said. "We didn't have Oakland's depth. All our regulars had to be healthy all year. The reason why we won it last year (in '79 with the Pirates) was because we had depth. The Oakland A's of 1972-3-4 were one of the greatest teams ever assembled in the history of baseball. And we made a run at them. But they were better than us. That's why we finished second. But we got the best out of our ballplayers. No, I don't think anybody would've made the difference. I think they had the best 25 ballplayers."

What about 1973, when the Sox led the A's by a goodly margin before Henderson tore up his knee and Allen broke his leg—both injuries wrecking those players' seasons? "Once again," Tanner said, "when you don't have the depth, you pay the price for it. And all they ask is, 'Did you win or did you lose?' They don't care about this guy or that guy being hurt. Like two years ago with Pittsburgh, I think we could've won it (Willie Stargell and Rennie Stennett, on their way to great years, were sidelined for long periods), but we didn't have the depth. Last year we had the best 25-man roster I ever had. And that's why we won. We had versatility, a strong bench, a strong bullpen.

"When I was with the White Sox, we didn't have 25 players capable of doing the job if someone got hurt. That's why we finished where we finished."

Yet, there was and still is a feeling of negativism about Chuck Tanner's stay in Chicago. The 1974 club helped produce that feeling. The team—bolstered by the acquisition of Ron Santo, the addition of a talented youngster in Bucky Dent to plug the hole at shortstop, plus the return from injuries of Allen and Henderson—never did get going and plodded home fourth, a .500 (80-80) ballclub. With two weeks to go, Allen announced he was quitting the game, although he came back the next year to play for the Phillies. And Santo, forced to play out of position (he toiled mainly at second base that year when he wasn't the designated hitter) and finding American League pitching not exactly to his liking, followed up Allen's retirement declaration with one of his own.

Tanner took Allen's retirement speech at face value. "He came to me first and told me he was gonna retire," Chuck told me. "I said, 'Ah, c'mon, just stay—we're gonna play the young kids going down the stretch.' He said, 'Nah, I just can't take it anymore.' " Take what, I asked. "He didn't go into detail," Tanner said. "He really meant it, because he lost about $25,000 in salary. He gave it up and he really did retire. I thought it was gonna last. He was really sincere about it. When he tells you something, he means it. Then he decided to come back the next year but, of course, you know, we just couldn't take him back. That's when we traded him (to the Braves for $5,000 and catcher Jim Essian)."

Minus Allen in '75, Tanner seemed to look the other way rather than address what appeared to be half-hearted efforts by Henderson, Melton, May and others. One of his players, Tony Muser—who had been anointed as Allen's successor at first base during the winter and was suddenly dumped from the opening-day lineup when Tanner decided to put May at that position—blasted the manager publicly and revealed that Chuck's rah-rah method of running a ballclub was beginning to wear thin with several members of the team.

The building negativism was no more obvious than at the home opener against Texas, witnessed by barely 20,000 on a fairly nice day. Rookie outfielder Nyls Nyman, a lefthanded hitter, delivered a run-scoring single to give the Sox a lead but was lifted his next time up because the Rangers had switched to a lefthanded pitcher, Jim Umbarger. Tanner sent up Jerry Hairston with the bases loaded to bat for Nyman, and the crowd began booing—and the boos weren't for Hairston, a switch-hitter who had shown in his previous two years in the big leagues an ability to hit righthanders well but an utter inability to hit lefties. The booing grew much louder after Hairston rolled out weakly to kill off the rally. The Sox lost in extra innings.

It was also that season that Tanner angered many by sending young slugger Lamar Johnson back to the minors just before Opening Day, instead purchasing 37-year-old Deron Johnson from Boston to serve as designated hitter. Deron was coming off a big .171 year, so the announcement of his acquisition was greeted with wild enthusiasm. Next, Tanner picked up 36-year-old Claude Osteen to be the club's fourth starter, and the over-the-hill left proceeded to go 7-16. It was a gloomy summer, made bearable, however, by the laughs provided when Tanner repeatedly attempted to convince people that players like Rich Hinton, Bill Gogolewski, Lloyd Allen, Danny Osborn, and Pete Varney really DID belong in the major leagues—and when new catcher Essian spent a month on the team without even getting into one game.

After the 75-86, fifth-place finish of '75, Bill Veeck bought the club from John Allyn and named 67-year-old Paul Richards to manage, at the same time promising Tanner a front-office job for one year, after which Chuck would be brought back to replace Richards. Tanner listened politely, but said no thanks, and signed to manage Oakland.

"I knew one thing," said Tanner. "I had to be on the field. He (Veeck) said he didn't want me to leave, but that Paul Richards was like a security blanket for him, which I understood. There was no animosity—but I have to make my own decisions and do my own thing and I'm a manager and I want to manage. I was too young to get out of managing. I wanted to stay on the field.

"So Finley offered me a job and I took it. He got on the phone with one of the writers and said, 'Well, what did they do?' The writer told him, 'They hired Richards.' So he said, 'Well, tell Tanner to call me right away.' This was right after the press conference. So I called him and we got together. He said he wanted me, made me an offer, and I accepted."

So the Tanner era in Chicago, which had begun with so much promise, ended in unfulfillment. Attendance, which had climbed from less than 500,000 in 1970 to 1,316,527 by '73, had fallen to 770,800 in '75. The pennant, which seemed so close in '72 and '73, now seemed further away than when Tanner had first arrived. Nonetheless, Chuck looks back on his five years in Chicago as a period of success.

"The one thing I know," he said, "is that when I was with the Chicago White Sox, every year at the end of the season we knew that we got the best out of all our ballplayers. And it might have been one of the greatest jobs ever done in baseball, as far as taking a team that was really down and out and making them respectable. And we did it with trades—we didn't have the money to do it—and by maneuvering players and changing the style of baseball, being aggressive and having a good attitude. And I was just as proud of the job we did with the White Sox as I was when we won the world championship with the Pittsburgh Pirates last year. Because I know what we did."

After unloading some more tobacco juice, Chuck continued his stirring defense. "But see, people don't give you credit for that. They give you credit for where you finish. And if you don't win it, you're no good. But I disagree with that. But see, if you sit down and try to explain how injuries hurt you and all that, they say, 'Aw, he's just crying. He didn't win.' That's right. So I don't even try to explain it. All I know is, we did the job.

"We had to bring up players like Jorge Orta, who'd never played pro ball; Bee Bee Richard, who had had half a season. Others, like Forster and Johnson and Gossage, we brought up from Class A ball and had them going against these veteran clubs with a lot of experienced ballplayers. That's why I know we did maybe one of the best jobs ever done in baseball. And I think after I left Chicago and went to

Pittsburgh, it started to sink in and people have begun to realize the job we did in Chicago. And they appreciated it more after we were gone."

In a few minutes, I would be gone, wondering to myself if he and I had been watching the same team those last two, disappointing seasons in Chicago. Apparently, I concluded, we had not.

RAY BERRES:
Director, Reclamation Projects Dept.

In 11 years in the major leagues, Ray Berres hit .216 and blasted all of three home runs. But somewhere along the line, it had occurred to me that Berres, the White Sox pitching coach for almost 20 years beginning in 1949, might well have been the single biggest reason for the White Sox' 17-year string of first-division finishes.

Pitchers would come from other clubs to the Sox labeled as losers and suddenly, as if by magic, they would become winners. The list was remarkable: Harry Dorish, Saul Rogovin, Marv Grissom, Bill Kennedy, Bob Keegan, Don Johnson, Jack Harshman, Bob Shaw, Frank Baumann, Juan Pizarro, Johnny Buzhardt, Ray Herbert. And then there were the oldtimers, cast adrift by other teams who figured they were washed up. The veterans would resurface with the Sox and immediately become effective again. Examples abound: Joe Dobson, Virgil Trucks, Dixie Howell, Gerry Staley, Ellis Kinder, Turk Lown, Warren Hacker, Jim Brosnan, and Don Mossi.

At first, it was explained that this was because of the brilliance of Paul Richards. Then Richards left, and still it went on. Marty Marion suddenly became a brilliant handler of pitchers. Then Marion left, and still it continued. Now it was Al Lopez who was the brainy magician

Ray Berres

with the pitchers. Lopez left and the pattern remained. Then, we were told, it was Eddie Stanky who had built such a formidable group of pitchers.

All the while, Ray Berres stayed in the background, far out of the spotlight. I decided that he would have to be dragged, kicking and screaming, out of the background, so I drove up to his Twin Lakes, Wis., home, just across the Illinois-Wisconsin state line, to discuss pitching mechanics and to reminisce about some of the fellows he had helped during his long stay in Chicago.

It was like learning at the feet of an aging professor who knew all there was to know about his given subject. "There's a reason," he began, "for wildness. Say I'm a righthanded pitcher and I'm supposed to pitch a righthanded hitter down and away, and invariably the ball goes up and in on him. There's something I'm doing wrong and normally it's in my timing—it might be some silly quirk. Maybe because I'm not staying balanced, not waiting 'til I get to the fulcrum point before I release the ball.

"It's the same thing as a golf swing. There are no two things as closely associated, in my mind, as a good pro golfer's swing and a good pro pitcher's delivery. They're together. If I swing my club a little bit off—there it goes, a slice. Same with pitching. If you release too soon, it's got to go out there—up and in to that righthanded hitter we were talking about.

"I've had a lot of luck with some guys I couldn't convince at first. They thought I was nuts or something. In spring training, kids who'd never seen me before. I'd say, 'All right, I'm gonna tell you where the ball's going before you ever throw it.' They wouldn't believe it. And I'd say, 'High away, high away. You can't throw one low and away.' 'How do you know?' 'Well, there's several little things that happen . . .'

"See, these are things I happened to see and learn when I found out I wasn't gonna be a star. I said, 'Well, then, I have to have longevity.' One of my minor league managers, Clyde Milan, had told me when I played at Birmingham, 'Ray, you'll never be a star, but you'll always have a job, as long as you're as observant and cooperative as you are.' I couldn't beat out those good hitters, so I had to learn to do other things. But it wasn't until my later years that I started to assert myself

113

on some of these things. Before that, I used to keep it to myself. I figured, 'I'm not a star—nobody's gonna listen to me.'

"I always used to say there's a reason for everything. It's what you do initially. A bad beginning means a bad ending. I always traced things back to why and where you were committing this thing. And it was usually in the initial motion. Like in the case of Tommy John. I saw Tommy John when he was with Cleveland. He had kind of a funny quirk in his motion. And everything would go high and away to righthanded batters. We had a chance to get him in the deal with John Romano (in January 1965) and I said, 'Gee, if we can make just a little correction, and Tommy will accept it, he'll be a winner.' "

In spring training, the work began. "I told him, 'Tommy, if we can only get you to do this—wait 'til you come from back here before releasing. Do what's natural but just wait a little longer. Wait until your arm gets on its way up—now you can do what you want with the ball. You can throw it down or you can throw it up and in.' It took a long, long time. He couldn't get the idea of laying back and waiting."

Finally Berres, knowing what an excellent golfer Tommy was, decided to try a new way of getting through to him. After a workout one day at Sarasota, Ray got out his golf clubs and decided to hit a few balls. Noticing Tommy looking on, he purposely sliced several in succession. "Tommy walks up and says, 'Gee, Ray here's why you're squirting 'em over there.' And I say, 'You do it.' And he got up and he hit a ball. I told him to hit another, and when he got up to the top of his backswing, I said, 'Hold it!' And he stopped and he held it. And I went and put a ball in his hand. I said, 'Now, throw it.' And he threw it just as pretty as you please. He said, "Is that what you're trying to get me to do—to wait 'til I get up here and then go?' I said, 'Yeah, it's as simple as that.' He said, 'Good Lord.' I said, 'See, you've got a quirk back here—you have to wait until you undo that before you can release the ball.' "

Gary Peters, another excellent Sox lefty, had a different problem. "Gary would turn his back to you—he was a long-armed guy—and he wouldn't get around," recalled Berres. "So everything would squirt out wide (to righthanded hitters) or he'd force his arm through and there'd go a wild pitch. We didn't know what to do with him. We wanted him to come at you with his right shoulder pointing at you. We had to tell the catcher, 'If you see his numeral, holler at him. Try to keep him from turning the back to you.' We'd have a helluva time with him. And he'd revert back to his old way every once in a while. It's natural. In the stress and strain of a game, you always revert back to what you did as a kid. Unthinkingly. And if you're not stopped right away, you really get into a bad habit. We finally got him cured by having him drop his throwing arm before he reached that tuck point in his delivery—so his hands wouldn't be together.

"Ray Herbert was another guy we'd have to sit on unmercifully. When we got him (from Kansas City in '61), I told him, 'Ray, all your life you've been a .500 pitcher.' He said, 'Why? Because I haven't been on good clubs?' I said, 'You've been a .500 pitcher because half the time you're right, half the time you're wrong. You get too many pitches inside to righthanded hitters. And the ball you want to get away from righthanded hitters—particularly the curveball—you're bouncing in the dirt. I've been watching you for a long time, and I feel I know what you're doing. And when I tell you, you're gonna laugh at me. But I'll tell you what. Either you'll agree to do it our way or we won't be able to use you.' "

Then Berres told Herbert what he'd been doing wrong. When the righthander would bring his arms up over his head during his windup, he'd unconsciously bring his head forward, as if he were ready to have his picture taken. "We called it the Spaulding Guide look," Berres laughed. "Looking pretty. But he'd do that, and the body was sneaking forward. So there was only one way for him to go. And he'd get beat inside."

So Berres stressed the importance of balance, of not letting the body go one way while the arm was still going another way. Herbert was a good pupil: He was 9-6 for the Sox the rest of the '61 season, won 20 games in '62, and led the league with seven shutouts in '63.

Another 20-game winner who had heeded Berres' advice a few years before was Billy Pierce. "Pierce was very cooperative," Ray said. "The only thing about him, he'd get going too fast. The adrenalin kicks up and you're not aware of this. We had to slow down his delivery. We figured with Pierce, if we could smooth out his delivery a little bit and slow it down, his control would improve. And you can check it out.

Look at all those walks he had his first couple years with us and then look at the next year and the year after that. (Billy walked 112 men in 171 innings in '49 and 137 in 219 innings in 1950. In '51, he cut the walks to 73 in 240 innings and then walked 79 in 255 innings in '52.)

"But Billy would've been much more effective if he'd have driven those hitters away from the plate more than he did. He wouldn't knock anybody down—he was too much of a gentleman. He accidentally hit one of his best friends, Johnny Groth, in the head during a game one day. Gus Zernial was then with Philadelphia and they came in for the next series, and Gus said, 'Hey Ray—what's this I read about Billy conking Johnny Groth in the head?'

"I said, 'Yeah, Gus, Billy's not gonna let you big strong bastards dig in on him anymore.' 'You really mean that?' I'm only kidding, but I said, 'Yeah!' And don't you know, the first pitch Billy throws to Gus that day is a fastball that gets away from Billy—and down goes Gus . . . "

But Pierce simply wasn't a headhunter. "We didn't really have any in all the years I was with the White Sox," said Berres. Sox pitchers didn't even go in much for retaliation, unless the situation absolutely called for it. "Ryne Duren of the Yankees would invariably pop Jim Landis," Ray remembered. "So we got tired of that one day and when he came up to bat, Lopez brought in the little Cuban lefty, Rodolfo Arias. He told him, in Spanish, 'I want you to waste the first two pitches outside, and the next one I want you to stick in his ribs. We've got to stop this.'

"First time, Arias missed. Duren looked over at our dugout and Lopez yelled, 'That's right—we mean it! You can't keep hitting Landis like that.' So the next pitch, he got him. But that's the only time I can recall Lopez retaliating. We'd try to push you back, but we wouldn't retaliate."

Ray Berres would, however, preach. "I always worked towards a delivery that was conducive to throwing strikes. I preached delivery and keeping the ball low. If you have the proper delivery, the pitch will be low or you'll have command of it. My argument was, you can never practice theory unless the mechanics of pitching are ironed out. To tell a guy to throw a ball low and away, and it goes high and inside, there's something wrong with the mechanics. Pitching should

116

really be simple.

"I used to tell pitchers, 'Look, if you did something radically wrong, you wouldn't be here. But by making this little adjustment, you could be a lot better than you are. It's my opinion—you don't have to take it. But it's my observation.' Like Johnny Buzhardt. His elbow once in a while would stay in close to his body, and his arm wouldn't get high enough. And you could just see the top of his hand was like on the side of the ball. The ball would stay parallel to the ground right at a certain height. I'd say, 'John, stay back long enough so that you don't come to the plate with the elbow tucked in and hanging down—stay back until you get the elbow up and across on that plane.' Once he got on top, boy, he was a real good pitcher with a good, live fastball. But he would have that tendency to drop down every once in a while. A lot of times pitchers will do that when they get tired."

There were other signs of weakening Berres would look for in his pitchers. "I kept looking for an old habit of yours to pop up during a game," he said. "You might've been going along three, four, five innings real well. Then all of a sudden this habit of yours starts sneaking in and all of a sudden it becomes a spot where, 'Geez, I've either got to change him or I have to go out and get him.' And this is how we worked on the phone between me in the bullpen and Richards or Lopez or whoever in the dugout. I'd probably see things from the back of the pitcher that they couldn't see from their angle.

"I'd keep a chart just to convince you that this was the point in the game where you started to go back to that bad habit of yours. I could show it to you in black and white. I'd have the pitches marked 'good,' 'good,' then maybe an 'Oops!' when that habit would pop up. The guy would say, 'Geez, I'm still throwing good.' But after you see that his delivery has changed, it's time to get him out of there. Lots of times we took guys out in the seventh or eighth inning, knowing that they're getting by luckily. If it's too close a ballgame and there's power coming up, you can't trust the luck.

"Another thing I never believed in was a lot of unorthodox deliveries. That kind of delivery's gonna fool the poor hitter most of the time but it's not gonna fool the good hitter most of the time. The best thing is to see a pitcher get in a groove where he can throw a fastball 80 to 90 percent of the time where it should be thrown. And if you can't do that, you're gonna struggle. Then you're gonna have to overpower someone. But now supposing the pitcher gets this good delivery and he's going along real well, and he's getting hurt by just one particular hitter. So all of a sudden, maybe he's got two strikes on this guy, and he's gonna sidearm him. I'll bet you 90 per cent of the time, if you watch it, the subsequent pitches are balls. He's either gonna get it in a bad spot or he's not gonna get it in the strike zone at all. He takes himself out of the groove and he can't get it back. Oh, I've seen it happen so often. He'll either wind up walking the man, losing the next man, or getting the ball in a bad spot and out of the park it goes. Oh, we watched for that so closely in the seventh, eighth, and ninth inning."

That was the time to bring in the relief. The man turned to in the early '50s was usually Harry Dorish, a chunky righthander who chalked up 29 saves in 1952-53 after picking up a trick pitch—the slip pitch—taught by Berres. "We were rained out in Chicago about three days prior to the opening of the '52 season," Ray said, "and so we worked out in an armory. I was fooling around with a pitch, throwing to Richards one day, and I threw it to him and it sunk and the ball hit Richards in the shin. He said, 'Hey, what is that?' I said, 'I dunno, I've been throwing it on the sidelines for years.' He said, 'Do you suppose you could teach it to Dorish?' I said, 'Well, let's try.'

"And all of a sudden, he got it—real quick. It's like a palm ball. You get it back in your hand and it just kinda drops off—where the palm ball is just kind of a straight change. When you threw this pitch, it slipped out of the hand, so it had no spin. And if it did have any spin, it would have like a screwball spin. And you had to throw it hard or it wouldn't get up to the plate. And that's where the deception came in. When Dorish got it, he had guys all over the league swinging at bad balls. One day in Detroit, he goes in and, geez, he does a helluva job. They're swinging at bouncing balls. And this was the start of it. Everybody around the league's going, 'What the hell is this thing?'

"We tried to keep it quiet without mentioning what it was, or otherwise they'd be looking for it. But he was phenomenal. Batters would swing at it and it'd be dropping in the dirt. Boy, would he bark my shins warming him up—I was too proud, I guess, to wear shin guards. After all, this was only the bullpen. But then he slowly started to lose

118

it. How he lost it, in my book, was he'd get ready to go in, approximating his game speed, and then he wouldn't be called on. So he'd stand around out in the bullpen, staying loose, and he'd just sort of pace himself. And he got in the habit of throwing it easy. And I said, 'Harry, you can't do that—you're gonna start doing it in a game. And if you throw it that way, nothing happens. The optical illusion isn't there, the velocity isn't there, and all of a sudden you lose it.' "

Later that decade came Gerry Staley, the hero of the '59 pennant-clinching victory, and ex-Cub Turk Lown, who had grown enamored of his blooper pitch, which Berres forced him to discard. "We took the blooper away from Turk because every time he threw it, it would take him at least two pitches to throw another strike. So we took it away from him entirely. Made him mad, but it made him more successful. He got in two or three more years in the big leagues where he otherwise wouldn't have gotten 'em.

"One day in '59—we had an off-day Monday and this is a Sunday game in Yankee Stadium—Turk Lown is loosening up in the bullpen so he doesn't have two-three straight days' rest without throwing. And oh, is he firing. I'd never seen him faster in my life. So we're starting to get in a little trouble so I go over to the phone. 'Hey, Al, if you need somebody quick, grab Lown. Boy, is he ever firing.' 'Good—I need him right now. Mantle's coming up with the bases drunk.' So I yelled, 'Hey Turk—you're in there.'

"He goes in and Al meets him at the mound. 'Ray tells me you're throwing nothing but aspirin tablets. I want you to throw nothing but hard stuff to Mantle. Don't throw him any of those blooper change-ups, or he'll hit that facade in right field. If you can, get it in on him a little. But just go to your fastball.'

"He struck him out on three straight pitches to end the game. And when he came in, Al says, 'Attaboy, Turk—that was a great job.' Turk says, 'Hey Skip, I wanted to throw him that blooper so bad.' Lopez says, 'If you had, you'd have been out of here on the next plane.'

Another relief pitcher who made a name for himself under Berres' tutelage was Sandalio "Sandy" Consuegra, a little Cuban righthander with excellent control who one year (1954) established a winning percentage (16-3 for .842) that remains unsurpassed in Sox history.

"Consuegra had a fastball and a little slider—didn't have much in the way of a curveball," said Ray. "His deception came by following a guy in like Rogovin, with the big, long arms and the big delivery—and now here comes little Consuegra. So he was hard to time. But he had good control. He kept it down most of the time and off the plate."

The mere mention of Sandy's name brought back a flood of happy memories. "He was the funniest guy you ever saw. He was a comic. Anything he did, he made you laugh, because his language was broken, you know. Sometimes you didn't know what you were laughing at. But he could imitate. He'd imitate Hitler. He'd put a little mustache on and plaster his hair down. He'd imitate pitchers. Like Donovan, when he'd bend down to get the sign from the catcher, he'd stick his butt out. And if he couldn't see the sign the first time, he'd stick his butt out even more. And that would make that little Con-suegra laugh. And then that little bastard would do it in a game, just to make you laugh. Or he'd be warming up in the bullpen and he'd do it and yell to me, *Berre—Oye, Berre—quien es?'*

"That 16-3 year he had. Several times he'd be in the shower, and we'd be a run behind and we'd pinch-hit for him and come back in our half-inning to go ahead or win it. It was one of those years."

Near the end of the year, Sandy came down with a problem that almost cost him the league percentage title. "He was in the hospital, 'cause he'd been itching like hell with the hives. One day, one of his Cuban friends must have shown him in the paper that he needed two or three more innings or something like that to get his 154 innings to qualify for the championship. So geez, here he is. He shows up in the clubhouse, all spackled up and everything. I say, '*Que pasa?*' He says, '*No pasa nada*—me ready.' 'Are you sure?' 'Yeah, me ready.' So he goes down to the pen and he goes in to relieve and does a helluva job. He immediately wants to go back to the hospital again, and he tells Marty Marion, 'Me eetchee.' Marion says, 'You itch here with us until the end of the season—then you can go home and itch all winter.'

Marion's predecessor, Paul Richards, had disapproved of Sandy's antics earlier that same season. "In spring training, Sandy was messing around, cutting in front of fellows who were doing their running, doing all sorts of nutty things," Berres recalled. "And finally he got stepped on. His Achilles tendon was spiked badly—almost torn off.

120

Richards was madder than hell. Sandy had to go to the hospital and get the stitches. The next day, his leg's all bandaged up and he's gonna sit and watch practice. Richards says to him, 'Hey, get your uniform on.' He says, *'Por que?'* Richards was still mad at him, so he made him get the uniform on and he looked funnier than hell with that foot all bandaged up and a plastic bag on it. Richards had a picnic table brought out and he made Consuegra sit on it and throw, just to keep his arm in shape while the foot was mending."

Berres didn't challenge Richards on the handling of that situation. "I was fortunate to work for managers like Richards and Lopez, who had made a study of pitching like I had," he said. "When Marion came, that's when I started to have more free rein. It was fun working with Paul. I was always in the position where I could come up to him and express to him what I saw and why I thought something happened. Next time we had an opportunity the two of us would work together with a particular pitcher. Lopez was real fine, too. If you told him you had an idea, he'd say, 'Well, fine, let's try it. Nothing ventured, nothing gained.' "

It was just such an attitude that enabled Berres to help make a winner out of Bob Shaw and, a bit later, Juan Pizarro. "I happened to see Bob throwing in the bullpen at Detroit," Ray told me, "when he was still with the Tigers. And everything he was throwing was a promiscuous pitch. But finally I happened to see him throw a pitch— his last, disgusted throw as the game was ending—where the ball went zip. It really moved down. And he didn't even notice it. I said to myself, 'Geez, there's a young kid, pretty good stuff—even though it's all over the place.' It so happened that I picked up a Detroit paper the next day, and Bob Shaw had been optioned to the minors, he'd refused to report, and had quit and had gone home. So we got to talking. I said, 'Geez, if you ever get a chance to get him, let's take a chance on the guy. Let's see what we can do.' Nobody seemed to be interested. I said, 'He's young, he has a good arm. I happened to see him do something that, if we can get him to do it repeatedly, I think he'll be of some help to us.'

"When he came to us, I told him what I had seen. I told him, 'You'll be here and you'll be given the same chance everybody else has been given. And if you do it our way, you can help us and help yourself.

We believe this. Are you willing to go through this transition?' And he said, 'Well, yeah, if you can prove to me that my way is lousy, sure, I'll go the other way.'

"So as time went on, we'd sit and talk. And every time a pitch would get away from him, I'd explain to him why. It was timing again. He'd go to the plate with his arm dragging alongside his right leg. He'd drop the ball down by his right leg. By the time he got his arm up to the focal point of his delivery, his body was already gone. His leverage, everything, was spent. Consequently, he had a late delivery with his arm, so the ball was flying all over the place.

"And he said, 'Geez, you're after me on every pitch.' I said, 'I have to stay after you so you don't continually make this kind of delivery.' So all of a sudden, he got what we were driving at. And he went to extremes with it. It was funny. He was really conscientious about it because he saw how it helped his control, he saw the movement, he saw how it helped his breaking ball. One day, Lopez and I were in a cab driving down Michigan Boulevard and Al says, 'Hey, Ray, look at your protege.' Bob's walking along Michigan looking in the windows and practicing that delivery. Whenever there was a mirror or a reflection, he'd practice it. And all of a sudden he got it, and boy, what a pitcher he was for us in '59."

And what a pitcher Pizarro, the smokin' lefty from the Milwaukee Braves, became once Berres got hold of him in 1961. "Pizarro pitched with an arched back and a rushed delivery and consequently all he could throw was one fastball after another and his best pitches—with the most velocity and most movement—were up out of the strike zone. Well, you might as well throw it out the window. It took a long time to convince him to change his delivery just a little bit. I told him, 'This is what's hurting you: Unless they chase your bad, high fastballs, you're not gonna accomplish anything. You're not gonna pitch here until you make the change. But I'll tell you what. We'll make you a promise that we'll stay with you and give you enough time to develop this and we'll give it enough time to prove either we're wrong or you're wrong.' And that was satisfactory with him.

"He was in the bullpen one day in May and all of a sudden he threw a ball, one of his last pitches, just before the game ended—when he wasn't gonna be used. I said, 'Hey, do that again.' He said, 'Why?'

'Just go ahead and do it. Throw it down to the wall down there.' The catchers had already left. So he threw it. 'Here's another—do it again,' I told him. And he did. I called a catcher back. 'Now throw it a little harder, a little harder, a little harder. Throw it to approximate your game speed.' Finally he said again, 'What's hard about that?' 'The hardest part was getting you to do this. Now throw your slider. Now your curve.' And they were all real good. He'd gone from arching his back and rushing to the plate like that to just laying back and throwing it. And when he got it, he said, 'Why didn't you tell me?' I said, 'My God, every day I'm telling you!'

"The next day, we were way out of the game and I called Al and said 'Al, stick Juan in there so we can see if he'll do in a game what he's doing right now.' So he says, 'OK, send him in.' He went in and had two real good innings and he says, 'Hey, that's easy. Look—I'm not even sweating.' "

Pizarro's success story began unfolding. He would wind up 14-7 that season, 12-14 after a bad start the next year, then 16-8 and 19-9 the following seasons. But even Pizarro needed to be watched closely. "He started a game at Yankee Stadium, and all of a sudden he got out of kilter and went back to his old ways and started walking one guy after another. And then he gives up a long triple to right-center to Hector Lopez—he hit it nine miles. I said, 'What are you doing? Sleeping with this guy? You making him look good at our expense?' Just to get him mad, see. So out of the game he comes, and Al was half-burned. He thought it was just carelessness. But he hadn't realized Juan had gone back to his old ways.

"Anyhow, the first game was over and Al said, 'Juan, go down to the pen for the second game.' Juan came down and said, 'I don't know why I'm down here—I was so lousy in the first game.' I said, 'Well, maybe you might not be lousy anymore.' Sure enough, we get in a situation where we need Juan. Boy, he gets in that real good groove. I call Al: 'Boy, he's got it.' 'Send him in.' And he does a great job and he wins that second game.

"After they get out of kilter, what do you do? Keep reminding them or let them get worse? I felt I was conscious-bound and duty-bound, both for my sake and the pitcher's sake, to tell him."

And that's why he was such a brilliant pitching coach, why Frank

123

Lane considers his bringing Berres in 1949 as one of the best deals he ever made in his long career of dealing. Looking back, it's interesting to speculate on what kind of manager Ray would have made had he chosen to go that route. "I was offered a few managerial jobs," he disclosed, "but I always turned them down. It wasn't meant to be. I'm not the type. I could hire, but, doggone it, I couldn't fire. My greatest satisfaction came in helping somebody if I could. I got more of a kick out of that than anything."

Judging from the list of pitchers helped by Ray Berres, he must have gotten an awful lot of kicks.

IN MEMORIAM: NELSON FOX

I can still hear the voice of Tates Johnson—"Whitey"—the field announcer at Comiskey Park:

"Batting in the second position, Number Two, the second baseman, Nelson . . . Fox . . ."

Then there'd be the roar of approval from all those thousands of fans who loved, as I did, that little guy with the big plug of chewing tobacco in his left cheek. The little guy with the big bottle bat, the fellow who was the guts of the White Sox for so many years, the man who looped dozens and dozens of base hits into short left-center to keep countless rallies alive.

He was part of Chicago's summers from 1950—after Frank Lane had gotten him from the Philadelphia A's for the immortal Joe Tipton—until 1963. He departed in a trade during the winter of '63-'64 to Houston, where he was reunited with one of his first Sox managers, Paul Richards. But Nellie left behind him a record of accomplishments no White Sox second baseman will ever again approach.

He was the American League's Most Valuable Player in 1959—the first Sox player to get that award. He batted .375 in the World Series that year. Twelve times he was named to the A.L. all-star team. Four

Nellie Fox arrives at home plate after a rare home run—this one a game-winner in the last of the 11th against Washington in September 1960. Greeting him are Al Smith (16), coach Don Gutteridge (39), and batboy Bill Sather. [FIELD ENTERPRISES INC. 1960]

times he topped the league in base hits, reaching a peak of 201 in 1954. In a four-year stretch beginning in 1954, he scored 111, 100, 109, and 110 runs in successive seasons. Only once did he strike out as many as 18 times in a season—that for a guy who was averaging 700 plate appearances a year.

In the field, he topped American League second baseman 10 times in putouts. Six times he led them in fielding percentage and assists, and five times he was the leader in doubleplays. And he always led them in games played. He led everyone in that department, so seldom did he miss a day. One string of consecutive games ended at 274 in August 1955 when Marty Marion gave him the day off in Baltimore. Nellie started another streak the next day, this one lasting 798 games until Sept. 4, 1960, when illness forced him out of the lineup. He had played in 1,072 out of a possible 1,073 games. His durability was remarkable for a 5-9, 160-pounder who was constantly being sent flying by big hulks intent on breaking up doubleplays at second base.

"I remember pitching against the Yankees one night in Chicago," "Tricky" Dick Donovan said. "And Bob Cerv was on first. He'd played college football. About 6-2, 215 or so. Legs and arms like Alley Oop. Just a real big guy. There's a ball hit to Aparicio in the hole, over to Fox for the force—and Cerv knocked Nellie out into short left field.

"Nelson was pained, sore—my God, it took him about four or five minutes to make it back to his position. Cerv came up next time with a guy on first. Nellie called time and came into the mound. 'Tricky, do me a favor.' I said, 'Nelson, anything. You name it.' 'How 'bout putting one up under that S.O.B.'s chin?' I said, 'Nelson, consider it done.'

"Next pitch, I put one high and in tight. Cerv went down, the bat went up in the air, the ball hit the bat, and it bounced back out to me for an easy 1-4-3 doubleplay. Nellie came over to me in the dugout and told me, 'Tricky, you're my friend for life.' "

He was everyone's friend. But no one was closer to Fox than Billy Pierce, his roommate for 11 years. Pierce's eyes were smiling as he remembered his old buddy. "Nellie was a tremendous competitor," he began. "He was a holler guy on the field, but he was actually a quiet fellow off the field. He didn't like to mingle with crowds and he didn't like big cities too much. His favorite thing to do when the season was over was to go home (to St. Thomas, Pa.) to hunt and fish. He'd get lost in the woods out there in the wintertime.

"But he was always giving 1,000 per cent. He was a ballplayer who you'd say, with his size and speed, had just average talent. But what he got out of it was all-star talent. He never had the greatest arm in the world. He never had the greatest speed in the world. But he was still an all-star."

Pierce remembered spring training of 1951, when new manager Richards—figuring that the .247-hitting Fox of 1950 would have to be vastly improved if he were to remain a regular—made Nellie his No. 1 project. Richards brought in Joe Gordon, the former star second baseman of the Yankees and Indians, to work with Fox on the mechanics of making the doubleplay. Richards' hitting instructor, Doc Cramer, persuaded Nellie to change from a thin-handled bat to Cramer's model—the bottle bat. Richards himself counseled Fox on the fine art of bunting, which would help Nellie add several points a year to his batting average.

"So there was some learning to go along with Nellie's hustling," said Pierce. "But Nellie had that determination that few fellows have. At night, in the room, he'd say, 'You know, I threw that one time at bat away.' In other words, he'd already have two hits and he'd kind of relax the next time up. We'd be way ahead in the ballgame and maybe he'd let up. He'd be angry at himself for wasting that time at bat.

"A fellow would be throwing bullets out there—Herb Score or somebody like that. Nellie would come back to the dugout and say, 'Aw, he don't have anything.' Other guys would come back and say, 'He must be crazy.' But nobody could ever throw the ball by Nellie— nobody."

Not even Pierce, who finally got a chance to pitch against his ex-roomie in '64 when Billy was with San Francisco and Fox was with Houston. "He bunted once and got thrown out on a pretty good bunt—it was a real close play—and oh, he griped," Pierce laughed. "Because he didn't like to bunt anyway unless he got a hit. Then he hit a line drive and a guy caught it. He wanted to get a hit off me so bad. So I always kidded him: 'You're 0-for-2 against me.' "

Fox kidded Pierce a few times, too. "I remember once I was pitching and they were hitting the ball pretty hard off me," Billy grinned. "And

128

one ball happened to hit our third baseman, Freddie Hatfield, in the leg. They went into the dugout to work on him, and I threw a few warmup pitches to stay loose—and then I look up and Freddie hadn't come back out. Marty Marion had sent Sammy Esposito out to play third. I hadn't thought Freddie had been hurt that bad.

"Nellie came over to the mound and I asked him, 'Is Freddie hurt bad?' And he said, 'No, no, he's OK—Marty just feels that since Freddie's got four kids, it's much safer to have Sammy, the single guy, play third while you're pitching.' "

Foxie didn't kid, though, when he was back out at his position— or even when he was busy playing cards with his roommate back at the hotel. "The coaches," Pierce reported, "would never have to run a bedcheck on us because they could hear Nellie's yelling all over the hotel. If he was winning or losing, he'd be hollering all over the place. The only time the coaches would ever call our room would be to tell us to please quiet down so they could get some sleep."

One person who knew Nellie almost as long as Pierce knew him was broadcaster Jack Brickhouse, who was doing Sox games on WGN-TV when Fox came to the Sox for the 1950 season. That season saw Nellie playing second fiddle to regular baseman Cass Michaels and, for a short term after Michaels' trade to Washington, to newly acquired Al Kozar. Eventually, Nellie won the job from Kozar and began his steady rise toward stardom.

"He always had that plug of tobacco in his cheek," Brickhouse remembered, "and his wife, Joanne, used to bawl him out about it: 'It looks terrible on television.' We had a running gag, he and I. He accidentally called me Bob one time in an interview. He had me confused with Bob Elson, which can happen once in a while. Bob's working radio, I'm working television.

"So Nellie thought that was funny. So he started doing it a lot— calling me Bob all the time. I said, 'You keep that up, I'm gonna call you Al Kozar. So after that, we had a running joke. He called me Bob all the time, I called him Al all the time. It went on for quite a while."

So did the ribbing Fox took from his teammates for his woeful lack of power—he hit only 35 home runs in his entire career. "One time we had a lot of fun with Nellie was opening day '59 in Detroit," chuckled Jungle Jim Rivera, "when he hit the home run in the 14th inning to win it—which was the only home run I think I ever saw him hit. But everybody in the dugout got towels and were holding them up, and as he came in, I wrapped one around him and gave him a hug and said, 'Man, if I could hit the longball like you, Nellie, I'd be in the Hall of Fame.' "

Once, Al Smith recalled, it was Nellie's turn to be the welcoming committee for a home run hitter and he wanted no part of it. "I hit the first home run that set off the new scoreboard in 1960," Smitty said, "and Fox was the next hitter. And he wouldn't shake my hand at home plate. The sportswriters saw that and wondered if there was something going on between me and Nellie. But I told them what had happened:

"Here's all this noise and fireworks going off and music blaring. Lights flashing. It seemed like it went on for five minutes. And Jim Bunning's the pitcher. Nellie says to me as I come down the line from third, 'I'm not shaking your hand—I don't like this. 'Cause I'm going to get knocked down.'

"Sure thing, Bunning's first pitch is high and in and Nellie goes down."

Usually, though, Nellie followed someone like Luis Aparicio in the lineup, so there was little fear of knockdown pitches. Looie hit homers about as often as Fox did. Bill Veeck remembered the Sox' 1-2 punch of 1959. "Our offense that year, it seemed to me, was Aparicio would walk and steal second, Fox would single him in, and then we'd wait three more innings."

It was Veeck who gave Fox a "night" that same season, and 38,000-plus turned out to see Nellie showered with all manner of gifts. "We gave him a boat that night," Bill Veeck said, beginning to smile. "There was no water, of course—except for a little creek—within 100 miles of his home. Ultimately, he sold the boat and bought some land he had wanted. We would've given him the land, of course, but you can't tow a piece of land into a ballpark."

That he deserved such a "night" was only too obvious. Everyone knew he was the heart of the ballclub, a leader respected by all. "I remember Fox on the road in '59," said Jack Kuenster, who covered Fox for seven seasons with the old Chicago Daily News. "When we'd check into a hotel on an offday, the players all of a sudden would start dispersing all over town. Nellie Fox would always say, 'Don't forget to get your rest—get back in at a decent time.' He tried to set that standard for them."

Pete Ward, who broke in with the Sox in '63 when Fox was playing his final season in Chicago, revealed another way in which Nellie set the standard. "Nellie Fox in '63 took as many groundballs as anybody who has ever played infield. And he was near the end of his career. But he was out there working his ass off every day.

"That year, I was going through one of my fielding slumps. And I'd made one of the most routine plays anybody could ever make for the third out of an inning. Any high school kid in the country could've caught the ball and thrown the guy out. Well, I caught the ball and threw the guy out. Nellie Fox came running across from second base on his way to the dugout like it was the greatest play in the world and we'd just won the seventh game of the World Series. He was leaping in the air, whistling away. But he wasn't showing me up at all. It was just his way of having some fun and relaxing me a little bit."

Nobody, however, could ever get Fox to relax—if he wasn't playing. "He was a guy who loved to play," said Al Lopez, who got to manage Nellie for seven years after managing against him for six years in Cleveland. "Even if he wasn't feeling good he wanted to play. It finally got to where I couldn't take him out, because if you kept him on the bench, he'd be a pest. He'd be bothering everybody. I'd say, 'Well, let him play if he wants to.' "

But eventually the day came when Nellie could no longer play. And then, some years later, the day came when he could no longer live.

Jacob Nelson Fox was born on Christmas Day, 1927. Cancer of the lymph nodes claimed his life on December 1, 1975. He was just 47 years old, my first childhood hero to die.

"It's a shame," Jungle Jim Rivera said, shaking his head in sadness. "But I guess God wanted him. It was his time."

IN MEMORIAM:
SHERMAN LOLLAR

The news came 18 years and two days after the White Sox had clinched their only pennant since 1919: Sherman Lollar, star catcher and silent leader of the Sox for a dozen summers, was dead at age 53, a victim of cancer. Now two members of the 1959 American League championship team had lost their battle to live.

The memories remain alive, though. Sherm Lollar, with the No. 10 on the back of his uniform shirt, out at the mound counseling a pitcher in a jam. Or slugging a long home run over the leftfield wall and out onto Sam's Parking Lot at old Municipal Stadium in Kansas City. Or throwing out still another would-be base thief with a perfect peg to Luis Aparicio at second.

Sadly, the memory most White Sox fans will carry of Lollar is Sherm being gunned down at home plate in the last of the eighth inning of Game Two of the '59 World Series. Lollar was at first and Earl Torgeson was at second with none out and with the Sox trailing Los Angeles 4-2. Al Smith doubled up the alley in left-center to send Torgeson home easily, but the notoriously slow Lollar, waved in by third-base coach Tony Cuccinello, was an easy out at home—thanks to a perfect relay, Wally Moon to Maury Wills to John Roseboro.

Sherm Lollar

"But," Jack Brickhouse reminded me, "you can't blame Lollar. It's not Sherman's fault. He ran as fast as he could. Like the old story about Ping Bodie. He was thrown out by about 25 feet trying to steal second once, and Bugs Baer wrote about it: 'Well, Ping had larceny in his heart, but his feet were honest.' "

No, it would be a mistake if Sherm Lollar were remembered only for being thrown out at home plate in the World Series. He was a solid major leaguer who knew how to play the game. He was a player who improved the skills he had by constant hard work—hard work having been part of his makeup since the days he had labored as a mule skinner in the lead and zinc mines around Baxter Springs, Kan. His was an Ozark background—he was born in Durham, Ark., and eventually settled in Springfield, Mo. From that background developed a quiet doer who performed his job without complaint and, while doing so, earned the respect of everyone around him.

"Sherm's success," Al Lopez said, "was that the pitchers liked him personally—and they respected him. That's a great thing to have going for a catcher. It's tough to be pitching and having to worry about what a catcher's gonna call. If a catcher's got a reputation of being a rockhead, the pitcher's gonna have to worry that much more."

But Lollar was no rockhead. Like Lopez, a great catcher himself in his playing days, Lollar knew what to call and when to call for it. "He handled pitchers well, he was unflappable," Brickhouse recalled. "Ideal, I suppose, to be employed by Lopez. You could just see these two quiet men, the old catcher and the new catcher, thinking like catchers and handling pitchers so well."

Bill Veeck remembered, among other things, that relationship between Lollar and Lopez when he spoke at Lollar's funeral. "His wife (named Connie, as is Lopez's) asked me to deliver the eulogy—I'd never delivered one before. And I mentioned to all the people in the church—it was full, of course, with people spilling out into the street—that they were smarter than I. It hadn't taken them as long to recognize his true worth as it had me, because I had traded him twice. It wasn't until I fortunately inherited him in Chicago that I began to recognize how important he was.

"And I said that Al Lopez had continuously told me that Sherm was like having Lopez himself out there catching. Sherm and he agreed on

95 to 99 per cent of the pitches. It was like having a manager out there on the field."

Veeck first traded Lollar off the Cleveland Indians' roster after the 1946 season, sending him to the Yankees in a deal that brought to Cleveland lefty Gene Bearden (who would help win Veeck the '48 pennant by winning 20 games). After Sherm had drifted to the St. Louis Browns, Veeck sold the Indians, bought the Browns, and then traded Lollar to the White Sox in Nov. 1951 in one of Frank Lane's typical, eight-player blockbusters. He hit a home run his first time up with the White Sox and went on to play a major role in the club's slow climb toward a pennant.

But he didn't establish himself as an everyday player right away. His first Sox manager, Paul Richards, cut his catching time to 107 games in '53 and 93 games in '54 while giving opportunities to the likes of Red Wilson, Matt Batts, and Carl Sawatski, the stout ex-Cub. It wasn't until Marty Marion was named manager late in '54 that Lollar was pronounced the No. 1 catcher. By that time, though, Sherm had already been accepted by his Sox teammates as part of the team's nucleus, had been nicknamed "Dad" because of his slow temperament and his slow movements, and had shown off his wry sense of humor.

"Lollar was easy-going—and he ran the same way," laughed Jungle Jim Rivera. "He never talked a lot, but he was a dry-humor type of guy. One day in '53 we were playing Detroit and Bill Summers was the plate umpire. I was sitting on the bench that day, wasn't playing. They had a lefthander, Billy Hoeft, pitching against us. And Gene Bearden was pitching for us. And Summers was calling some bad balls, and Lollar's giving Summers hell all day, and Summers isn't even paying attention to him.

"So finally, they're coming off the field toward the dugout after the game, and we're still in the dugout. And Lollar says to the other umpires, 'Hey, will you take this guy home? He's got to be blind. Take care of this poor guy or he won't even make it back to the hotel. And make sure his wife picks him up at the airport, I'm worried about him.' All that without ever cracking a smile. You had to laugh."

Once the entire team was laughing at Lollar. "Earl Torgeson was on second, Sherm was on first," remembered Billy Pierce. "And how it happened I'll never know, because Sherm never would try to steal a base, anyway. But for whatever reason, Sherm all of a sudden lit out for second base. And Torgy's standing on second and he looks down at Sherm and says, 'Hey, Dad, what are you doing here?' "

All Sherm could do was look sheepish. Seldom, though, did he have to apologize for his actions. Four times during his stay with the Sox—in '53, '56, '60, and '61—he led league catchers in fielding. Three times he led in doubleplays. Seven times he was named to the A.L. all-star team. His RBI totals increased from 34 in 1954 to 61 the next year, to 75 in '56 and to 84 in both '58 and '59. He drove in 70 in 1957 even though he missed more than 40 games because of a broken wrist. As for the long ball, he topped the club with 20 homers in '58 and led again with 22 in the pennant year of '59. And all through it he remained an unpretentious, down-to-earth man. A man Dick Donovan was proud to call a friend.

"Sherman and I spent a lot of time together," Donovan said of his Arkansas-born batterymate. "His friends were my friends. I remember when we'd go to Washington, we'd spend a lot of time in Sen. Fulbright's office. Lee Williams and John Erickson were two Fulbright aides and we all became good friends. Sherm introduced me to another senator—from Rhode Island—Theodore Green, 92 years old at the time."

Sherm wasn't quite that old when he called it quits after the 1963 season. But he was 39, which was old enough. Later, he managed in the Oakland A's farm system—everyone always figured he'd make a good manager someday—but never in the White Sox organization. He made it back, however, to Comiskey Park for the 10-year reunion of the pennant-winning team in 1969. He was not there for the 20-year reunion. Nor was Nellie Fox. That's when it all finally struck home for their longtime teammate, Al Smith.

"It didn't really hit me that they were gone until the reunion, when Nellie's wife and Sherm's wife embraced," Smitty said. "That's when I realized, 'OK, yeah, they're not here anymore.'

"But you know, when you talk about '59 and those days, Sherm and Nellie still seem so alive."

Their memories will so remain.

BILLY PIERCE:
Fastballs, sliders and Ed FitzGerald

I met Billy Pierce for lunch at D'Filippo's, an Italian restaurant at 37th and Ashland, maybe a mile and a half west of the ballpark where he had spent all but four of his 17 big league seasons. He had come from his office at Continental Envelope, just a couple blocks away, and he approached the restaurant with those short, fast steps I had watched him use so often as he went out to take the Comiskey Park mound.

We shook hands and a waitress led us to our table. We sat down and I mentioned to him that he had been the starting pitcher in the first game I had ever attended in person—that July 1954 game against the Yankees, the game he had had to leave—leading 5-1—because of a split nail on his throwing hand. And I told him how Mickey Mantle had won it 7-5 with a three-run homer in the ninth.

"I don't remember that one," he said, "but I remember one like it." He began telling me about a game he pitched against the Yankees in Chicago in 1952, the night Jim Rivera first wore a Sox uniform. Pierce went into the game with an 11-7 record, and five of the seven losses had been to the Yankees. In those five losses, his teammates had backed him with awesome support: a grand total of seven runs. But

137

Billy Pierce

this night, it seemed, things would be different. The Sox led 7-0 at one point and 7-3 when manager Paul Richards excused Billy for the evening in the seventh inning and brought in relief ace Harry Dorish to wrap it up.

"I had pitched with two days' rest," he remembered, "and Richards said, 'Bill, go seven innings and we'll let Harry mop up.' So Harry came in and in the eighth inning, he got 'em out. Ninth inning, I'm in there taking a shower, feeling good, and listening to the game on the clubhouse radio. Then there were a couple of walks and a hit, and an easy groundball was hit to Hector Rodriguez at third, and he booted it. And that set the stage for everything else."

Still, there were two out. Two men were on base, but the Sox led 7-4. Richards called for lefty Chuck Stobbs because Joe Collins and Irv Noren, a pair of lefthanded hitters, were the next two New York batters. Collins walked to fill the bases.

"Then I remember Irv Noren fouling off about 10 pitches before finally drawing a walk," said Pierce. "And then Mantle hit a home run with the bases crammed. And we lost the ballgame. Frank Lane was so mad, Rodriguez never played another game for us."

Lane didn't forget Stobbs, either. That winter, Frank shipped him to Washington in a deal for pitcher Mike Fornieles. So Stobbs' career with the Sox lasted but one season. Pierce was a different story: He joined the team in 1949 and stayed on through 1961, winning 186 games—a record for Chicago lefties. He was Lane's first acquisition, coming to the Sox from his hometown Detroit Tigers for a catcher named Aaron Robinson. Billy remembered the circumstances surrounding the deal as if it were yesterday.

"I'd been with Detroit all of '48 and I had won three and lost none. And there was a thing in one of the Detroit papers saying that only five players on the club were going to stay—they had come in fifth, they hadn't gone too well. This was in October. The story listed Johnny Groth, Hoot Evers, I think Hal Newhouser too. Anyway, I was one of the five listed. And I thought to myself—you know, being a hometown boy—'Oh, that's nice. I'm gonna stay here.'

"And it wasn't a month later that I was driving over to my girl's house, and there was music playing on the radio and they cut in— 'We have a sports note . . .' That's how I found out I'd been traded to

Chicago. And right away, I was disappointed, because of what I knew of Chicago. We'd come in here for games in '48 and there wasn't any crowd, the stockyards were in full bloom, and the lights were kind of dingy, like they hadn't been cleaned in years. But it turned out to be a break for me because I came over to a ballclub where I got the opportunity to pitch. You have to have a chance. Later, I was told by Lane that the Tigers had wanted to give him Ted Gray (another lefty) instead of me—Teddy and I had gone to the same high school in Highland Park, Mich. I was also told by Lane that the next day the Tigers tried to call off the deal.

"But it was a jolt. Chicago had had a terrible year in '48 (51-101) and of course Detroit being the hometown, I was always charged up—that was my team. That's why I signed with Detroit. By being in the Esquire Magazine all-America boys' baseball game in New York in '44 (he was named the game's most valuable player and was presented the trophy by Connie Mack), there were several clubs I could've signed with. But Detroit was my hometown team."

Soon Chicago would be his adopted hometown, and Chicago would adopt him as one of its own—just as it would with Minnie Minoso, Jim Rivera, and Billy's roommate of 11 years, Nellie Fox. Pierce's success wasn't immediate. He was 7-15 in '49 and improved to 12-16 in '50, and among those dozen victories was a one-hitter against the Yankees. Then he lowered his earned run average from 3.99 to 3.04 in '51 and to 2.58 in '52, winning 15 games each of those seasons. But he didn't really become a great pitcher until 1953, when he added a third pitch—the slider.

"I was talking to Ted Williams one day, and Williams was one of Pierce's greatest admirers," Frank Lane had told me. "And Williams said, 'That little guy you have, he's got to come up with a slider.' I said, 'Well, if I tell him that, he won't pay any attention. You tell him.' "

The next time the Red Sox came to Comiskey Park, Pierce was protecting a one-run lead in the ninth with two on and two out. The Boston batter was Ted Williams. Pierce threw what looked to Williams like a fastball. He swung, but the ball broke at the last second, and Williams, instead of getting all of the ball, got just a bit of it and popped out to end the game. Williams told Lane, "I've got to learn to keep my mouth shut."

"I was basically a fastball pitcher until I came up with the slider in '53," said Pierce. "Then I was still a fastball pitcher but I threw a lot of sliders and fast curves. The slider's a controlled breaking ball and you're more of a pitcher with the slider than you were before. Most fellows, when they have just the fastball and curve, are just throwers. But the slider makes you a pitcher because, on 2-and-0, 3-and-1, or even 3-and-0, you can throw a breaking ball and put it for a strike."

With the new pitch, Pierce was superb in '53. He went 18-12 with a 2.72 ERA and led the league in strikeouts with 186. He threw $39\frac{2}{3}$ consecutive scoreless innings in one stretch and even held the Yankees scoreless for $23\frac{1}{3}$ straight. All told, he pitched 271 innings, after having pitched 255 and 240 the two preceding years. Maybe he should have expected what would happen the following spring in Tampa, Fla.

"I went to throw a ball hard," Billy remembered, "and it just about killed me. And it never did get better. But I found out after about three weeks going to different doctors that I could try to pitch it out. So I put some real hot stuff on my arm and I went out there and, no matter how much it hurt, I had to throw harder and harder and harder and I finally loosened it up. And I did that for the next 10 years, from 1955 through '64. Every time I started I had to do that to a certain extent. I had an adhesion in the arm and, just like with a knife, I had to cut it, tear it. But that first spring training, I didn't know what was happening. I thought, 'My God, maybe this is it. Who knows what's gonna happen?'

"Finally, after I got it loosened up later on, I pitched a little bit that year. I didn't have that great a year, won nine and lost 10. But it started feeling much better and then in '55 they pitched me kinda sparingly—once a week, once every six days—and I had a real good year (15-10)—had the best ERA I ever had (a league-leading 1.97). In fact, I had a record of 5-6 at the all-star break but I was still picked to start the all-star game."

The won-lost record was misleading because, as usual, the Sox offense was sputtering. Before that '55 season was over, Billy would lose four 1-0 games. "In fact, I lost two games to Cleveland 1-0 within a week of each other," he laughed. Other than the frustration of those

1-0 defeats, though, 1955 was a year of success. "It worked out great—the rest did me good," he said. "Then in '56 and '57 I pitched a lot of innings again and won 20 games both years."

Then came his greatest game. On a June evening in 1958, he retired the first 24 Washington batters as the Sox built a 3-0 lead after eight innings against Russ Kemmerer. The game moved to the ninth. Pierce retired Ken Aspromonte and then Steve Korcheck. One more and it would have been a perfect game. Washington manager Cookie Lavagetto, who had broken up Floyd Bevens' no-hit bid in the ninth inning of the fourth game of the 1947 World Series, sent up Ed Fitz-Gerald to bat for Kemmerer. Pierce remembered the rest all too well.

"FitzGerald was a first-ball, fastball hitter. So we threw him a curveball away. And he hit it down the rightfield line for a hit. It was hit well—it was a good hit."

Billy retired Albie Pearson moments later to get the shutout victory, but the smallish crowd of 11,300 was still screaming its hatred for FitzGerald, who had wrecked the fans' dream of seeing a perfect game. Pierce, however, held no animosity. "I didn't feel that badly about it—really not that badly. We were in a little slump and I was just happy to win the ballgame. It didn't mean that much—at the moment. In later years, I wished probably that it had happened. It would've been nice if it had happened.

"But if you're in the game for 17 years like I was, you have a lot of things to look back on. You don't need that one thing. I can live without it."

The game itself had lasted a mere 1:46. "With Washington, we had some fast games. Another time I pitched and beat Washington in 1:32. In fact it was funny: The fellow who was running the concessions at the time said, 'Bill, take your time—you're costing me money. With Wynn, we get at least 2½ hours every time.' Wynn was a slow worker. So was Donovan. But I'd rather pitch a little faster. That was my trouble when I was younger. I tried to go TOO fast. And I'd get goofed up. You can't be too quick. Paul Richards was my manager and catcher at Buffalo, and he'd hold the ball, just to get me to slow down.

"But we had good success against Washington for some reason. We had good success against Cleveland. Even when they had that great team in '54, we broke even with them—we were the only team in the league to do that. But the Yankees would always beat us. We'd win some games, but they would always win more than we did (except in '55, when the teams split the 22-game season series, and in '59, when the Sox were 13-9 against New York).

"Of course they always had a little bit more than we did—a little more depth. And that made all the difference in the world. We tried to save pitchers for them and we'd lose other games because of it—because we didn't have the hitting to make up for it. The Yankees could overwhelm Philadelphia—later Kansas City—and some other clubs but we couldn't overwhelm anybody with our hitting so we couldn't spot our pitching. They had Johnny Kucks and Tom Sturdivant, who they could spot against certain clubs, and they could save Whitey Ford for the White Sox and Cleveland. Stengel could do it but our managers couldn't. We didn't have the depth. We always had to keep low runs because we didn't score 10-12 runs a game.

"The Yankees would go into Kansas City after beating us 2-1 and 3-2 and they'd beat Kansas City 8-6. We were the other way around. We'd get done playing those real tough games with the Yankees and because we didn't have the depth in pitching or the good hitting, we'd go to Kansas City and lose 5-4 or 4-3, all the time. That's what hurt us. We didn't have the depth."

But the Sox-Yankee games of the '50s will always be remembered on the South Side as maybe the most thrilling baseball games of the century. Especially the ones when Pierce faced the American League's other premier lefty of the era, Ford. Billy had an 8-6 record in head-to-head competition with Whitey, but he was always more concerned about facing the Yankee lineup than Ford.

"You had Mantle and Berra," he said. "Bauer was tough on left-handed pitching. Now you get past them, and psychologically maybe you tend to relax a little bit and Skowron would kill you. Bill was a good hitter. He gave the White Sox a lot of trouble. Mantle and Berra were the 3-4 men in the lineup and they probably beat us more games, but probably batting-average-wise, Skowron did as well against us as anybody.

"Gene Woodling would always get on base, too. They had a lot of good hitters. Mantle was almost an 80-point better hitter righthanded

143

than he was lefthanded, because he knew the strike zone. Lefthanded, he'd swing and miss the ball up above the letters and also the ball in the dirt. Righthanded, he wouldn't swing at those pitches. I wish he would have. But Mickey righthanded was probably as good a hitter as there was."

Put Pierce, I used to think, on a team with that kind of hitting and he might have won 311 games in his career instead of 211. In 1962, I got my wish, even though Billy's career was almost over. Ed Short and Al Lopez, out to rebuild the club, sent Pierce and Don Larsen to San Francisco for pitchers Eddie Fisher and Dominic Zanni and first baseman Bob Farley, who Bob Elson quickly sized up as a potential Mickey Mantle. Farley was gone before the season was three months old. (Later, the Giants also sent along pitcher Verle Tiefenthaler, whose last name, by some miracle, was somehow stitched in full onto the back of his uniform. That was the only thing memorable about the guy.)

The trade did not disappoint Pierce in the least. "Well, I'll tell you, I'd been here 13 years. And I had a feeling something might happen. I was player representative at the time and we all went to the winter meetings. You get premonitions. I told Eddie Short—and I'll always be thankful to him for this—'If I'm traded, I want to know first. I don't want to read about it in the papers or hear it over the radio.' And he called my hotel room one night and told me I'd been traded to the Giants. So I had a chance to call my wife. In fact, my oldest son, Bill— we were kinda leery about how he'd react. So my wife told him, 'Dad's been traded to San Francisco.' And his first reaction was, 'Oh, boy! Now I'll get to meet Willie Mays!'

"So it worked out quite satisfactorily. The White Sox had had a rough year in '61 (86-76 but 23 games out of first) and it turned out to be a break for me because we went out there to the Coast and right away won the pennant in '62 (Pierce chipped in with a 16-6 record). We had a good ballclub—a real good ballclub, actually—and I'm surprised it didn't win more often. Fellows like Mays, McCovey, Cepeda, O'Dell, Marichal, Kuenn, Haller, all the Alous, Davenport, Sanford. That was a good ballclub."

But the Giants couldn't beat the Yankees, either, although Pierce topped Ford 5-2 in the sixth game of the Series with a three-hitter. "I left Chicago, and I left the Yankees behind, and I go over to the National League and the first year I hit the Yankees in the World Series. And Whitey. That was an exciting two weeks for me—probably the most exciting I had ever had. Through all the years with the White Sox, winning the pennant in '59, pitching in seven different all-star games—all that was exciting. But in '62, we tied for the league lead, had a three-game playoff with the Dodgers, and then played a World Series that lasted seven games. And I was involved in everything. I won the first playoff game 8-0, then I relieved in the ninth inning of the last playoff game. I started two Series games and when McCovey lined to Bobby Richardson for the final out with Mays on third in that seventh game, I was in the bullpen warming up to go in to relieve in case we had tied it up. It was a very exciting time for me."

But for Sox fans, I said as a waitress cleared away what remained of our lunch, the '50s was the time that was the most exciting. "It was an exciting time for baseball," Billy said. "The '50s—it was the tops. Because there were so many good teams: New York, Chicago, Cleveland, Detroit, Boston." And the White Sox were always up there, drawing well and playing exciting ball. It was a time when the city loved the Sox and the Sox loved the city.

"We felt we were part of the city," he told me. "We were representing Chicago. We all felt that way. You'd go to an all-star game (Billy started two others besides the one in '55), you were representing your ballclub and your city and if you didn't do well, it made the whole city look bad. There was a lot of pride in the ballclub. There were a lot of guys who had to work hard to accomplish something. They couldn't play halfway and still do well. They had to go with everything they had.

"No, we had a good ballclub. Nobody ever said they beat us easy. They knew they were in a fight. Even the Yankees."

And when Billy Pierce was out on the mound, the fight was always that much tougher.

MINNIE MINOSO:
The Cuban Comet

Minnie Minoso was the White Sox' Jackie Robinson. Before the arrival of the Cuban Comet from Cleveland on May 1, 1951, every Chicago player had been as white as the team's sanitary socks. The fans cheered for players like Luke Appling, Cass Michaels, Don Kolloway, and Dave Philley. And Billy Pierce, Eddie Robinson, Gus Zernial, and Floyd Baker. All white faces in white uniforms.

But when Minnie arrived, the White Sox suddenly had their first black player. Things forever would be different on the South Side. A new kind of electricity swept through Comiskey Park. Minoso's blackness was in stark contrast to the whiteness of his new White Sox uniform. There was a certain air of confidence about him as he took pregame warmups before that afternoon's game with the mighty New York Yankees.

Then the Sox came to bat in the first inning against Vic Raschi, New York's three-time 21-game winner. With one out, Paul Lehner—acquired in the deal that brought Minnie to Chicago—singled to right. Up stepped Minoso. Raschi threw and Minnie swung, and the ball took off to straightaway center, disappearing over the old bullpen fence, 415 feet away. He could not possibly have made a more

Minnie Minoso, just reacquired on waivers from the Washington Senators, gets his old uniform back from clubhouse man Sharkey Colledge during spring training, 1964, in Sarasota.

147

dramatic debut.

"That was one of the greatest days in my life," Saturnino Orestes Arrieta Armas Minoso told me, in his broken English, in his office at C & K Distributors in Chicago, where he works in public relations. "That day, I never forget. It helped that I finally know I have regular position. In Cleveland, I was on the bench, play maybe two-three times a week. Some guy get hurt, I go in and play.

"But when I come over here, left field or third base or whatever, I know I'm in the lineup every day."

That first day, Minnie was stationed at third base. Unfortunately, it should be added. Because, just a half-inning after his brilliant break-in with his bat, Minnie diminished it by a less-than-brilliant breakdown with his glove. With the bases loaded and two out, he let Mickey Mantle's groundball go right through his legs, allowing the tying runs to score. The Sox went on to lose, 8-3.

But they won 20 of their next 23 to take over the league lead, and Minnie obviously was one of the big reasons for the surge. His hitting, his speed, his daring—it all rubbed off on his new teammates, who were completely captivated by the newcomer, regardless of his race. All of which proved Minoso right: He himself had not been worried at all about becoming Chicago's first black baseball player.

"No, I was not scared," he said. "Because in baseball, I never was scared of nothing. I thought I was like in my own home. I never scared. I just went up there, knowing I had to show the people.

"Paul Richards (Minnie pronounced it Paw Reechard) gave me good welcome myself over here. When I got here, Chico Carrasquel told me that Paul Richards had a meeting and said, 'He's gonna be here and this guy's gonna help the ballclub. And I don't want anybody do nothing against him. I don't care if he's black or brown or what color. As long as he helps the ballclub, the White Sox are gonna have him.'

"The people, the fans, made me feel at home, completely. So after that I figured I had a home here for a hundred years. It's true. The people gave me good welcome. And no matter if, sure, I make a mistake—I usta play lousy like anybody else. But the only thing I would do would be to give you 100 per cent every day. So I'm happy now because I did that. Because in the job that I do, a lot of people, they tell me, 'Minnie, I remember when you did this or did that . . .' And no one ever has told me, 'Minnie, one day you pushed me away or gave me bad expression because I wanted your autograph.' No, it's always, 'You always would give autograph, no matter what time.' So these things make me feel happy."

Naturally, he didn't win the fans simply by giving 100 per cent all the time and by signing autographs for everyone. He also performed on the field. He was second in the league that first season to champion Ferris Fain with a batting average of .326. He hit 34 doubles, 14 triples, 10 homers, batted in 76 runs, scored 112, and stole 31 bases. The Sporting News named him the American League's Rookie of the Year. But, racial prejudice being what it was in 1951—a year in which a mob in Cicero took to throwing rocks through one dwelling's windows to let the black family inside know they were not welcome in the neighborhood—the Baseball Writers Association of America gave their Rookie award to Gil McDougald. McDougald hit 20 points below Minnie, had 11 fewer doubles, 10 fewer triples, 13 fewer RBI, 17 fewer stolen bases, batted 130 fewer times, and played in 15 fewer games. But McDougald played for the New York Yankees and, more importantly, was white.

The injustice never seemed to bother Minnie, however. He just went on performing. His batting averages for the next 10 years read like this: .281, .313, .320, .288, .316, .310, .302, .302, .311, and .280. He drove in 104 runs in 1953, 116 in '54, 103 in '57, and 105 in '60, when he was 37 years old. In his 11 years as a big league regular (a head injury in '62, after he'd been traded by the Sox to St. Louis for Joe Cunningham, limited him to 39 games and he never again would be a full-timer), he averaged 98 runs scored a year. Over the same span, he averaged 170 base hits, 29 doubles, seven triples, and 89 RBI. He seemed indestructible. Nothing could stop him—not taunts from rival dugouts, not beanballs, not anything.

"Some managers used to holler at me, tell me they are gonna hit me (with pitched balls), and then they do it," Minoso recalled. "There was Jimmie Dykes. Everytime we play Philadelphia, gee whiz, he cuss me out and he tell me he's gonna hit me. He didn't do it in Chicago. He's afraid of the people, because they in my corner. And because he used to play here. But in Philadelphia, they used to give me hell."

The Yankees' Bob Grim gave him more than hell. One day in May of 1955, the big righthander beaned Minnie, giving the Sox star a hairline fracture of the skull and sidelining him for more than two weeks. But Minnie, who crowded the plate and annually led the league in getting hit by pitches, never did feel any ill will toward Grim.

"In this case, I always said before and I say it now, things like this happen in baseball. But I don't think Bob Grim threw baseball intentional to hit me. Probably, you know, he gonna pitch me close and the pitch was a little wild. But I never had it on my mind that he do it on purpose—even though it almost killed me. No, I have no feeling against any pitcher who hit me."

Not that he forgot who that pitcher was. "Willard Nixon hit Minnie in the head one day in Boston," Paul Richards remembered. "We tried to get Minnie to leave the game and he wouldn't. Next time up against Nixon, he tripled against the centerfield wall on the first pitch. Next guy up, Al Zarilla, hit a little flyball to Dominic DiMaggio in short center field. Our third base coach, Jimmy Adair, saw Minnie getting ready to tag up, and hollered 'No! No! No!' And Minnie yelled back, 'Too late—me gone!' And he slid in with the winning run."

Another time, in 1956, he was struck on the right big toe with a pitch thrown by a Baltimore lefty named Don Ferrarese, later a teammate of Minoso's on the Indians and White Sox. He would be sidelined, the doctor said, indefinitely. Two nights later, he hobbled to the plate in a makeshift shoe and doubled during a game-tying 11th-inning rally in the opener of the miraculous four-game sweep of the Yankees that drew 125,433 pennant-starved fans to Comiskey Park.

"The pitch, it broke the toe, and I have to cut out the shoe," Minnie told me. "They say, 'Can you play?' And I say, 'Well, look, I think I be able to play.' They say, 'No, I don't think you can play.' I say, 'Look, I play, but you gotta buy me two pair new shoes.' It usta cost maybe $25. And they say, 'All right,' So I cut out my shoe, you know, and I play."

"But wasn't the pain terrific?" I asked.

"Well, a little bit," he said, "but you know, in this case—it kind of hard to explain to somebody, what you feel sometime, you know—but you do it, especially when you are in love with it. Somebody ask,

'Why you do that? You no have to do that.' But I have to keep-a moving, myself."

He'd been on the move ever since his father took him out of school at age 14, handed him a machete, and put him to work out in the sugar cane fields of Perico, a town in the Cuban province of Matanzas. He formed a plantation baseball team shortly thereafter, became its manager, and eventually found his way to a semipro team in nearby Havana. From there, it was on to the professional team in Marianao, for whom he batted .301 and was named that league's Rookie of the Year for 1945. That won him a contract with the New York Cubans of the Negro National League for 1946, and two years later, Bill Veeck— then running the Cleveland Indians—signed him to a contract. He spent the '49 and '50 seasons (except for a brief look-see with Cleveland at the tailend of '48) with the Indians' farm club at San Diego, where he ravaged Pacific Coast League pitching to earn promotion to Cleveland in '51.

But by then Veeck was out of the picture at Cleveland, luckily for Frank Lane, who was able to whisk Minoso away from the Indians in a three-club deal involving seven players. It was also Lane (Minoso still calls him "My Daddy Number Two") who, as Cleveland general manager, persuaded the White Sox to part with Minnie in the winter of 1957-58. The deal made all the front pages of Chicago's newspapers and brought shock to Minoso.

"I feel like the whole world was over for me," he said. "Like my city—you know it's my city because I'm still living here—had put me out. Like when you leave a place where you were born and raised. You feel funny. I never believed it, that I was traded. But it was true."

And so, when the White Sox were clinching the American League pennant in Cleveland Sept. 22, 1959, Minnie was playing left field in the uniform of the Indians. His old teammates—fellows like Billy Pierce, Nellie Fox, Sherm Lollar, Jim Rivera, Luis Aparicio—were finally going to be champions. But not without a fight from Minnie. "I tell you," he said. "I wanted to see them in the World Series. But this was my profession. I wanted to see them win in the right way. Not because they were my friends."

He would rejoin his friends the next season, after Veeck—now in charge of the White Sox—got him back from Lane in another seven-player transaction over the winter. Minnie couldn't have been happier. He proved it on Opening Day, before 41,661, when he first hit a grand-slam homer into the centerfield bullpen (shades of '51) and then, leading off the last of the ninth, hammered a shot into the left-field stands to beat Kansas City 10-9.

There would be two other victorious returns. The Sox picked him up from the Washington Senators in the spring of 1964 and, on the night Dave Nicholson hit his home run over the Comiskey Park roof, Minnie delivered a pinch homer with two men on to help the Sox win the second game of a twi-nighter with the A's, 11-4. It was to be his last major league home run, but it wouldn't be his last major league hit.

That would come a dozen years later, after Bill Veeck brought Minnie back to Chicago as a coach. In September 1976, Veeck put Minoso on the active list and one Sunday afternoon in Comiskey Park, Minnie went up to the plate to face a California Angel pitcher named Sid Monge. The California Angels hadn't even existed and Monge was all of 20 days old when Minnie had first stepped into that same Comiskey Park batter's box 25 years earlier. Minnie took Monge's first pitch for a strike. Then he lined the next one into left field for a single to become the oldest player in baseball history to collect a base hit. He was 53 years of age.

Last September Veeck activated Minnie again. This time, in two at-bats, he failed to hit safely, but he had appeared in at least one game. That made him the only man ever to play major league baseball in five different decades. He was, and is, a truly amazing individual.

"That Minoso," Dick Donovan had said, grinning. "He was something. Lopez or Marion would bawl him out for missing a sign, and Minnie would kinda shrug his shoulders and say, 'No comprendo.' But if you told him, 'Hey Minnie—you left a five-dollar bill on the table,' he'd say, 'Which table?'

"But he was a great team player. He'd be getting hit by pitches just to get on base, or he'd be hit-and-running and giving himself up to help the team when he could've been up there swinging for home runs."

Thirty years ago, Bill Veeck sat in the pressbox at Comiskey Park, look down on the field at Minoso, and said, "There's the ballplayer

I like most to see."

Minnie Minoso is pushing 60 now. In 1980, he was still the one player a lot of White Sox fans wanted most to see.

That says a lot about the White Sox of 1980, perhaps.

It also says a lot about Minnie Minoso.

JIM RIVERA:
Out of the Jungle

The first hint you get that "The Captain's Cabin" really is Jungle Jim Rivera's place is when the waitress brings you the menu. There, on the cover, is a caricature of a lefthanded batter with the familiar No. 7 on the back of the uniform. In the corner are the words, "Your host: Jim Rivera."

It is here, in Crooked Lake—a small resort community just outside Angola, Ind.—that Rivera, the most colorful of the colorful Go-Go White Sox of the '50s, has made his home. We visited him in the midst of a summer in which more customers than ever before had treated themselves to Jim's Special, a 16-ounce rib steak; jumbo Brazilian shrimp, dipped in batter; and the seafood platter, featuring jumbo shrimp, scallops, frog legs, and crab legs.

"Best summer I've had in 14 years," he was saying. "We turn 'em away. So I guess that's a good sign."

We were sitting in the restaurant's cocktail lounge, downstairs from the main dining area. The lounge has been christened "Screwballs of America, Inc." Jim Landis had indicated that such a name was appropriate for anything run by Rivera. "Rivera was the leader as far as our comics went," Landis had told me. "A sportswriter would be talking

154

A dapper Jungle Jim Rivera comes charging onto the field during the 10th anniversary reunion of the 1959 pennant-winning team, July 20, 1969 at Comiskey Park.

155

with him like we're talking now and he'd have a bat in his hands—
and the bat would be hitting this guy's knee. Continuously. He'd be
hitting it a little bit harder and harder, until finally the guy would yell
out in pain. It finally dawned on the guy that Rivera was just playing a
game with him."

Some said Rivera was a screwball on the field as well, what with his
arm-flapping to wave off other outfielders and with his belly-buster,
head-first slides. More, however, called him a hustler. Landis, in
almost reverent tones, said: "That Rivera—he just played his tail off."
Even at age 36, when most ballplayers have stopped being ballplayers,
Rivera was busy stealing 21 bases. At age 36, even Maury Wills stole
only 29. Luis Aparicio stole 8. Rivera, it would appear, never really
did slow down. His style of play wouldn't allow for it.

"In the first place," he began, "you gotta love something. As a kid, I
always played everything, but I was never that good at anything. So I
always tried to go a little harder, and by hustling, I overshadowed my
lousy hitting or whatever. And it paid off, 'cause when it came time to
choose up sides, they always wanted me. So that made me feel good.
Even later, when I went to spring training with the White Sox, I felt
like it was a big thing to me, to make the club. Even though I was a
regular the year before, I still hustled. 'Cause that's what the manager
wanted. And that's what the people liked."

Jim, born Manuel Jose to Puerto Rican parents in 1922, had been
hustling for a long, long time anyway. "I was born in Manhattan, on
112th Street, right there in Harlem. I didn't stay there long, though.
My mother died when I was a little kid (six years old). My father had
remarried so I was sent to an orphanage across the Hudson. And being
there with 70 or 80 other kids, that's when you start the hustling,
trying to beat everyone out of everything. I always wanted to be the
fastest runner, the best hitter, everything."

The head-first slides came later—much later, after 10 years in the
orphanage, a job hustling telegrams for Western Union, and a WPA
job that he had to walk six miles each day just to get to. "One day in
the minor leagues, I was trying to stretch a double into a triple, and I
decided to go in head-first. I was thrown out, but it was close. And I
said to myself, 'Gee, the umpire took his time to see whether the third
baseman tagged me on my hand or up higher on my arm.' See, when

you slide with your feet first, they just wave at you with the glove and they'll call you out, if they tag you or not. So I started going in head-first all the time after that and before you know it, I liked it. And I got a lot of calls that way."

He got enough of them in 1953 to lead the American League in triples with 16. "Sixteen triples," he repeated proudly. "That's unheard-of on grass. With astroturf, I'd have had 30."

He WAS 30 as a rookie in 1952. He didn't start playing organized baseball until 1949, when he hit .335 at Gainesville, Fla. One reason for the late start was his stay in the Army, which was made a bit longer because of a trip to the federal prison in Atlanta. Rivera, Army lawyers charged, had raped the daughter of the post commander at Camp Barksdale, La. Off to jail he went (he was sentenced originally to life imprisonment but, after several reductions, only served 4½ years), even though the charges had been reduced to attempted rape when a somewhat belated examination proved the girl, an Army nurse who had been caught returning late to quarters after a date with Rivera, was still a virgin.

Bill Veeck later told me, "In a regular court of law, they'd have thrown out the case (after it was proved the girl had never, in fact, been raped). But no. They now charge him with attempted rape. But this is what happens when you get involved with the commandant's daughter.

"But when I was trying to get Jim from the White Sox (when Bill was running the Browns in the winter of '51-52), I decided to try and document what had happened to him. I tried to get a transcript of the court-martial. And a very strange thing: It was missing. They had all 50,000 or so of the ones before it and another 50,000 after it, but just this one was missing. So I asked Stu Symington, who was our (Missouri's) senator and a very dear friend, if he could help. And all of a sudden, they found it.

"I took a copy and gave it to the publisher of the Post-Dispatch and I gave another copy to the publisher of the Globe-Democrat and I said, 'You make a decision on this—I want you to understand I'm going to hire him. But I want you to know the background on this.' But there was never any mention of the true story in the St. Louis papers.

"Now there was a fellow, a preacher, who had a church about five blocks from the ballpark. Had a Sunday morning radio program. And he came in one day and said, 'Look, you're gonna sponsor our program, aren't you?' And I said, 'No. Why?' 'Well, otherwise I'm gonna do a piece on Rivera.' I said, 'Let me tell you something: If you weren't a man of the cloth, I'd pop you right now. I'll give you one minute to get out of here. And I do hope you do a program on Rivera. And I'm gonna call the papers and tell them to come and cover it. But if I were you I'd be very certain of my material.'

"He did the program but he didn't come out and say anything. He implied it but said nothing that you could get him on for libel. We taped it, of course. And the press did cover it but nobody ever wrote anything about it. Now, about 12 years later, this same fellow is convicted and sent to the pokey for raping three girls in the choir. Talk about poetic justice."

But the die had been cast by the court-martial: Rivera was a badboy, not to be allowed to violate the purity of organized baseball. Finally, the Gainesville club owner, Earl Mann—perhaps less hypocritical than his fellow baseball men—signed Jim to a contract after watching him play ball for the prison team and working to secure his release. Pensacola then bought him from Gainesville, and Rivera hit .338 with 20 homers and 135 RBI for his new team in 1950. People were beginning to forget Rivera's reputation.

Seattle of the Pacific Coast League gave Pensacola $3800 to get him, and Jungle Jim proceeded to burn up that circuit in 1951: 40 doubles, 16 triples, 20 homers, 112 RBI, and a .352 batting average. During the season, the White Sox shelled out $65,000 to get the contract of Rivera, who was to report to the Chicago club in time for spring training the following March. But Veeck had other ideas.

"When the season's over," Jim remembered, "I go to Puerto Rico to play in the winter league. Now, while I'm over there, Rogers Hornsby, my manager in Seattle, gets hired by Veeck to manage the Browns. Now he says, 'What do you need? What can I get you?' Hornsby says, 'I want an outfielder by the name of Jim Rivera, if you can get him.' So they deal with the White Sox, and the White Sox needed a catcher, so they give them Sherm Lollar. Now in the meantime, the Browns get Clint Courtney to catch. OK, they're all set.

158

"Now I go to St. Louis, I report to spring training, I'm playing there, and in July, the White Sox get me back, for Ray Coleman and J.W. Porter and cash. Richards put me in right away, in center field."

It was a memorable night, that Tuesday, July 29, 1952. There were 38,967 fans on hand at Comiskey Park to see the Sox and Billy Pierce go up against the league-leading Yankees, who rallied from a 7-0 deficit to win 10-7 on Mickey Mantle's grand slam in the ninth. Rivera was given Coleman's old uniform shirt with a No. 39 on the back. Coleman, along with his .215 batting average, already had been sent packing to St. Louis, but not everyone in the stands was aware of it.

"I'm out there in the outfield during batting practice, shagging flies and wearing No. 39," Rivera recalled. "I had just reported. And they're yelling, 'Get lost, ya bum! We don't want you!' They didn't know it was me. They thought I was Coleman."

They realized their mistake soon enough. Rivera, batting second in the lineup behind leadoff man Nellie Fox, singled and doubled his first two times up and homered the next afternoon. But just to be safe, the White Sox—or more specifically veteran outfielder Eddie Stewart— made sure Jungle Jim wouldn't have to undergo any more abuse from Ray Coleman haters. Stewart had been wearing uniform No. 7. He eventually surrendered the number to Rivera but, wisely, he didn't swap it for No. 39. Eddie wasn't deaf. He switched to No. 21.

"I said, 'Eddie, you don't have to do it.' He said, 'Well, you had No. 7 in the minors and with the Browns—you like it, go ahead.' I'd never asked for No. 7, not even in the minors. They just gave it to me. And then whenever I went after that, I always took 7. Superstitious? I guess so . . . "

His uniform number became as familiar as the whispered allegations of Rivera's adventures with the ladies, his celebrated batting hitch, and his circus catches. His reputation still sullied by the Army court-martial, Rivera had to wade through another annoying period of mudslinging when, in the final week of the 1953 season, a Hyde Park woman brought rape charges against him. The charges were phony, the grand jury declined to vote an indictment, and Rivera was cleared. But baseball commissioner Ford Frick decreed that the White Sox were responsible for Jim's behavior and that they could not trade or sell Rivera for at least one year. The Sox were pleased with Frick's pro-

159

nouncement: Rivera hit a career-high .286 the next season.

The batting hitch is something he still can't explain. "We were talking about that a couple of weeks ago," he said, "with a guy up in Coldwater, Mich., where I play golf. He said, 'Jim, did you ever feel the hitch?' I said, 'No—even though I know I'm doing it, I don't feel it. I'm watching the ball, ready to go into the ball. I'm not thinking about all this other stuff.'

"But every Monday, they used to show films upstairs (at Comiskey Park). Richards would show 'em to me and say, 'Lookit, Jim—look what you're doing.' I said, 'I can't believe it—I didn't know I was that bad a hitter.' They tried things to correct it—like having me hold the bat a little lower—but nothing worked. See, I did it all my life. You can't change it now. I think if I was a young kid, they coulda corrected it, but . . . "

But it was a lost cause. At the 20th reunion of the 1959 club at Comiskey Park in September 1979, Rivera took his cuts against Bob Shaw, Gerry Staley, and Turk Lown. Even after all those years, the hitch was as pronounced as ever. Maybe that flaw explains more than anything his .256 lifetime batting average. And why he is mostly remembered today not for his hitting but for his head-first slides and brilliant catches, the most famous of which occurred in the fifth game of the '59 World Series against the Dodgers in the Los Angeles Coliseum. The Sox were leading 1-0 in the bottom of the seventh with two out and two Dodgers on base and Charley Neal up. Manager Al Lopez called time and sent Rivera out to right field, moved Al Smith from right to left field, and took leftfielder Jim McAnany out of the game. Neal hammered one of Bob Shaw's pitches into right-center but Rivera, getting a superb jump on the ball, hauled it down with an over-the-shoulder catch to save two runs and the ballgame.

"Lopez was a smart manager, no doubt about it," said Rivera, who had been used in a similar situation on Nellie Fox Night that season, Aug. 21 against Washington. With lefty-hitting Clint Courtney—by that time with the Senators—batting in the top of the eighth and the Sox a run ahead, Lopez sent Rivera out to play right field in place of McAnany and Jungle Jim responded by reaching into the first row of the rightfield seats after a tremendous leap to come up with Courtney's home run bid. "Took that one right out of the fans'

160

hands," he smiled.

"But I knew Charley Neal from the winter league in Puerto Rico, and his long ball is to right-center and left-center. And that's where the ball was hit, to right-center. And I never thought I had a chance to catch the ball—I'll be honest with you. Oh, he hit the heck out of it. But I just ran as hard as I could and stuck my glove out and there it was. And we won the game 1-0."

The victory enabled the White Sox to force a sixth game back in Chicago, but Rivera felt that all was lost, anyway. "That second game (at Chicago, when Sherm Lollar was thrown out by 20 feet trying to score all the way from first on Al Smith's eighth-inning double), we threw that one away. They (by "they," of course, he means third-base coach Tony Cuccinello) shoulda never sent Lollar home. See, we're still talking about it, 20 years later. I still get it from people here. People come in here and say, 'What in the hell were you doing? How come you weren't running?' I say, 'Hey, I'm not the manager.' It was just one of those things. It's a shame."

In a way, it's a shame Rivera had to wait until he was 37 and past his prime before he got a chance to play in a World Series. But the catch on Neal gave people who hadn't seen him in his prime an idea of what he had been like. And he did deliver a key blow in the pennant-clinching victory Sept. 22 in Cleveland. Smith's homer broke a 2-2 tie and Jim followed immediately with one of his own to help seal the triumph. "I hit it off Mudcat Grant, into right-center, into the old bullpen over there," he recalled. "I got a fastball, shoulder-high, boy . . . " And hitch or no hitch, the ball was gone.

Soon Rivera would be gone. He played in only 48 games for the Sox in 1960, and early in 1961 he was sold to the Kansas City A's—whose general manager, Frank Lane, had purchased him for the White Sox 10 years earlier. He hit .241 in 64 games with the A's and then opted for retirement. His career had spanned 1,171 games, all but 161 of them in a White Sox uniform. He is still proud to have been a member of the Go-Go White Sox.

"We scrapped. We gave 'em heck. But I'll tell you something. We were up against SOME team. And you've got to give them credit. They were the best team I ever saw in baseball. And that's the Yankees. I don't care what they tell you about the Cincinnati Big Red

Machine and all that. Those guys couldn't even play with the Yankees. They were tough. Super ballplayers. They had pitching, defense, running, everything."

He pointed to the large TV in the corner, above the bar. "I see a lot of ballgames here—you should see the antenna on the roof. I get the Tigers from Michigan. I pick up a station from Ft. Wayne that does the Reds games. And I can get Chicago, too."

The White Sox?

Jungle Jim Rivera smiled and nodded his head. "I'm still a Sox fan. Oh yeah. Always will be. 'Til I die . . . "

RON JACKSON:
The Tallest Insurance Man in Kalamazoo

I was showing Billy Pierce a list of people I was planning on talking to for this project and his eyes lit up when he came to Ron Jackson's name.

"You know," he told me, "I always said that Ronnie was handled wrong. He would've been better than Dave Kingman—a lot better. No question. He had tremendous power. There was one guy who really gave him trouble. And that was Whitey Ford. And I'll be darned but that seemed like the only pitcher Ronnie'd ever get a chance to play against."

On our way up to Mackinac Island, my wife and I stopped off in Kalamazoo and drove to Jackson's insurance office. His car pulled up at almost the same moment as ours, and I knew it was him as soon as he got out. At 6-7, he had been the tallest Sox player I could ever remember. So he wasn't—and isn't—the sort of fellow who could quickly lose himself in a crowd.

We sat down in his office and he told me about his days as a basketball star at Western Michigan and how he had played against such pro stars as Jack Twyman and Al Bianchi. And how there had been a chance he might have become a pro basketball player instead of

Ron Jackson reaches for throw during infield workout at spring
training, 1955, in Tampa.

a pro baseball player had not the White Sox come up with an offer that Jackson found impossible to turn down. Frank Lane had indicated the amount was in the neighborhood of $75,000, big money in those days—it was 1954—and bigger money than pro basketball was paying at that time. He had been watched closely by longtime Sox scout Pete Milito and also by Chicago manager Paul Richards, who took an immediate liking to the huge first baseman—especially after Paul had watched Jackson blast a few tape-measure home runs in a workout at Comiskey Park.

"Richards was the guy who really wanted me—probably he was the main reason they signed me," said Ron, who signed a bonus contract on June 15, thus making him ineligible for option to the minors until June 15, 1956. (In those days, a player signing for more than $4,000 was declared a bonus player and was forced to spend two years with the major league team.)

"I'm sure it was his decision to sign me. I don't know that for a fact, but he was the one who really negotiated with me. Although it really wasn't much of a negotiation. He just asked me what I wanted and I advised him of that. He said he'd see what he could do and then they signed me. They were the first ones to offer what I had in mind at the time, which was still with a year left in college. If I'd waited 'til graduation, I'd have probably waited for the highest offer."

He didn't have to wait long to see some action with the Sox, who were battling for first place with the Yankees and the Cleveland Indians. Richards sent him up to pinch-hit one night at Comiskey Park against the Philadelphia Athletics and Jackson responded the way any scared 20-year-old would have: He popped up to the catcher. "But my first start was against Baltimore in Chicago and my last time up I hit a home run into the upper deck off Duane Pillette," he recalled. "Helped us win the game."

He hit three more homers that first season—one a game-winning shot into the upper deck off Cleveland's Bob Lemon—and hit .280 as Richards worked him into 40 ballgames. Injuries to regular first baseman Ferris Fain and to veteran backup Phil Cavarretta helped Jackson to get the playing time he did get. "Fain got hurt my second week with the club," said Ron, "and Cavarretta went in and did a real good job but then he got hurt—pulled a leg muscle—and then they put

165

me in."

Richards liked what he saw of the big guy, but he liked even more what the Baltimore Orioles were waving in front of his nose. The Orioles were offering him big money to become both their manager and field manager. Richards had brought the Sox out of the second division and into pennant contention and now it was time to move on to a new challenge. His resignation was announced Sept. 14 and coach Marty Marion was named to replace him. It turned out to be a bad break for Jackson.

"Baseball," he said, "seems to be like other things. You like to be able to point to areas of your success. And Richards had some vested interest in me. And the fact that I would be successful if he was there to do anything about it would have been a feather in his hat, as far as developing a player. But I meant nothing to Marion. I meant nothing to Al Lopez. And so, for my own particular advantage, it would've been a better situation for Richards to have stayed in Chicago or for me to be traded to Baltimore—which Richards later tried to do several times, but the White Sox wouldn't let me go. There were a lot of clubs interested in me originally, but the Sox just let me sit. We had a real good ballclub at Chicago. I'd have been better off if Chicago had been a poor ballclub. It's tougher on a good club than a poor one for a young guy to get a chance."

He didn't get a chance from Marion, who went with veteran Walt Dropo as his first baseman in 1955 and '56 while Jackson got into only 40 games in '55 and another 22 the next season (before being sent down to Vancouver, where he hit .304). "Marion just didn't want to use younger players," said Jackson. "Even Aparicio was forced on him, I'm sure."

Lopez wasn't one of his biggest fans, either. The Senor sent Ron to Indianapolis in 1957, Jackson had a big year (21 homers, 102 RBI, and a .310 average), and there were high hopes at spring training in Tampa in '58 that the Sox, at last, had their own, homegrown slugger. Lopez publicly stated that Jackson was the team's big longball hope, especially in the wake of winter trades which had sent Minnie Minoso to Cleveland and Larry Doby to Baltimore. It turned out that Earl Torgeson and another oldster, Ray Boone, wound up playing first base most of that season.

166

"Lopez called me into his office and told me that if he let me play regularly, I would lead the league in strikeouts," Jackson told me. "I told him that if he knew anything about me, that he would see that historically I struck out a lot the first months of the season but that the strikeouts would go down as the season progressed. And I said, 'Let's point to another fact.' And he and I, we never hit it off very well anyway. But I pointed out to him that, at that point, I'd been up 100 fewer times than Sherm Lollar. I had two fewer homers and I had three or four fewer RBIs. And Lollar was leading the team in both departments. And I was hitting .274. But Lopez insisted I had to hit over .300.

"So I don't really think he gave me a full shot. I think he was obligated to give me a shot but I don't think he was really sticking with me to make it. He stuck with more enthusiasm with Jim Landis the very same year. A couple of years before that, they stuck, with enthusiasm, with Aparicio at shortstop—which obviously turned out to be a sensational decision to make. But I can recall sitting around listening to the older fellows on the ballclub saying about Aparicio, 'How long can they continue to go with this guy? He's killing us.' But the thing of it was, there was a commitment made by the ballclub to make him the shortstop. There was never that kind of commitment to make me the first baseman. That's all I'm saying. There's no reason Mr. Lopez had to like me. No reason I had to like him. But had I been with a different ballclub or with a different manager, then my fate might have been different. It helps to have someone in your corner when you need him. That someone, obviously, is either the manager or general manager or someone who says, 'This guy plays.' "

That someone wasn't in Chicago, however. Even Bill Veeck, when he assumed control of the club before the '59 season, wasn't going to tell Lopez he had to play Jackson at first base. It was off to Indianapolis again for Ron, who would be sent to Boston at season's end for lefty Frank Baumann. Baumann had the lowest earned run average in the American League in 1960, while Jackson was spending the year back in the American Association with Louisville and Indianapolis. Then, after hitting 25 home runs at Louisville in '61, he called it quits and went into the insurance business back home in Kalamazoo. The big first baseman with the upper-deck power was through at age 28.

"But I had good times in baseball and I wouldn't trade them for any-thing," he said. "It was a big thrill all the time. I've got to be honest. It was disappointing to do bad and it was delightful to do good. And you have to remember that I was a kid who had dreamed about playing big league baseball. So many of the guys I played with, they never cared about playing baseball as kids, never thought of it. I think Johnny Groth never even thought he'd play baseball. He'd been a softball player or something. Baseball was full of guys that really, that wasn't their aim in life, to be a big league ballplayer. A long ways from it. But it WAS mine.

"And I gave it ample time. I could've done some things differently, obviously. Maybe the two-year bonus rule didn't help. But still, when it's all said and done, you've got to come to the big leagues at the right time. If your number's not in there, or if they're not looking for someone of your particular type and quality, you're out of there. A guy my size—sort of an odd size for basball—put me on a bad ballclub and it at least gives them something to talk about. But the White Sox didn't need that. They were going for the pennant. We were a good ballclub. And don't think it wasn't fun to be a part of that."

DICK DONOVAN:
He Wouldn't Give Up the Ball

Dick Donovan, Marty Marion had said, was so afraid of what might happen that he refused to give up the baseball. It was Dick's first start in a White Sox uniform, and he had the misfortune of pitching the day after the Sox had tied a big league record for runs scored by pounding Kansas City 29-6. He should've known he was going to have to pitch a shutout to win. But he didn't.

The Athletics were on their way to a 5-0 victory when Marion made his way to the mound. "Marty was exactly right," said Tricky Dick when I got hold of him at his suburban Boston home. "I was scared I was going back to the minors."

Donovan had had enough of the minors. He had spent eight years in towns like Ft. Lauderdale, Evansville, Hartford, plus Milwaukee and Atlanta—then minor league cities. He had been up with the Boston Braves for brief trials three times, with the Detroit Tigers once. And now, he feared, he was ending Brief Trial No. 5. But Marion promised him another start within five days. Dick handed him the baseball and departed for the dugout.

Five days later, Marion gave the ball back to the big right-hander. This time, the opposition was far more fearsome: the Boston

Dick Donovan pitches batting practice during spring training, 1960, in
Sarasota.

Red Sox, a team Donovan had cheered as a youth back home in Quincy, Mass. True, Ted Williams, who had announced his retirement—he would return a month later, however—was not in the lineup. But Jimmy Piersall, Sammy White, Jackie Jensen, Norm Zauchin, and Billy Goodman were. Nonetheless, Donovan, pitching in Comiskey Park, went out and shut out Boston on four hits, 7-0, for his first big league victory.

"That first one was really special to me," he said, "because it was against the Red Sox, my hometown team." It was even more special for the White Sox, because it marked the first of 73 triumphs Donovan would pitch for them before being chosen by the new Washington franchise in the American League expansion draft after the 1960 season. Fifteen of the 73 came in that first year, 1955. After Donovan's conquest of the Red Sox, he defeated the old Senators in relief. On May 8, he shut out Detroit 1-0, exacting sweet revenge from the club that had cut him loose the previous spring. And on May 15, he blanked Washington again, 3-0.

On a staff which included some of the league's finest pitchers— Billy Pierce, Virgil Trucks, Jack Harshman, and Sandy Consuegra— Dick quickly became one of the aces. He was sailing along with a 13-4 record July 29 and was one of the main reasons the Sox were leading the Yankees, Indians, and Red Sox in the tight American League pennant race. (Among the four losses were a 1-0 setback at Detroit and a 1-0 defeat at Yankee Stadium.) That's when that good old White Sox bad luck struck again.

"We were in Washington," he remembered. "It was a Friday night. I went out with Lollar, Fox, and Pierce after the game, and I had some shrimp. That night, it hit me. I just thought it was a stomach ache. And it turned out to be appendicitis. I was examined by the Washington team doctor and I flew back to Chicago and I was operated on Saturday night at Mercy Hospital."

Dick would miss three weeks, during which the Sox managed to stay in the thick of things as Harry Byrd and Connie Johnson filled in for him as best they could. He finally announced he was fit to return to the starting rotation when the Tigers moved into Comiskey Park for a four-game series Aug. 19. Marion wasn't sure. He started Billy Pierce on Friday night, and Billy shut out Detroit 3-0 before 36,473.

171

The next day, Marion decided to give Donovan one more day of rest and nominated Bob Keegan to start in his stead. Keegan was no mystery to the Tigers, who shelled him out in the third—although the Sox, getting four hits apiece from Nellie Fox and Jim Rivera and three by George Kell, rallied to win 8-7.

Finally, after Johnson had blanked the Tigers 2-0 on four hits in the opener of Sunday's doubleheader, Marion figured it was time to give Donovan his start. All Donovan did was scatter eight hits and roll to an 8-2 laugher as 34,542 watched the home team move to within two percentage points of the first-place Yankees. But that was to be Dick's last happy day until the final weekend of the season, when he shut out Kansas City. In between, he would drop five straight decisions.

"I felt good that first day back," Dick remembered. "But you can't come back from a major operation that quickly. Once you have something like that, it takes a while. Your resiliency is gone. You just don't bounce back that quick."

But by next season, he had bounced back. He went 12-10, showed his batting skill by hitting .222 with three home runs, and pitched no-hit baseball into the eighth inning of the opener of that memorable four-game sweep of the Yankees in late June. He reached his peak, however, in 1957, his first year under manager Al Lopez. Dick wound up 16-6 with a 2.77 earned run average, walking only 45 batters in 220 innings. And eight of those 45 walks were intentional. In '57, he pitched two one-hitters—one against Cleveland in May and the other against Boston in July. But his best game was the one he pitched against the Yankees Aug. 29 in Chicago. Hank Bauer hit Dick's first pitch of the ballgame into the stands in left for a homer. The Sox tied it up and the game went into extra innings. You can guess the rest. Donovan's first pitch to the venerable Enos Slaughter in the top of the 11th was higher than Dick wanted it to be. Slaughter hammered it into the upper deck in right. Just like that, Donovan had lost his best-pitched game of his best season.

I asked him if the arrival of Lopez had had anything to do with his 1957 brilliance. "It was a combination of things," he said. "Ray Berres had been helpful, too. But Lopez was the best manager I ever played for. In fact, he was the best manager in baseball all during my career. But what really turned me around was when Whitlow Wyatt (his manager at Atlanta in 1954) taught me the slider. That was the pitch that made my career. The slider gave me the third pitch I needed to be a winner."

He was a winner in 1958, although it wasn't easy: He was 3-10 in the first half. The problems started on the second day of the season. Donovan led Detroit 4-2 with two out and two on in the top of the ninth. Frank Bolling hit a high drive down the leftfield line. The ball kept curving and kept curving, but it didn't curve enough. It struck the foul pole for a three-run, game-winning homer.

But Dick rallied to win 12 of 16 decisions in the second half of that season, and it seemed '59 would be a continuation of the same old Donovan success story. "But I got off to a slow start," he recalled. "Then I started going good, pitched two or three good games in a row. I felt great. I was caught up in all the excitement. (The Yankees') Bill Skowron had gotten hurt—he was incapacitated. And Herb Score was ineffective after a good start with Cleveland. We all felt we could finally win the pennant. And then I pulled a tendon in my right elbow in July."

Onto the disabled list he went, but he returned in time to do some clutch pitching. With the Sox in Cleveland the last weekend of August for a critical four-game series against the second-place Indians, rookie Ken McBride came down with tonsillitis. Lopez asked Donovan to pitch instead, and Dick responded with a 2-0, five-hit shutout and the Sox had a 3½-game lead. It was a typical, clutch Donovan performance, but what was remarkable about it was that he hadn't had the usual time to mentally prepare himself—something Dick was awfully big on.

"You didn't want to bother him the day of a game," Jack Brickhouse had mentioned. "I remember one time we were on the plane and Dick was supposed to pitch that night. I walked down the aisle past his seat and just happened to lean over and say, 'Good luck tonight, Dick.' Now what are you going to say to someone when he tells you 'Good luck'? You're gonna say, 'Well, thanks.' Right? Not Donovan. He looks up at me and goes, 'I wish you guys would get off that good luck baloney. Luck has nothing to do with it.' And on and on he went. On the day of a game, he'd bite your head off if you got him upset. That was the kind of intensity he put into his job. Any other day, a nicer, more congenial Irishman you'll never meet. But when he was pitching, boy, you were better off staying away."

Dick did his utmost to make the Dodgers stay away from home plate in the third game of the 1959 World Series, leaving the game in the seventh inning with the Sox trailing Don Drysdale 1-0. Chicago wound up losing 3-1. In the fifth game, before 92,706 in the Los Angeles Coliseum, Donovan relieved in the eighth inning—he got out of a bases loaded, one-out jam that inning—to combine with Bob Shaw and Billy Pierce for the first shared shutout in World Series history. But in the sixth—and final—game of the Series, he was pounded in relief, perhaps a harbinger of things to come.

Because in 1960, Tricky Dick ran out of tricks. Used mostly in relief, he was tagged for an ERA of 5.38 despite winning six times and losing but once. "I got off to a bad start and never could get going," he told me. "The year was just a complete wipeout. You can't have too many of those years, or you don't stay in the big leagues long. They'll give you one, but . . . "

The Sox wouldn't even give him one. They left him unprotected for the expansion draft and Washington snapped him up. He opened the season against, of course, the White Sox and though losing to them 4-3 went on to lead the league with a 2.40 ERA. In 1962, pitching for Cleveland, he came back all the way, winning 20 games for the first time in his career and leading the league in shutouts with five. But he was nearing the end.

"The things that I remember most, the things that come back to me now," he said, "are my first win in the American League, that game I lost to the Yankees 2-1 in Chicago, the game I relieved in in the Series and we won 1-0, getting caught up in the expansion draft and going to Washington, losing to the White Sox my first game, beating them 2-1 in 11 innings in Comiskey Park (in '64), winning 20 ballgames for Cleveland. Those things come to mind.

"But my happiest days," he concluded, "were in Chicago. After I left Chicago, it was all downhill."

Fourteen years with Bache Halsey's Boston office, a new career in real estate, and a happy marriage that has produced a son named Peter and a daughter named Amy—all that has followed his departure from Chicago. That part of it, I thought to myself, has hardly been downhill for Dick Donovan.

174

LUIS APARICIO:
A Candidate for
Cooperstown

After six weeks of calling Luis Ernesto Aparicio's office in Maracaibo, Venezuela, and getting little more in response than a secretary telling me, "*Lo siento mucho, pero no esta,*" I realized with some disappointment that I might never have the opportunity to speak with the greatest shortstop the White Sox have ever had. Mainly, I wanted to learn from him how he felt about the way the Hall-of-Fame voting had gone the last couple of years.

It had been shocking to most Chicago baseball fans. The first year he was eligible for the voting, Little Looie, now 47 years old and running a major insurance business in Maracaibo, had polled 124 votes. That wasn't too bad for a fellow in his first year of eligibility, and most people agreed that the next year or the year after would see Aparicio enshrined.

But last year in the voting, Looie, inexplicably, not only failed to equal his performance of the year before but he managed a mere 48 votes. Fans were dumbfounded. Why, even Ralph Kiner had been elected to the Hall of Fame a couple of years earlier. Lou Boudreau, a shortstop who might have been able to cover a quarter of the ground Aparicio routinely covered, had long since been voted in. So had

Luis Aparicio in the uniform of the Memphis Chicks during the 1955 season.

Ernie Banks, who played short on the North Side while Looie was playing it in far better fashion on the South Side. All right, Aparicio didn't hit 35 homers a year. But there IS more to this game than hitting, isn't there?

Like other Chicagoans, I had always figured Aparicio was Hall-of-Fame material. He was the finest shortstop of his time, playing 18 years in the big leagues, from 1956 through 1973. He led the American League in stolen bases years in a row (1956-64), stealing as many as 57 in 1964. He was tops among A.L. shortstops in assists six straight years ('56-'61) and in fielding percentage seven straight ('60-'66). True, he was not a great hitter, but his lifetime average was a respectable .262 and he reached a high of .313 for the White Sox in 1970. All told, he played 2,581 games at shortstop in his career and played them all with a style and grace not seen before and not seen since.

"I can't believe he didn't make it," Sammy Esposito had told me after Aparicio had failed to win election in his first year of eligibility. "Looie played a long time, too—18 years. Solid .270-.280 hitter. Best shortstop that ever played the game. Looie was unbelievable. He not only was flashy—he made the great plays—but he was also so steady. It's a combination you don't see that often.

"Carrasquel was almost in the same mold as Looie but I didn't think he had the range Looie had. Both of these guys were so steady, and all their throws were right there. Every time. I can't believe Looie didn't make it. These things amaze me."

They amaze Jim Landis too. "I haven't seen a shortstop yet who could top Aparicio. I don't care what anybody's gonna tell me. I've played behind him too long and I've seen what he has done. And I've watched others and I still watch others. But Aparicio was fabulous."

"Aparicio has to go down as one of the best shortstops of all time," Billy Pierce had insisted. "He would hit .275 or something like that, he'd steal bases, he'd run the bases, and he could field with anybody. Anybody."

He had one of the greatest throwing arms any shortstop ever had, too. Former Chicago Daily News baseball writer Jack Kuenster claimed that the play he remembers most from the '59 season was the Al Smith-to-Aparicio-to-Sherm Lollar relay to cut down runners at the plate. "There'd be an extra-base hit into the leftfield corner.

Aparicio would go out and plant himself on the foul line, get the relay from Smith, then turn and fire straight as an arrow to Lollar to get the runner trying to score from first. Aparicio's throw was always right on the money. I don't know how many runners they shot down like that in '59."

Not that '59 was the only year he performed brilliantly. He was something special from the day he was signed by the one and only Frank Lane. "I first heard about Aparicio from a fellow named Eddie Moncada, sports editor of El Mundo, a Caracas newspaper," Lane remembered. "He told me about this little guy who was a helluva player. I asked Chico Carrasquel about him and he said the same thing. So I started following him.

"I found out that Cleveland was already negotiating with him. At that time, any player who received more than $4,000 for signing was a bonus player—he had to be kept for two years by the big league club before he could be sent to the minors to play every day. I learned that Looie wanted $10,000 to sign. Hank Greenberg at Cleveland was trying to figure out a way to sign Looie without having to keep him at Cleveland for two years."

Greenberg didn't move quickly enough. He'd already been outfoxed once by Lane when the latter got Minnie Minoso away from him in 1951. Now Lane struck again. "Acting as vice-president of our Waterloo (Ia.) farm club," Frank told me, "I bought Aparicio's contract for $4,000. Then I gave him a bonus of $6,000 for reporting to Waterloo. See, it was just another way to skin a cat."

Aparicio did well for Waterloo in 1954, hitting .282 and showing off his magic glove and rifle arm enough to earn promotion to Memphis and an invitation to the Sox training camp at Tampa in 1955. Looie's name popped up in a few exhibition box scores that spring but new manager Marty Marion knew that the 21-year-old needed at least another year in the minors. So Aparicio spent the year at Memphis and helped the Chicks win the Southern Association championship. So well did he perform that, at season's end, the White Sox shipped Looie's countryman, Carrasquel, to Cleveland in a deal for centerfielder Larry Doby. The door was wide open for Aparicio. Next spring, Looie fought off the challenges of veterans Jim Brideweser and Carl "Buddy" Peterson and won the starting shortstop job.

"We came out to spring training that year feeling, well, the kid was our shortstop," said Marion, himself an all-star shortstop for the Cardinals throughout the '40s. "The kid could throw real good, but he couldn't make the doubleplay too good, and every time he'd field a groundball he'd run halfway to first with the ball. But we worked with him a lot and finally we got him to throw the ball.

"Also, he always had great range—even then. He'd go out into left field and backhand the ball. But when he'd make that backhanded play in the hole, he could never throw anybody out. I said, 'Hell, you might as well let Minoso field the ball—you're not doing any good with it.' So we got him to where he could come on in and charge the ball and turn toward third base on that play in the hole. And he turned out to be a helluva shortstop.

"But early in his first season, he was going pretty bad and I put him on the bench for three days. I let him sit. I told him. 'You're too nervous, kid. I'll put you on the bench. Watch from there—it'll do you good.' But when I put him back in there, I never did take him out again."

There was no reason to. Looie was on his way to becoming the American League's Rookie of the Year. The 5-9, 155-pounder was making plays even Carrasquel had never dreamed of making, he was showing unanticipated hitting ability with his .266 average, and he was upsetting the opposition with his speed on the basepaths. He stole 21 bases that first year, moved up to 28 in '57, and to 29 in '58, and then swiped the unheard-of total of 56 in '59, when he tied the club's all-time record set by Wally Moses in 1943. It was Aparicio, then, who almost singlehandedly brought back the stolen base as an offensive weapon. The last time a big leaguer had stolen so many bases was in 1944, when the Yankees' Stuffy Stirnweiss had stolen 55. The closest anyone had come to that figure during the intervening 15 years was Willie Mays with 40 steals in 1956.

Looie kept getting better and better—hitting .277 in 1960 with 51 steals and .272 in '61 with 53—until 1962. His average that year slipped to .241, his stolen bases dropped off to 31, and, some argued, his range afield was diminishing as well. Balls that used to be gobbled up by Aparicio were now starting to get through. Manager Al Lopez had words with his star shortstop on more than one occasion toward season's end. Fearing a repeat of the case of Carrasquel, who had played indifferently in his last year in Chicago and whose career had

179

not lasted nearly as long as everyone had anticipated, the Sox un-loaded Looie to Baltimore in January 1963.

Aparicio immediately proclaimed that the White Sox would not win another pennant for another 40 years (they had waited 40 years for their last one). The Sox management was so stung by "The Looie Curse" that they retaliated with a low blow: They gave Aparicio's No. 11 uniform to newly acquired Dave Nicholson, the sultan of swish. But Looie didn't care. Within four years he was helping the Orioles win the pennant and a world championship. Two years later, the Sox swallowed their pride and reacquired Aparicio, and though the team finished ninth, Looie led Chicago in hits, runs scored, doubles, and total bases and was named once again to the Sporting News American League all-star team.

At age 35, he batted a solid .280 in '69 and followed up with that .313 in '70. It was during that season that he was honored by Sox fans on July 19, Luis Aparicio Day. In keeping with the way things went for the White Sox that year, it rained throughout the ceremonies. It was during that same period that rumors popped up claiming Looie was about to replace kindly old Don Gutteridge as White Sox manager. Aparicio, it was said, would instill some pride into this sorry group of Chicago athletes who were posing as major league baseball players. The rumors kept spreading until September, when Gutteridge was fired and replaced by Chuck Tanner.

Somehow, I sensed almost instantly that Aparicio's days in Chicago were numbered. Not three months later, while I was at Ft. Lewis, Wash., learning the finer points of firing an M-16 and the meaning of the dying cockroach position, the news came that Looie had been traded once again by the White Sox. This time, he was going to the Boston Red Sox for second baseman Mike Andrews and a young shortstop also named Luis—Luis Alvarado. (The similarities between the two Luises ended with their first name.)

The trade didn't bother me at all. At least I knew Looie was going to be able to close out his career with a good team. The career ended after the '73 season and I sat back and began waiting for the day when I could brag about all the times I had gone to Comiskey Park to watch Luis Aparicio, the Hall-of-Fame shortstop, make plays no one had ever seen before.

I'm still waiting.

SAMMY ESPOSITO:
The South Side Utility Co.

For seven years, Sammy Esposito was the No. 1 utility infielder in the American League. The "experts" used to say that Sammy could have been a regular with any other club in the league—except the Yankees. As I walked up the stairs to his office in Case Center on the campus of North Carolina State University, I wondered if Esposito himself wouldn't have wanted it differently—wouldn't have wanted to be a regular for someone else rather than a benchwarmer for his hometown team, the White Sox.

"I was naturally not very happy about not being able to play every day," said Sam, who in his 14 seasons as head baseball coach at N.C. State has won four Atlantic Coast Conference championships, has never had a losing season, and has sent Mike Caldwell and Tim Stoddard on their way to big league careers. "But I think I was smart enough to know that it was a good situation.

"We were a winning ballclub, I was playing in my hometown, they treated me well—Chuck Comiskey was great to me—and I liked playing for Al (Lopez) and I know he appreciated having me on the ballclub. I talked to Greg Pryor at the reunion of the '59 pennant-winning club) in 1979 and he said, 'How could you do what you did all

Sammy Esposito at Comiskey Park in 1952, just after signing with the
White Sox.

those years with the White Sox? I couldn't have been able to stand that.' 'Well,' I said, 'No. 1, I played for a winner. That isn't true now. And that's tough.'

"When you're not winning, and the guy ahead of you is hitting .240, you deserve a shot at playing. I was in a little different situation. I was primarily a shortstop and a second baseman and I was playing behind two guys (Luis Aparicio and Nellie Fox) who will probably be Hall-of-Famers. My only chance at being a regular would have been at third base, and I played some there. But I knew you couldn't play Aparicio, Fox, and Esposito in the infield at the same time and get enough production with the bat. Both those guys were singles and doubles hitters and you've gotta have someone at third base who's gonna drive in some runs and give you the long ball once in a while."

Sam leaned back in his chair and mentioned that Pryor had told him that he was having difficulty accepting the utility man's role. "That's another factor that's so important for a utility man—that he accepts his role like I did. Although I wanted to play every day, I accepted my role as a utility man. And Al knew I was ready to play every day I was with 'em. Seven or eight years, I never missed a day. I was there early, I left late. Kept my mouth shut, didn't complain. It's a nice feeling to have someone like that.

"I might not have done the job every day, but you knew I was there. And the young people today, they get very impatient. And I tried to tell Pryor some of these things, but he kept saying, 'Yeah, but you guys were winning. And you were playing behind great players.' "

Sam never figured he'd be playing behind anybody when he signed with the Sox in 1952 out of Indiana University, where he'd been starting guard for a team that would win the NCAA basketball title in '53. He had been an outstanding shortstop at Fenger High on the South Side and also at Indiana and the Sox had him tabbed as the future replacement for Chico Carrasquel. "When I got drafted by the Army in '53, I had played at Waterloo and I was considered the best shortstop in their minor league organization," Esposito remembered. "They were thinking of me eventually taking over for Chico. And I got out of the Army in '55 and I didn't even go home. I joined the Memphis club in Mobile on a Sunday morning before a doubleheader. I got off the train and got a cab to the ballpark. I had played the year before in the Army but I hadn't played at all yet that year—this was in May.

"I got to the ball park just as Memphis was taking infield practice. And I was standing by the dugout there, waiting for Jack Cassini, the manager and second baseman. And I'm watching them practice, and I see this little guy at shortstop, bouncing around, making throws and everything. It was Aparicio. And I said to myself, 'Uh-oh, I'm at the wrong place here.' So they come off the field and I introduce myself to Jack Cassini. He says, 'Oh, yeah—run down there and get dressed. By the way, what position to you play?' I immediately said, 'Third base.' I'd never played third base in my life. But I knew Jack was the manager and the second baseman and that Looie was over at short. And I'd seen someone over at third who I didn't know, so I thought, well, that's my only chance to play. Jack said, 'Hurry up and dress—you're in there.'

"So I played the doubleheader at third and had a terrible day. Had a couple of errors and didn't get a hit. But at least I was smart enough to know I wasn't ever gonna be the White Sox shortstop—not after seeing Looie play. He was just dynamite."

Aparicio and Esposito went up to the White Sox together in 1956, after helping Memphis win the Southern Association championship. "We were down seven or eight games with three weeks to go to Birmingham, the Yankees' farm," Esposito remembered. "We had a nine-game series with them, won all nine games from them and won the pennant with about three games to go. Cassini got beaned with about six weeks to go and they sent Ted Lyons, who was trouble-shooting for the White Sox, down to manage us the last six weeks. And Ted was a Hall-of-Famer, a great pitcher for many, many years, but had never been on a winner. He'd win 20, 22 games every year and the White Sox would finish last. And then he ended up managing us to a championship.

"I'll never forget the day we won it. It was in Memphis. Ted and Looie and I—and a kid named Dutch Dotterer, who later caught for Cincinnati—we did a little celebrating that night and there we were, walking down the street at 3 in the morning, arms around each other, still with our uniforms on."

Esposito had hit .281 for the Memphis club in '55, but he'd never approach that figure in the majors. When he did play, it was generally for late-inning defense. And when he did get a chance to start, he'd often find himself being lifted for pinch-hitters in clutch situations. "I remember once in '57 I'd gotten two hits my first two times up in a game against Cleveland and driven in four runs," he told me. "I was really feeling good. Then Cleveland went ahead 6-4 and the bases were loaded my third time up. And Lopez pulls me and sends Ron Northey up to hit for me. He comes past me swinging a couple of bats and says, 'Out of the way, bush—let the old man do it.'

"I was really hot. I threw my bat down and walked right past everybody in the dugout and went right up to the clubhouse. As I'm going up, I hear a roar from the crowd. I run back down to the dugout and Northey had just cleared the bases with a double. I couldn't be angry at Lopez after that."

Not that he wouldn't have a run-in or two with the friendly Senor after that. Sammy roomed with Jim Rivera, which was like inviting Lopez's constant scrutiny. "We were in Kansas City," Esposito recalled, "Jim and I used to play a lot of gin together. And we finished a Sunday afternoon game early and we went back to the hotel and we had something like a 6:00 train back to Chicago. It was like 4:00 and Jim said, 'Let's catch a cab to the train station, we'll get on our car and we'll play some cards there until the team gets there.'

"So we're playing gin, I'm having a beer. Jim didn't drink. Did you know that? He didn't drink. Anyway, we're playing and we forgot what time it was, but we weren't worried because when we got there, the porter told us this was the White Sox' car. Next thing we knew, the train next to us is pulling out. We look up and we see some familiar faces through the window—the White Sox train was pulling out. We jumped up and ran out of our car, but by that time the train was gone. It finally dawned on us that the guy had given us the wrong train.

"So first we checked to see if there were any flights out of there, but we couldn't get on a plane. So we checked on trains and they told us there was a train to Chicago going out of there in 40 minutes that would beat the White Sox train back to Chicago but would arrive at a different station. So we said, 'Let's get on that.' We couldn't get a sleeping berth so we had to sleep in the coach, and we're bouncing around all night. But we got our story straight. When we got in, we were gonna get a cab from the Dearborn Street station to the Union Station, where the Sox train was going to get in. Then we'd go to the platform and just mix in with the guys as they got off. And Lopez would never know."

The plan seemed foolproof, except for one thing. Lopez knew.

"It hadn't dawned on us that when the White Sox got on the train in Kansas City, our bags were out on the platform. Lopez had walked past and said, 'Whose bags are these?' And Bernie Snyderworth (traveling secretary) said, 'Esposito's and Rivera's.' 'Well, better take 'em on—they missed the train.' So Al knew we'd missed the train. So we're standing there in Chicago waiting for our bags and he walks by and says, 'That'll be $200 apiece,' and kept right on walking.

"So the next day we had an afternoon ballgame and we got to the park early and Jim said, 'Let's go in and tell Al the truth. It won't hurt.' You know, $200 was $200. So we explained the whole thing to Al. And he said, 'You know, I'm going to give you your money back, because anybody who could make up a story like that deserves to get their money back.' "

Rivera, Esposito said, was a man of action. "I'll never forget the time Rivera decided to steal home. Billy Pierce was hitting. Jim just decided out of the clear blue that he was gonna go. And he always slid head-first. You never slide head-first into home—you take a chance hurting your head or at least jamming your fingers. But he took off and about the time he slid home, Pierce took one of the best cuts he ever took in his life. But he swung right through the ball—and also missed Jim's head by less than a foot. I don't know how he missed him. And Jim's safe at home, he gets up, dusts himself off, and walks into the dugout like nothing happened. And we're all on the floor dying."

Esposito felt like dying one early September evening in 1960. An illness had ended Nellie Fox's consecutive-game streak at 798, so Sammy was called on to start in his place. The Sox were playing a night game before 36,732 at Comiskey Park against the Yankees, whom they trailed by just 3½ games. Early Wynn had a 4-1 lead in the top of the eighth with New York runners on first and second and one out. Moose Skowron hit a doubleplay ball right at Esposito, who booted it for an error to fill the bases. Yogi Berra then singled to drive

186

in two runs, making it a 4-3 ballgame. Then pinch-batter Johnny Blanchard lifted a flyball to right-center, but Jim Landis and Al Smith collided, the ball dropping off Smitty's glove for a two-run double. Now it was 5-4 and Lopez came out to wave in reliever Gerry Staley from the bullpen. Then the fun started.

"I'm standing out at second talking to Looie and all of a sudden this guy comes out of the stands toward me. And he said he bet a lot of money on us and I'd just blown the game. And some punches were thrown. It was a very embarrassing situation for me."

The fan's name was Willie Harris, and he was quickly subdued by the park police, who had him taken to the nearby Deering district station where he was booked for disorderly conduct. "I was sued by this guy afterwards. Some lawyer got with him and they brought this lawsuit. Of course, it was thrown out of court. They sued the White Sox, too. They figured they could get some money out of it. But he had come out onto the field, so he was in the wrong right from the start. But that was a most embarrassing time for me. What made it more embarrassing was losing the game. I had a tough time getting over that. It was a tough night for me."

It might have been tougher if Wynn had still been around at game's end. "Wynn—and Dick Donovan too—were hard to play behind," Esposito said. "They kept you on edge. You know, you worried about doing something wrong behind them because they were just different guys when they pitched. They'd shoot daggers at you if you booted one. They were so intense the days they pitched.

"I remember Early's first year with us. I had started the game and somebody pinch-hit for me, and I was up in the clubhouse. I took a shower and then I was watching the game on TV. And Early got knocked out. He came up there and I was just relaxing, sitting up there watching the game. And he used to tear clubhouses up. He picked up a chair and threw it against the wall. Then he looked at me with that look. So I picked up a chair and threw it against the wall. Then he said, 'Well, that's better. Let's have a cold one together.' "

Sammy had plenty of cold ones the weekend of June 22-24, 1956—the weekend the Sox swept four straight from the Yankees. Just a rookie hitting a "lusty" .191 at the time, Esposito had the big hits in the Friday night contest, doubling in the tying runs as a pinch-hitter

187

with two out in the 10th and then looping a single just out of Phil Rizzuto's reach to drive in the winning run in the 11th. A crowd of 48,346 had seen a hometown boy make good.

"That Yankee game was exciting," he remembered. "They were still the tops then. All those names, their great record. To have played a part in beating them—especially as a rookie—was a great feeling for me. But what made me feel just as good was the fact that I played darn well in the other games, too (he started both ends of Sunday's double-header as the third baseman and leadoff man and went 3-for-9). It was a nice weekend for me. We had tremendous crowds. Those were exciting days."

They made up for the exciting days he had missed by signing with the Sox four years earlier. "When I signed I was playing basketball at Indiana," he said. "I was gonna be captain of the national champion-ship team the following year. Branch McCracken, my coach, and Frank Lane were really good friends. When I decided to sign with the White Sox, I did it without calling Branch up because I know he would have talked me out of it. But I thought it was a good time to sign. The money wasn't that stupendous, but it was pretty good money for that time.

"But the reason I signed was because if I had stayed in school and finished up my last two years, then gone into the draft, I'd have been 23-24 years old by the time I got out of the service. By that time, I'd have been too old. So I had to make a decision to play pro baseball or not to play it. So I signed and then called Branch. And Branch was very upset. He said, 'I know Frank Lane very well. I'm going to call him.' I said, 'Branch, it's too late—I'm getting on a bus to Waterloo, Iowa.'

"I went back to school that fall and he didn't really have much to do with me. At least until they won the national championship, because that really got me out of his doghouse. He was all right after that. See, I'd ended up starting my sophomore year from the start of the Big 10 season 'til the end of the year. We had Bobby Leonard, Don Schlundt —we had a great ballclub. I had reservations about not playing with that group for the next two years. But I had to go into pro baseball at the time I did. But basketball was really my game. Everything came so naturally to me. I had a much easier time playing basketball than baseball."

But baseball had been in his blood ever since he was old enough to ride the "L." He didn't take it to Comiskey Park, however. "I was a Cub fan," he told me, smiling. "I lived on the far South Side and I remember many a day my mother would pack me a lunch, I'd get on the 'L' and head to the North Side and spend the whole day out there. I was definitely a Cub fan."

With that, I fled.

JIM LANDIS:
It's in the Well

Hard-hitting, slow-footed outfielders, to me, have never seemed right wearing the White Sox uniform. Fellows like Gus Zernial, Rocky Colavito, Richie Zisk, and Wayne Nordhagen were hardly quintessential White Sox outfielders.

On the other hand, men like Jim Busby, Jim Rivera, Mike Hershberger, Ken Berry, and Jim Landis were. They were outstanding defensively, fleet of foot, and inconsistent with the bat. It was because of players like them that I've always gotten more of a kick out of a game-saving, diving catch or a game-saving throw to the plate than a game-winning home run in the bottom of the ninth.

All were, at one time or another, Sox centerfielders. But none played there longer, or more brilliantly, than Landis. He could run, he could throw, and he could catch any catchable ball—and some that were beyond the Comiskey Park bullpen fence and thus rightly judged uncatchable.

Jim Landis, despite good offensive years in 1958, '59, and '61, never will be remembered for his bat. But he wasn't as bad a hitter as he showed his rookie year ('57), when he struggled to finish at .212. Nor was he as bad as he showed in the first two months of the '58 season,

190

Jim Landis leaps to take home run away from Detroit's Bubba Morton during 1961 season. Landis' catch preserved a shutout for Frank Baumann.

when he was rolling along at a .180 clip while critics questioned manager Al Lopez's decision to stick with the 24-year-old from the Bay Area.

"I know he had a lot of confidence in me," Jim told me. I had met him at Chicago's Downtown Marriott, where he was awaiting the 20th anniversary reunion of the 1959 American League champs. "Here I'm hitting .180 and I'm still playing every day. I'm more than grateful. He never said anything like, 'You'd better do something or else.'

"It may sound corny, but I think I was in awe of the whole situation. You know, it's a dream come true. You're in the biggies—a little faster than I realized. I'm here. And it took me a while to finally say, 'Hey, I belong here.' I was stagestruck—very much so. I wasn't down on myself or anything—but it was just getting that start. I felt I was gonna hit something anyway. But even later, I always played scared, in the sense of, 'Hey, I don't want to leave here. This is it. This is what I really want.' It may sound funny, but I did play scared, because of wanting something so badly. You know, it's all you ever wanted since you were nine years old, and there you are."

He wasn't scared, however, in the outfield. "Maybe I'd hurt myself once in a while," he said, "but if I didn't, then I'd be shy of the fence anyway, so I probably wouldn't have made some of the catches I did make. You couldn't be afraid of a fence. Sometimes they thought I was crazy. But I think the intent had a lot to do with it. I always felt this: It may sound a little cocky but you had to feel this way—there was no ball I couldn't catch. That to me was real determination and if you don't have that, you're not a good outfielder, first of all. You've GOT to have that feeling and I just felt, 'I'm gonna catch it.' "

It's surprising, then to learn that Jim had originally been signed as an infielder out of Contra Costa College in Richmond, Cal., by Bobby Mattick, then a Sox scout and now the manager of the Toronto Blue Jays. "And I played third base my first year in pro ball in Wisconsin Rapids," he said. "I didn't realize myself I could run pretty good."

Neither did the White Sox, but they were quick to realize their mistake. So at spring training in 1953, at Phoenix, the Sox decided to make an outfielder out of the lanky, kid third baseman. "They felt, 'Anybody who can run that good, let's try this.' " Actually, it was

Johnny Mostil, then chief of the Chicago scouting department and himself a one-time standout Sox centerfielder, who made the decision. "He thought I could be an outfielder and he really worked me," Jim said. "I've said it many times, how much I owe him. He just worked my tail off. I was the one out there after everyone had left. In fact, a couple of times, Paul Richards had to come out there and tell him, 'Hey, that's enough.' But we really went at it. But all I can say is, it really paid off."

There was some natural ability involved, too. "I always felt a little cocky about the knack I had of getting a jump on the ball. There are some things you work on and there are other things that are just there—and that was one of them. I felt I could always get a good jump on a ball."

He needed that good jump one day in New York in 1959, when Mickey Mantle drove an Early Wynn fastball almost 460 feet to center field. Landis, off with the crack of the bat, finally caught up with the ball back by the monuments of Yankee greats Miller Huggins, Babe Ruth, and Lou Gehrig—monuments placed in the deepest part of the Yankee Stadium outfield because no one was ever going to hit a ball that far, anyway. Bob Elson always called it one of the top three catches he had ever seen.

"You play a guy like Mantle extra deep anyway," Landis said. "Especially in that park, 'cause it was 461 to center and 430 to left-center and 400 to right-center. If he got it between you, it was an inside-the-park homer. It was a gigantic place. If we'd have been in Comiskey Park and he'd hit it that far, it'd be in the bleachers. I wouldn't have had to worry about it.

"Anyway, I just kept running and running. I was about five feet from the monuments when I caught it. You look back and say, 'My God, you hit the ball that far and you don't get anything for it?' If I'd hit a ball that far and somebody had caught it, I think I'd shoot him."

Landis never did hit a ball that far, although he did knock 22 home runs one season. But he did, after that slow start in '58, develop into a hitter dependable enough to bat third in the lineup in 1959. That year, he followed up his .277 average of '58 with a .272 mark—nothing spectacular but nonetheless better than what had been anticipated two years earlier. His biggest hit of the season may well have been his

193

ninth-inning single at Yankee Stadium July 17 that drove in the only two runs of the night.

But it was in the field where he excelled during the pennant-winning season. He led all A.L. centerfielders in putouts with 420, gunned down 10 runners on the bases, and made just three errors. And his catches saved several games, among them a 2-1 victory over the A's one evening in Kansas City. With the bases loaded and two out in the last of the ninth, pinch-hitter Dick Williams drilled a low liner to center—a sure base hit. But Landis, getting his usual great jump, sprinted in, dived for the ball, and caught it just before it hit the ground.

"But you can remember everybody doing something special that season," he said. "And you can remember enjoying it. And I've seen it this week in the papers here, other people like Shaw and Staley being interviewed. Everybody keeps coming back to the same thing: It was such a tremendous group of guys. It really was. It was fabulous. And you don't realize it at the time, but we had a really good ballclub.

"It was at our 10-year reunion that it really, really hit me. What a fantastic group and that hey, this really was a good club. Better than I really thought at the time. People say, well, we eked in, the Yankees had an off-year. But if we look back, which I did myself, you say, 'Hey, we weren't that far out of first place every year anyway.' So we eked in one year. Maybe one year we were three games out. I know another year, '64, we lost by a game to the Yankees. So I think things were a lot better than even I myself thought at the time."

The spirit, however, was never better. "That '59 ballclub, we could have 10-12 guys go out to dinner together, sit around and really have a good time. Today you'll find one or two. The conflicts and the jealousies—none of this we had. It was tremendous that way. And we had comics, especially Rivera. And then guys like Donovan, who was a comedian and he didn't know it. I used to sit down at the end of the dugout and laugh. And he'd be dead serious. Here's what he did: Every time he pitched, he had his jacket and a towel next to him on the bench, but they had to be folded perfectly. Both of them. And he'd take I don't know how long to do it. They'd be folded nice as it was but he'd refold the jacket.

"And the area, the ground, in front of him in the dugout had to be spic and span. Rivera would be four or five people down from Dick and he'd be throwing spitballs in front of him—constantly. And Dick, not knowing he was having a game played on him, he'd keep picking 'em up and clearing the area."

It was a fun time and a fun club, a long way from the dreams of a young boy from the Oakland suburbs. "Growing up out there, we had Coast League ball," said Landis. "Some great ballplayers, and Casey Stengel managed at Oakland and Billy Martin played for him. People like that. It's a funny thing, but my ambition as a kid was to play in the Coast League. That was the big leagues to us."

He never fulfilled that ambition. But his oldest son, Craig, has. Craig Landis, signed out of Vintage High School in Napa, Cal., by the San Francisco Giants after being their first-round draft pick in 1977, spent the 1980 season with Phoenix of the Pacific Coast League. His average hovered most of the season around the .275 mark—not a particularly overpowering mark by Coast League standards.

"But," Jim Landis had said, smiling, "he's becoming a very good outfielder."

It figures.

AL SMITH:
Showers of Suds

People who remember Al Smith don't seem to remember him for the pennant-clinching home run he hit in Cleveland in 1959. Nor do they remember him for his run at the league batting championship in 1960. Nor for the fact that he was the first player to set off Bill Veeck's exploding scoreboard.

No, most people remember him for two things: the cup of beer accidentally dumped on him during the second game of the 1959 World Series, and his futile attempt to rise to the occasion on "Smith Night" that same year. I smiled at recollection of those two "events" as I drove to Brainerd Park on Chicago's far South Side, where Smitty had been supervisor since 1976. When I arrived at his office and reminded him of them, Al was smiling, too.

"At first I was angry," he said when I asked him his reaction to the unexpected shower in that World Series game. "I thought somebody had thrown the beer at me. But the umpire down the line told me that a fan had lost it trying to catch the baseball." (The baseball had been driven off the bat of the Dodgers' Charley Neal for one of Neal's two homers that afternoon.)

The Chicago Tribune ran an eight-sequence photo spread the next

Al Smith gets drenched by a cup of beer as fans above him follow the path of Charley Neal's home run during second game of the 1959 World Series. Note the fan in the upper left-hand portion of the picture making the catch on the baseball. The fan who dropped the beer is in the first row, directly above Smitty. [PHOTO COURTESY CHICAGO TRIBUNE. PHOTO BY RAY GORA]

morning of Smitty's brush with the brew. Smith laughed when he saw it, but he would soon see it again. "That winter," he said, "Ira Hutchinson and I were working together as a team, selling season tickets. We went to this one steel company up on Commercial Avenue. We walked into the office area and all these people start laughing at us. I thought maybe my fly was open or something. I looked, but it wasn't. I looked at Ira, but he was OK, too. They led us into the office of some vice-president in charge of public relations, and here's this big blowup on the wall of the photo sequence of the beer being spilled on me. The guy who spilled the beer was this vice-president. Now we knew why all those people had been laughing."

People had been booing, not laughing, on Smith Night that season. That was when Bill Veeck, in an effort to get White Sox fans behind the leftfielder and off his case, decided to let everyone named Smith, Smit, Smythe, etc., into the leftfield stands for free, just by showing some kind of identification. The idea was great, but the results weren't. Sure, Veeck had the fans BEHIND Smith, but that didn't necessarily mean they were FOR him.

"Veeck was trying to get me to win the people over," said Smitty, who, hampered by a bad ankle, had hit just .252 in '58 (after coming from Cleveland with Early Wynn for longtime South Side hero Minnie Minoso) and was doing even worse in '59. "But that night, I hit into two doubleplays, struck out, flied out, and dropped a flyball.

"I remember I had my milkman out there that night. He was a Polish fellow. I went out there to autograph some of the fans' tickets before the game started. And I saw him out there and said, 'How the hell did you get out here?' He'd gotten somebody's tax bill, had the name "Smith" on it. That's how he got in. I told him, 'Well, you be my bodyguard out here tonight.'

"But they booed just like they always did. Which is fine. As long as they didn't come out on the field, I didn't mind. See, Minoso was run, run, run. I wasn't like that. I'd catch the ball, but I'd catch it my way. I was slow at it—I'd run when I got ready. That was the type of ballplayer I was. They thought I wasn't hustling.

"A sportswriter said, 'Al, do you hear the boos?' I said, 'Of course I do.' 'But you never turn around and look at the crowd.' 'What for? They pay their money. They can do what they want. Just don't come down where I'm at. I'm still getting paid the 1st and the 15th.' That's the way I looked at it. 'You don't have a good year, you don't have a good year. You don't hit, you don't hit. But when I hit, turn it around. You write about me, the fans will come over.'

"And when I finally started running and feeling I could really go on my ankle again, it was the latter part of July (in '59). So it was almost two years since the day I'd hurt it originally."

That had been the final day of the '57 season, when Smitty, then with the Indians, slid into home plate at Briggs Stadium in Detroit and jammed his ankle. "A bone chip developed," he said, "but they'd told me the ankle wasn't broken, so I went home to Chicago figuring the ankle would get better. In November I was traded to the White Sox— Frank Lane was running the Indians and he wanted Minnie back with him and Lopez wanted me and Wynn back with him. The trade didn't bother me. I was glad to come here, 'cause my home was here.

"But what did bother me was I went to spring training and I wasn't able to maneuver my foot. I didn't really have any spring training at all. I could hardly run. But they never told the sportswriters that. I played more than 130 games that year on that bad ankle, but I paid for it. I got it from the fans, but my leg wasn't good. I wasn't much of a replacement for Minnie."

Then came '59. Smitty was reunited with the man who had originally signed him for Cleveland—new Sox owner Veeck. "I'd played for the Cleveland Buckeyes in the Negro league. Veeck sent Hank Greenberg and some of his scouts to look at (pitcher) Sam Jones. And they saw me. That was in 1948. They signed me near the end of the season. They couldn't decide where to send me, because they didn't have many clubs in their organization where they could send black ballplayers. They had Oklahoma City in the Texas League— couldn't send me there. They had San Diego in the Pacific Coast League, which would've been all right, but they didn't want to start me that high. They finally sent me to Wilkes-Barre (Pa.). I was the fourth black player signed: Jackie in the National League, Doby, Satch, and me."

The latter three all had been signed by Veeck. But now, in '59, Veeck wanted to own the contract of another favorite of his: Washington slugger Roy Sievers. And if it meant the loss of Smith, well, you have to give up something to get something. "We were in Washington early in the season, and the Senators and White Sox were talking trade," Smitty remembered. "And I was in the deal—or so I've been told by a reliable source. And they were in Al's office talking about this deal. And Al finally said, 'No—this is the guy I want at the plate when the chips are down.' Chuck Comiskey was pushing the trade—and I found out about it.

"Well, that year I broke up about 14 or 15 ballgames with home runs or base hits and I threw out five or six guys at home plate. And when I hit the home run to win the pennant in Cleveland, Chuck Comiskey was there in the tunnel after the game, waiting for us. And I walked right by him. Then he came into the clubhouse, and I still didn't talk to him."

On the plane ride back to Chicago, however, Smitty was so happy that even Comiskey was an old friend again. "Early Wynn, Klu, and I stood up all the way on the flight back from Cleveland," he laughed. "I shouldn't say this, 'cause I could get in trouble with the FAA. But we landed standing up. We never sat down. First you're high from winning the game for the pennant. And then you're high from the champagne."

For Smitty, it was Pennant No. 2. He had played on Cleveland's 111-game winner in 1954 and had led off the second game of the World Series with a home run off Johnny Antonelli. "The first pennant was exciting, being my first one," he said. "But that club, you know, so many great ballplayers. You start talking about Feller, Lemon, Wynn, Garcia, Rosen, Doby, Wertz. And there were only three rookies, really: Mossi, Narleski, and myself.

"Here, every guy really did contribute something. That's what made the pennant here just as good. If someone said, 'Is there one guy on this club you could just push off to the side and say, Hey, you can do without this guy,' you couldn't do it."

No, the White Sox needed every player on their 25-man roster. Nothing came easy to a team that played 50 one-run ballgames and won 35 of them. "It got so that by the end of July and the first of August, we figured we couldn't be beaten. If we were down a run or tied going into that last inning, it was a feeling we had on the bench: 'One run's not gonna beat us.' We had a feeling that our guy was gonna walk—especially if Aparicio was coming up. If Aparicio walked, hell, he was gonna steal second. And then Fox would bunt— he was probably the best bunter I ever saw.

"Or, if Aparicio gets on, they can't throw too many breaking balls to Fox, 'cause Aparicio's stealing. And if you come in on Fox at third, expecting the bunt, he'd slap it by you. Now we have runners at first and third. Now all we worry about is, 'Hit a flyball, somebody!' And we'd get that damn flyball.

"But we had a feeling on the bench that we were gonna win. Lopez sat down at the end of the bench, and there was a towel next to him. No one sat on that towel. We all said, 'That's where Jesus Christ sits.' "

The good fortune ran out, however, in the World Series. The pivotal game was the second one, the pivotal inning the eighth. With Earl Torgeson at second and Sherm Lollar at first with no outs and the Sox down 4-2, Smitty doubled to the wall in left-center. Torgeson scored easily, but third base coach Tony Cuccinello—ignoring a time-honored baseball teaching that says, 'Never have the first out of an inning thrown out at third base or home plate'—sent home the lumbering Lollar. Sherm was out from here to McCuddy's.

"But that's the kind of baseball we played," Al said in defense of Cuccinello. "We played the running game that year. At that time, there was nobody out. I was up there to bunt. We were trying to get runners over to second and third. I bunted and fouled it off. Bunted again, and fouled it off. Now in a situation like that, you and I can sit up in the stands and say, 'How come he's not using a runner for Lollar?' But Lopez doesn't sit there and say to himself, 'Hey, Al's gonna hit a double into the gap.'

"But still, all our scouting reports said (leftfielder Wally) Moon didn't have a good arm and (shortstop Maury) Wills didn't have a good arm. Nothing like Aparicio's. But Moon gave Wills a perfect throw and Wills made a perfect throw to the plate. And Lollar was out by six or seven steps. But where did I wind up at? I wound up at third base with only one man out."

So the Sox still had the tying run at third. All that was needed was that flyball—or a wild pitch, a passed ball, a balk, or an error. But Billy Goodman, batting for Bubba Phillips against Dodger reliever Larry Sherry, struck out and Jim Rivera popped out, leaving Smith stranded at third. The Sox lost 4-3, but Smitty was just hitting his stride. In 1960, after moving to right field to make room for the re-acquired Minoso in left, Al finished second to Boston's Pete Runnels in the league batting race with a career-high .315 average. In '61, he hit a solid .278 with 28 homers and 93 runs-batted-in, and in '62, playing mostly at third base, he hit .292 with 82 RBI. But that would be his last season with the White Sox, who sent him and Aparicio to Baltimore for Pete Ward, Ron Hansen, Hoyt Wilhelm, and Dave Nicholson.

"One of the reasons I left Chicago was they wouldn't give me the money I wanted," said Smith, whose peak salary from the White Sox was $42,500. "I was asking for a $9,000 raise and we were about $2,500 apart. I said, 'Well, OK, let's split it. You take the $1,250 and I'll take the $1,250. And then you can give me a car so my wife can take it to spring training.' 'Cause they could write that off. But no, they wouldn't do it. Now, they don't even talk about $9,000. You hit .240 or .250, you'll make $140,000."

Al Smith was born 20 years too early to make that kind of money. But he is rich in other ways, because of the 15 years he gave to the kids in his programs at Brainerd and, before that, at Ogden Park. "When a kid comes back and tells me he's going to college here or he's got a good job there and thanks me for helping him, it makes me feel like I've contributed something. That's a good feeling."

Every bit as good a feeling as hitting a pennant-clinching home run.

GERRY STALEY:
A Sinker to Vic Power

For any White Sox fan old enough to recall it, the one shining moment in his memory is that night in September 1959, when Gerry Staley came in with the bases loaded and one out in the bottom of the ninth at Cleveland's Municipal Stadium and got Vic Power to hit the doubleplay ball to Luis Aparicio at short that ended the game and clinched for Chicago its first American League pennant in 40 years.

I'll never forget it. Many Sox fans must have always felt that the failure of the White Sox—especially their failure in the clutch, when the key ballgame or the pennant was on the line—was nothing more than an extension of their own inadequacies. So looking back, it must seem a miracle now that Aparicio didn't bobble the ball for an error, or throw the relay peg 20 feet over first baseman Ted Kluszewski's head to allow the tying runs to score.

But Looie, bless him, didn't choke. His pickup was clean, his throw was true, and the Sox had their pennant, at long last. And the one-pitch hero had been Staley, who couldn't have dreamed—three years earlier, when he had first been purchased from the New York Yankees—that someday he would be the hero of a White Sox pennant-clinching victory.

203

Gerry Staley

"Marty Marion was the manager of the White Sox when I first got here in '56," said Gerry, who was in town for the 20th anniversary reunion of the 1959 championship club when we met at the Continental Plaza Hotel. "He'd been a teammate of mine with the Cardinals, and I would imagine that was one of the reasons I wound up with the White Sox.

"I'd played with Marty and Marty knew what I could do and what I couldn't do. And we had Howie Pollet on the staff and Del Wilber, another old Cardinal, was the bullpen coach. New York had some young fellows on their staff who they didn't have any options left on, so they couldn't option them out. I was expendable and their young fellows weren't."

So Marion, who therefore deserves a bit of credit for the '59 pennant, convinced Chuck Comiskey and John Rigney to purchase the then-35-year-old righthander from the Yankees. Marty put him to work immediately, starting Staley in the second game of a Memorial Day twin bill at Cleveland—where he was destined to have his biggest moment three years later. Staley, as he would be 38 times in his tenure with the Sox, was the winning pitcher.

"The year that Marion was there," Staley said, "I started a lot of times (10 of his 27 appearances were starts). Then the next year, Lopez came and he figured he needed some people in the bullpen. They were loaded with starters—Pierce, Harshman, Donovan, Wilson, Keegan. He needed to work somebody into the bullpen, and he needed somebody there who wouldn't take too long to warm up, and who wouldn't come up with arm trouble if he threw a lot. Well, I'd never had arm trouble, and—after one or two pitches—I'd be ready to go in."

The bullpen wasn't necessarily a brand-new environment for Gerry, despite his being an ace starter for several years in St. Louis— where he won 10, 13, 19, 17, and 18 games in successive seasons. "I used to start between 30 and 35 games a year with the Cardinals," he said, "and even then I'd help out in the bullpen between starts if they were a little short out there."

And all the while, he was throwing the pitch that would make him such a standout reliever for the Sox—the sinkerball. "I threw it all those years—and the slider, and the changeup," he said. "Then, in later years, I came up with the knuckleball. I needed an extra pitch, 'cause you lose a little off the sinker and besides that, if you have just the one main pitch, they're gonna stand up there and wait for it. So you've got to show them something else once in a while."

But the sinker was his bread and butter. "The harder you throw it, the straighter it goes," said Gerry, "If you're throwing real hard—and you're not tired—you don't get that little extra turn. It's going a little bit too fast." It was going slower in '59, when Staley made a league-leading 67 appearances, causing the fatigue necessary for an effective sinkerballer. "If it's going a little slower, it's gonna fall from lack of speed."

The pitch made Staley exactly the kind of reliever Lopez needed. He had hard-throwing Turk Lown—Staley's roommate and, like Gerry, an ex-National Leaguer—to bring in when he needed the key strike-out. Staley was the man Lopez went to when he needed a doubleplay. The situation arose more than once in '59. One such memorable spot came on a Saturday afternoon in July at Yankee Stadium. The bases were loaded with just one out and Hector Lopez at bat with the Sox leading 2-1 in the bottom of the ninth. Staley threw one pitch, a sinker, and Lopez grounded into a short-to-second-to-first twin killing. That was the ballgame.

Then came that night in Cleveland. The Sox, before 54,293, led 4-2 going into the last of the ninth. Bob Shaw, in relief of starter Early Wynn, opened by getting Woodie Held on a popup. Then Jim Baxes singled off Shaw's glove. Jack Harshman, the ex-Sox pitcher who had hooked on with the Indians, lined a single to right. And Jimmy Piersall followed with a smash off Nellie Fox's glove, loading the bases. Out of the visitors' dugout came Al Lopez, who signalled for Staley. Staley knew what he'd have to do.

"As a reliever, you're coming in to close ballgames with men on base," he said. "So you've got to keep the ball low so they don't hit it out of the park. In the spot I came into that night, the situation is that you're gonna try to make the guy hit the ball on the ground. That's all you can do. You're not out there to—well, yes, you'd like a strike-out—but your main purpose is to get him to hit the ball on the ground so there is the possibility of a doubleplay. Make sure you throw the ball where you have that possibility."

206

I asked him if he had thrown Vic Power a good sinker. "Well, evidently," he said, laughing. "When he hit it, I knew it was on the ground. And that it was headed in the right direction—to Aparicio. As long as he fielded the ball clean, we were at least gonna get one out and we'd still be one run ahead."

Looie, of course, did better than that. He got the doubleplay, and that set off a wild victory celebration at the scene as well as back home in Chicago, where Fire Commissioner Robert Quinn—a lifelong Sox fan—ordered the city's air-raid sirens turned on. Cub fans feared a surprise attack by the Russians. Sox fans knew better.

"That game relieved all the pressures for all of the fellows on the club," Staley recalled. "And after all these years, we'd finally made it into a World Series. That's everybody's goal, to get to the World Series. I'd missed the Cardinals' pennant in '46. I first came up in '47. And I'd joined the Yankees too late in '55 to be eligible for the Series. I threw batting practice for them in the Series, but I couldn't even sit in the dugout during the game. So I'd just go back to the hotel and watch the game on TV."

But in '59, he was a participant, and a busy one. He pitched in four of the six games, saving one and losing one when Gil Hodges homered over the Chinese Wall at the Los Angeles Coliseum in Game Four. His earned run average for the Series was 2.16. In 1960, his 13 victories tied him for second on the staff with Frank Baumann, Early Wynn, and Shaw—all starters. He appeared in another 64 games that year and in many ways was more effective than he had been in '59. He pitched just one inning less than he had the year before, walking the same number of men (25) and allowing 17 fewer hits. And, he was named to the American League all-star team.

But the next year, at age 40, the Staley magic began to disappear. After going 0-3 for the Sox in 16 games, he was traded along with Shaw and outfielders Wes Covington and Stan Johnson to Kansas City for pitchers Ray Herbert and Don Larsen, third baseman Andy Carey, and outfielder Al Pilarcik. A 15-year career was nearing an end.

"I went to Kansas City and then finished up with Detroit in '61—I was with the Tigers for the stretch drive," he said. "At the end of the year, I had a chance to coach with Portland. Kansas City had a working agreement with them, and it was nice for me. I could live at home—I lived only 15 miles from the ballpark. So I went with them for one year, '62, and then I quit."

He quit baseball, but he didn't quit working. He got a job with the Clark County park system in his hometown of Vancouver, Wash. "I've been with them for 16 years," he told me. "I'm getting ready to retire. I'll be 60 next year, you know."

When he said that, 1959 suddenly seemed like ancient history. Has it really been that long since that night in Cleveland?

BOB SHAW:
Ray Berres' Disciple

Many people think the White Sox never would have won the one
pennant that they did win in my lifetime had it not been for the
pitching of Bob Shaw. I don't know. You figure the law of averages
would have guaranteed the Sox their pennant eventually, anyway.
Nevertheless, there is no discounting the 18-6 record and the 2.68
earned run average Shaw, until then an unknown 25-year-old,
contributed to the Chicago cause in 1959.

I sought, then, to speak with this handsome fellow who, two years
after his heroics of '59, would be pitching for the 10th-place Kansas
City Athletics and who, seven years after that, would be calling it
quits after a big league career that had lasted 10 years and brought him
108 pitching victories.

I found Shaw in West Palm Beach, Fla., in the sales and leasing
office of a proposed building project called Cedarbrook Office Park
and Plaza. He was, I quickly learned, doing what he had been doing
for a number of years—working in building and real estate. "I've been
down here almost 18 years now," he said. "I own small shopping
centers, stores, office buildings. This project right here, I'm just
project director. There are eight partners, and I'm just taking it right

Bob Shaw

from the beginning: zoning, architectural, leasing and managing.

"We're about ready to get off the ground. It's going to be an office park and a shopping center. We have about 13 acres. Basically, I build my own projects and manage my own projects. But this thing, I'm just helping them, because I wasn't too busy and they asked me to help them out."

Years earlier, in 1958, he said, he had asked the Detroit Tigers to help him out. The response was negative. "I had played in their minor league organization 4½ years," he said, "and then I went to Cuba to pitch in the winter league and was the most valuable player there in the Caribbean World Series—I beat Puerto Rico 2-0 to win it. Then I came back and the Detroit ballclub was in last place in May and they weren't using me and they decided to send me out. I had talked to them about some things and the answers I got I didn't particularly like. So I just made up my mind that my future really wasn't with the Detroit organization. When they told me they were gonna send me down, I just told them I was going to go home and that I hoped that they would trade me.

"And so I did—I went home, and I was home a couple of weeks. And that, even though I was losing money at the time, was the greatest decision I ever made in my life."

Because Shaw, along with first baseman Ray Boone, was sent to Chicago June 15 for pitcher Bill Fischer and outfielder Tito Francona. "My whole career turned around," he said. "I started to pitch pretty good—mostly long relief—and the next year I ended up starting after a month or so and was 18-6. But I owe a great deal to Ray Berres. And to Al Lopez."

Berres got the righthander to throw more three-quarters than he had been. "I threw too much from the side, which is bad," Shaw said. "Because if you break the ball parallel to the bat, you're gonna get hit more often. Also, you put more strain on your elbow and shoulder. What he basically taught was quite simple: You've got to break your hands, get the hand out of the glove, keep your weight back, get your arm up. It wasn't all that elaborate. Just basic fundamentals and he knew 'em and there are really very few people in the country who know what they are.

"Lopez brought me along slowly. That's the failure of many

211

managers. They get a kid who shows some promise and they dump him right into a start. I think that Al brought me along. Now, he also had other, veteran pitchers, so it was a twofold thing: No. 1 was to bring me along slowly and try and work me in. And No. 2, if one of the others faltered, which is what happened in '59, to give me an opportunity to start."

He made the most of that opportunity, which presented itself May 13 in Boston after Dick Donovan had gotten off to a slow start and Ray Moore had proved ineffective. Shaw, mixing his sinking fastball with his slider, shut out the Red Sox on five hits. "You get the chance to start, you do well, it gives you confidence, it makes you feel good," Shaw said. "But the things that I learned from Berres allowed me to be consistent—and that's the name of the game. In order to be a good major league pitcher, you have to be consistent. You have to go out there and do a good job just about every time out there."

Which is what he did all through that marvelous '59 season. Shaw downed the Yankees 2-1 July 18 in Yankee Stadium. He earned the Sox a split in a key Aug. 23 doubleheader by shutting out the Yankees in front of 44,250 fans and five days later beat Cleveland 7-3 in the opener of a four-game series at Municipal Stadium—a series the Sox would sweep to go 5½ games ahead of the second-place Indians. A game he didn't start—a Thursday afternoon contest in early June—stands out in his memory just as much, however.

"I was pitching in the 17-inning game that Earl Torgeson won with a home run against Baltimore," Bob recalled. "As a matter of fact, there were two outs and there were two strikes on him, because I remember saying, 'Oh, gee, I gotta go out there again.' Because I'd already pitched seven or eight innings. But he popped it. And, boy, normally you jump up. But I was so tired, and it was a real hot day. I just sat there and said, 'Dear Lord, am I ever glad he hit it."

He was saying the same thing after Vic Power hit the doubleplay grounder that clinched the pennant at Cleveland Sept. 22. "Early Wynn, my roommate—I learned a lot from him, about business, about wearing mohair suits—he started that game and I came in and pitched the last three innings. But I did a stupid thing. I loaded 'em up for Staley. I didn't want to, but I think I got a little excited, knowing we were that close to clinching it."

212

The World Series against the Dodgers was next. Shaw pitched the second game and lost 4-3, thanks to two home runs by Charley Neal and one by pinch-hitter Chuck Essegian. And he started the fifth game and, though needing relief help from Billy Pierce and Donovan, was the winning pitcher in the thriller played before a record 92,706.

"Well, I like to remember the good parts," Shaw grinned, "that beating Sandy Koufax 1-0 before the largest crowd in history. But you have to go back to that second game, when Tony (Cuccinello) sent Sherm Lollar in from first on Al Smith's double. And Wally Moon threw to Maury Wills and he relayed it to John Roseboro to cut down Lollar. Yeah, I guess you could call it a mistake, but that's part of the game.

"Neal hit two homers off me. He hit one to left field—that's the one where Smitty got the beer dumped on his head. And he also hit one over the centerfield fence. And obviously, whatever I say now sounds like an excuse, but it was ironic that we were pitching him away. Both balls he hit out were away, off the middle of the plate to the outside. And a few years later, I went over to the National League (with the Milwaukee Braves) and he was with the Mets. And if I'm not mistaken, I don't think he ever got a hit off me. Now maybe he was starting to go downhill, but I jammed him with fastballs and he just never hit me at all. And both the balls he hit off me in '59 were breaking balls to the outside part of the plate. Now I like to think I was following our scouting reports, whatever we had heard about him. But of course, that's water over the dam. But you've got to have an excuse—right?—when somebody hits two home runs off you in one game. It can't possibly be your fault."

We both laughed, and I asked him about that fifth game. "Yeah, I pitched well and all that stuff," he said, "but I have to consider myself lucky. Koufax, that day, was unbelievable. He was throwing out of those white shirts. No question, I wouldn't dare put myself in a category with Koufax. Super, super pitcher. You talk about a fastball rising, and a curveball. His were just explosive. And out of those white shirts, he really was almost unhittable.

"But we got runners on first and third in the third inning, and Lollar hit a groundball and they went for the doubleplay, and we got the one run. You can't fault their decision. In that ballpark, you don't figure

213

you're gonna have a 1-0 ballgame—not with that fence in left field just 250 feet from home plate. I did a little after-dinner speaking that winter in Chicago and I used to kid and say that when I reached real far back for the good fastball that day, I'd scrape my hand on that fence."

Shaw's thanks for his brilliant pitching and his after-dinner speaking for the White Sox was hardly what he expected. Owner Bill Veeck's general manager, Hank Greenberg, sent out Shaw's contract that winter with what amounted to a slap in the face. "Maybe because Hank had been a hitter, he sure didn't want to give any money to any pitchers," Shaw said. "I'd made $10,000 in '59 and after I was 18-6 with a 2.68 ERA and finishing third in the Cy Young award voting—and at that time there was only one Cy Young award—the offer I got from Mr. Greenberg was for a $5,000 raise."

I told him he had to be kidding.

"I wish I was," he said. "So I held out for quite a long time and that's one of the reasons I got off to a bad start that next season. Finally I signed on April 4 for about $22,000. See, back in those days, the owners definitely had the upper hand. I didn't have an attorney. I didn't have arbitration. I couldn't go before this committee or whatever. It was well-thought out, well-planned, by Hank and Bill. The logic was, offer him very little, then hold off, hold off. They knew darn well you're gonna play baseball. So they've got the upper hand. And, in my case, I hurt myself, because they knew I trained hard—running, calisthenics, preparation. I was always in shape. So that worked against me, because they still knew, even though I was at home, I'd by working my fanny off."

So Shaw finally reported to spring training at Sarasota, where he found a different-looking group of White Sox. Instead of fellows like Bubba Phillips, Norm Cash, Earl Battey, John Romano, and Johnny Callison, Bob found Minnie Minoso, Roy Sievers, and Gene Freese. "I'm assuming it was Bill's (Veeck's) decision," he said, "but they went for power. And that ballpark is not designed for power. It's designed for pitching, speed, and defense. So they picked up some power but they hurt themselves defensively. And they didn't really pick up much speedwise. They went for the power hitter to make the scoreboard go off. They created an attraction. And that was the exploding score-

214

board. And in order to make it explode, you have to get a little power."

But Shaw stops short of blaming his off-year in 1960 (13-13, 4.06 ERA) on Veeck and Greenberg. "You do have to realize, though, that only one pitcher on that club—Billy Pierce—won more ballgames than I did. The other thing is, there were no 20-game winners in the American League that year. Look it up. So, maybe if management hadn't traded away some of those players, I may have been 16-10. And for me, that would've been a heckuva year. But the answer is obvious: I did not pitch that well.

"But two things happened, and you're the first to know about this. And when I was a pitching coach, I always tried to tell anybody who had had an outstanding year, that it's very important for an athlete—in particular a pitcher—to keep himself physically active. Because here you've been going, pitching 250 innings, and now all of a sudden you stop. At least later on, I played golf and I'd swim during the winter. But I didn't even play golf that winter. I was single, I stayed in Chicago. I was working for the ballclub, I was selling meat, I was working for a housing development, I did after-dinner speaking. But I didn't do anything physically. And I don't know if it was calcium or what, but I actually got clicks in my shoulder—I'd make circles with my arm to try to eliminate them. I kind of learned a lesson of life: Don't completely inactivate yourself after being extremely active.

"So that's part of it. That plus not going to spring training earlier, not getting the money I thought I deserved. I think the combination of those two things didn't allow me to do as well as I might have done. But every time you talk about that sort of thing, it sounds like an excuse. But what I'm telling you is factual."

What also is factual is that Shaw, in Al Lopez's doghouse and pitching less-than-impressive baseball, was traded in June of 1961 to Kansas City as part of an eight-player trade. "I wasn't happy leaving the White Sox," he said. "But every time I've been traded, I made more money. And I was 12-14 for a 10th-place ballclub. So I did come on to do quite well. And I was very happy to beat the White Sox when I pitched against them."

He was happy to beat Lopez, too. "I had gone to give a talk. And a guy who was sitting next to me asked me a lot of questions and he became very obnoxious. And somehow or other it got back to Warren Brown (of the Chicago American) and there was an insinuation that I was drunk. Which wasn't true because I didn't drink that much—I just wasn't a drinker.

"Al called me in and said that he had heard this story. And I had told this guy off. This guy had been rude and he had been drunk. The story had come back to Al that I was the guy who had been rude and drunk. Which was not true. But I wasn't pitching very well at the time and I think that Al didn't believe me. And we got into some words— because he was wrong. And Warren Brown picked that up and from there it started to get written that I was having problems with Al. I think it all stemmed from that one incident. Other than the fact that I was caught out one night after curfew and it cost me quite a bit of money. But that didn't have anything to do with it. The argument we'd had over the other thing was more responsible for it."

Shaw, however, didn't carry a grudge. In fact, he claims it was Lopez who was at least partially responsible for planting the seed for the book "Pitching," which Bob had published by Viking Press in 1969. "Lopez and Berres, really, gave me the idea," said Shaw. "It's on the mechanics of delivery. If you don't have a sound delivery, you're gonna have problems. Either you're not gonna do well or you're gonna injure yourself. I would listen to Ray, and he'd make a statement about a pitcher: 'He probably won't last six innings,' or 'He won't have a curveball,' or 'He's gonna be high,' or 'If he does this, this is what's gonna happen.' It was unbelievable. Everything he said seemed to happen. His percentage for being right was astronomical.

"The more I listened to him and watched him, the more I learned and the more I became an advocate of what he was teaching. And then as I went around and continued on in my career, and even in coaching, I found out that the average pitching coach doesn't know what the hell he's talking about. Berres, he knew what he was talking about."

Shaw took Berres' teachings with him when he went to work in the organizations of the Oakland A's, the Los Angeles Dodgers, and the Milwaukee Brewers. After that, he left organized baseball to concentrate on his business interests, but still found time to teach baseball to his players in American Legion ball in West Palm Beach and nearby

Jupiter. Two summers ago he served as director of Jupiter's Boys Baseball Association and coached his son at the Bronco level (11 and 12-year-olds). For 1980, he said, he would go back to Legion ball.

"I refused to go any lower," he laughed. "I've been going downhill from the big leagues to the minors to Legion ball. I won't go any lower than bronco."

TED KLUSZEWSKI:
The Home Run
That Didn't Count

It has been little more than 20 years since one of the most unbeliev-ably depressing moments in White Sox history forever embedded Ted Kluszewski's name in the minds of Sox fans everywhere. Not that he hadn't already been there to a degree as it was. After all, Klu's heroics in the '59 World Series will never be forgotten.

But what happened in Baltimore's Memorial Stadium on the after-noon of Aug. 28, 1960 was so incredible that, even today, I get night-mares thinking about it. I had to seek out Kluszewski to see if the shock still remained with him as well, so, noticing that the Cincinnati Reds—for whom Klu toils these days as hitting instructor—were going to be in town to play the Cubs, I arranged to meet with the former slugger at Wrigley Field.

I met him in the Reds' clubhouse and together we walked out onto the field. I asked him if he remembered that day of horror. Of course he did. Together, we set the stage: The Sox, three games back of the sur-prising Orioles and one behind the second-place Yankees, were trailing 3-1 with two out and two on in the top of the eighth inning. Kluszewski was sent up to pinch-hit against righthander Milt Pappas by manager Al Lopez, who also sent Earl Torgeson and Floyd

Ted Kluszewski takes batting practice swings at Sarasota in 1960.

Robinson out of the dugout to warm up down along the rightfield foul line. Torgeson and Robinson would be entering the game defensively the next half-inning.

Just as Pappas was releasing his third pitch to Kluszewski, third base umpire Ed Hurley spotted Torgeson and Robinson warming up in what he felt was not the prescribed area for such duties. So he called time out. Pappas didn't hear him. Kluszewski didn't hear him. Nor, for that matter, did anyone else. The pitch was thrown, Klu swung, and the ball sailed into the rightfield seats for a three-run homer. The Sox led 4-3.

But wait a second.

Hurley was gesturing madly with his arms. He was waving the home run off. Kluszewski, though, didn't see him. He was busy running the bases.

"I hit it good," he recalled. "And I rounded first base and headed for second and I saw Jim Rivera, who was on base at that particular time, stopped at third. And I assumed, because I'd hit it hard—it was a line drive—that maybe they had called it a ground-rule double. Because it was hit in the area of the top of the wall, and maybe a fan had stuck his hand out and touched it.

"I didn't know what had happened until Rivera started back toward me and said, 'He called time.' I said, 'Called TIME? For what?' It was a real strange situation."

Was Klu crushed?

"Oh, completely. And then I had to go up and hit again. And I hit the ball good again. I hit a line drive to right-center, but it was caught. I didn't quite pull it enough. But it was strange. Hurley claimed Torgeson and Robinson weren't in the area where they were supposed to be warming up in and at the last minute he called time out. He was over at third and this was all happening at first base. So that was the argument more than that he had called time. Hell, he shouldn't have had his nose over on the sidelines. He should've been in the game."

Lopez and Nellie Fox had been thrown out of the game when the 15-minute bruhaha had ended. The White Sox had lost a little drive— and the ballgame, 3-1—and Klu had lost a homer.

"Nothing like that had ever happened to me," he said. "In fact, I'd never had a home run rained out in all the years that I played. That was the only time I ever lost a home run. But that was the turning point for us that season. We were three games back and if we'd have won we'd have been two back. But the way it worked out we lost the game so we were four out and we lost the next night and we were five out. We were a decent ballclub. We weren't quite as effective as the year before, but we were still capable of winning it. But that kind of turned us around. We were four back instead of two. It could well have been one, because you win that one and you go out and win the next one."

But it wasn't to be. The Sox finished third, thereby precluding any opportunity for Klu to repeat his record-setting feats in the '59 World Series. In that Fall Classic, he set a record for most runs-batted-in (10) by one player in a six-game Series, getting off to a glorious start by driving in five runs in the Sox' 11-0 opening-game rout of the Dodgers. He singled in a run in the first inning, homered into the first row off Los Angeles starter Roger Craig in the third, and then blasted a Chuck Churn fastball against the rightfield upper deck facade in the fourth. It was an amazing display for a 35-year-old man who many had figured to be over the proverbial hill.

"I would say that first game was my biggest thrill in baseball," he said. "It was the first Series game I'd ever been in. And I was playing. And you run out onto the field and you suddenly realize that this is the only game in the country and a lot of people are watching. In fact, up in the millions. And I got a big thrill out of it. In fact, even if I had had a bad series, it still would've been the greatest moment of my life. Regardless of how much you play, I think the World Series is really the epitome of what every ballplayer strives for."

And Klu, for all of his great years with the Cincinnati Reds in the National League, had never been in one before. It wasn't his fault. He had done his part. In successive seasons starting in 1953, the strong-man from southwest suburban Argo had hit 40, 49, 47, and 35 home runs, driven in 108, 141, 113, and 102 runs, and hit .316, .326, .314, and .302. In truth, he'd been frightening opposing pitchers ever since joining the Reds late in 1947. He stood 6-2, he weighed 245 pounds, and he cut off his sleeves so the pitcher could see how big and burly those arms of his really were.

"At first, I did that because the sleeves were restricting me from

221

swinging," the ex-Indiana University football player told me. "They could never make a uniform for me that would give me enough room. These new doubleknit uniforms give. But the old flannel ones didn't. I'd get hung up. So I asked them to shorten the sleeves on my uniforms, but they gave me a lot of flak. So one day, I just took a pair of scissors out and cut 'em off."

So there was a practical reason for the cutoff sleeves as well as a psychological one. "But after a while it became kind of a symbol," Klu grinned. "And it'd have to get pretty cold before I'd put a long sleeve shirt on after that."

Kluszewski's terrorizing of National League pitchers came to a rather abrupt end with the advent of back trouble late in 1956. "I hurt my back—it was a slipped disc—and it took until '57 to find out what I had. In '57, I hardly played at all (only 127 at-bats), and then they traded me to Pittsburgh. Looking back now, it would've been nicer if they had sent me to the White Sox then instead of me having to wait until '59, but you don't think about those things when you're playing."

He wasn't entertaining thoughts, therefore, of the possibility of a move to Chicago one late August day in 1959. He was sitting around his Pittsburgh apartment, minding his own business, when the call from the Pirate office came. He'd been traded to his hometown team, the White Sox, for veteran outfielder Harry "Suitcase" Simpson and a minor league infielder, Bob Sagers. Klu could not have been happier.

"The Pirates had had a fairly bad year and I'd played the first half of the season and then they had gone with the kids the last half," he said. "So I was sitting around on the bench, pinch-hitting, mostly. And I got the news that I was going to the White Sox. I was excited, very much so. Because what most people didn't realize was that I had never played in a World Series until then.

"In fact, I made it to Chicago that same day. Got the news in the afternoon and made it here that evening. My family—some of my brothers—they felt that I had finally made the major leagues, coming to the White Sox. I was a little of both—a Sox fan and a Cub fan. But Sox Park was a lot closer to Argo than this park, so the ballgames I saw were at Sox Park. Most of the family were Sox fans. Of course, in '59 they were ALL Sox fans. But none of them were there that first night, because they didn't expect me to get to Chicago that fast."

222

But he made it, all right, and was greeted warmly by his new team-mates, many of whom he knew well from the days the Sox and Reds had both called Tampa their spring training home. Clubhouse man Sharkey Colledge game him uniform shirt No. 4—the biggest he had (it had last been worn by 6-7 Ron Jackson)—and then scrounged around trying to find the bottom half of a uniform for the huge new-comer. "Our big problem was finding a pair of pants—they didn't have any big enough," Klu laughed. "What they finally did was they added about three inches onto the back of an old pair of pants and I was finally able to get into them. That was our big crisis during that evening. That's why I didn't get to take hardly any batting practice."

The Sox were playing Boston that Tuesday evening, and the crowd of nearly 40,000 knew to the man who that big fellow was coming out of the Sox dugout to pinch-hit in the last of the seventh. Kluszewski received a standing ovation from the hometown fans, promptly hit into a second-to-short-to-first doubleplay, and then, as he trotted off the field, he received another standing ovation. With a reception like that, Klu figured he owed White Sox fans something. So off to work he went. He took batting practice and more batting practice, trying to regain the old Kluszewski stroke. The home runs were slow in coming—he finally connected twice against Kansas City on Labor Day—but the line drives weren't. He averaged .297 for the Sox the rest of the season.

"You know, you don't play for a while, and hitting is such a fine art that you just kind of lose that little edge of getting that bat out there," he said. "Home run hitting is a type of thing where you have to commit yourself a little sooner. I was probably defensive for the first couple of weeks, just trying to make contact."

That helps explain why Klu's first 17 hits for Chicago were all singles. A 6-2, 245-pound slugger had put on a Sox uniform and had been transformed into a 6-2, 245-pound singles hitter. "But by World Series time," he told me, "I was back to about 70-80 per cent of my old swing. The back is kind of a crazy thing. Even though it hurts, the more you work at it the better off you are, because you're finally starting to loosen up. When your back is bothering you, you have a tendency to stiffen and everything shortens and you don't swing the bat the way you normally would. So the more I played the better I swung the bat and finally it culminated with the Series. I was hitting the ball as well as you could hit it by that particular time."

All of which brought hopes of a big 1960 season for Klu, who planned to play in as many as 125 games for the defending American League champions. But he got off to a slow start, his average hovering around .250 in early June when Lopez decided to go with Roy Sievers as his first baseman. It was back to pinch-hitting again for the big guy, who wound up getting into just 81 games that season. Lopez did put him back into the regular lineup Sept. 8, after Sievers had gone into a prolonged slump, and Klu came through with two singles and a game-winning double in a 5-4 victory over the Yankees—Klu's first start since July 4. Sparked by Kluszewski's resurgence, the Sox won six in a row and moved to within two games of the lead, but they would get no closer. Neither would Klu, whom the Sox left unprotected for the American League expansion draft shortly after the end of the season. He was selected by the Los Angeles Angels, destined to finish light years behind the pennant-winning Yankees in '61.

"It was understandable, being left unprotected by the White Sox," Klu said. "You get to protect only so many guys and you don't protect a guy who's 36 years old and at the end of his career. And I enjoyed it because I went to a new ballclub where I played a little bit. And I enjoyed my year out there. I hit 15 home runs and I only batted 250 times (263 official trips), so I was rather productive. But baseball was becoming a grind for me, so I just retired."

He returned in 1970 as the Reds' batting coach, and has spent the time since helping people like Pete Rose and Johnny Bench refine their skills and helping people like Davey Concepcion and Joe Morgan develop theirs. And he has spent as little time as possible replaying in his mind that home run that wasn't a home run.

ROY SIEVERS:
The Man Bill Veeck
Had to Have

On the telephone, Roy Sievers suggested that he come meet us at our hotel. "My daughter-in-law's sister is getting married tomorrow," he had explained, "and our house is kinda upside-down. I'll drive out and meet you."

"Fine," I had agreed. "There's a restaurant next door. We can sit and talk over there."

Directions were given and about a half-hour later, Sievers pulled up. As he got out of the car, I recognized him immediately. He had been a hero when he was the Sox' hard-hitting first baseman in 1960 at age 33 and I was a struggling pitcher-first baseman in the Oak Park Little League at age 12. On the day uniforms were issued, I quickly grabbed No. 5, Sievers' number with the Sox.

He was a hero because he could hit home runs. Players on other teams seemed to be able to hit them but White Sox players had trouble hitting them. Sievers hit 28 his first year in a Sox uniform but he should have had more: He had 21 by the first week of August and Bob Elson boldly announced that "Roy Sievers is a mortal cinch to break the White Sox home run record." Actually, it wasn't much of a record. It was 29, set by Gus Zernial in 1950 and equalled a year later by Eddie

Roy Sievers

Robinson. But because the club home run leader during the '50s generally was someone like Minnie Minoso with 15 or 16, the record of 29 seemed to me to be more indestructible than Babe Ruth's mark of 60. So when Sievers came within one of accomplishing the near-impossible, his high place in my estimation was guaranteed.

"I should've broken it, though," he said, as we entered the restaurant. "The last two games of the season, I hit about seven balls real good that I thought were going out. But the wind was really blowing in. None of them went out."

He was also a hero because of the way he hit the Yankees. When the White Sox took over the American League lead by winning three out of four in Yankee Stadium the weekend of July 22-24, 1960, it was Sievers who led the charge, driving in three runs in the Friday night 11-5 victory. A couple of weeks later, before 49,000-plus in Comiskey Park, the Yanks sent Whitey Ford against the Sox and Billy Pierce. Sievers hammered a shot on one hop to the 375-foot marker in left-center with two on in the first inning. The Sox were off and running to a 9-1 triumph.

"Ford tried to pitch me away and then come with the fastballs inside," said Roy, as a waitress arrived with coffee. "But I had pretty good luck against him and the Yankees. The more people you had in the stands, the more you got pumped up. I enjoyed playing the Yankees and the other top clubs."

He had spent so much of his career playing with the bottom clubs before tiny crowds that he couldn't have been pumped up too often. He played from '49 through '53 with his hometown St. Louis Browns, where he was the league's Rookie of the Year (in '49) and where he first met Bill Veeck. He then served a six-year term imprisoned in Griffith Stadium with the Washington Senators. But the six years were far from lost ones. He averaged 30 homers and 96 runs-batted-in during that span, which included a season (1957) in which he topped the American League in homers (42) and RBI (114) and another season (1959) when he fell off to 21 homers and 49 RBI. It was during that slump-ridden campaign that Veeck, then owner of the White Sox, made a stupendous offer for Sievers.

"It was fantastic," said Al Lopez, Sox manager at the time. "Something like $250,000 plus Washington could've picked four or five players from a list of about 10 players. I wouldn't have given the money for him, let alone the players."

His value diminished by the off-year of '59, Sievers came more cheaply in the spring of 1960. The cost this time was catcher Earl Battey, farmhand first baseman Don Mincher, plus $150,000. Veeck was ecstatic, and so was Sievers. The same could hardly be said for Lopez.

"The sad thing about it," recalled Sievers, "was when I got to the Chicago training camp at Sarasota (Fla.), I shook hands with all the players and they were real happy to see me. But then I shook hands with Lopez and he said, 'Well, it's nice to have you, but I don't know where you're going to play.' Well, Kluszewski had led 'em in the World Series, so I just said to myself I'd have to bide my time and wait. So Klu started off the '60 season at first base and didn't hit anything the first month. And I was in real good shape and I was swinging the bat good when I got the chance and I remember Nellie Fox saying, 'How can he keep playing that big Polack?' And I finally went in there and got hot and Klu never got back in there."

He wound up hitting .295 with 93 runs-batted-in to go with those 28 homers. The next year was more of the same: 27 homers, 92 RBI, and another .295 average. All of which bore out Bill Veeck's faith in the righthanded power hitter.

"Veeck was really a good man to play for," said Sievers. "He'd do things for the ballplayers the other owners wouldn't do. If you won a ballgame with a home run—especially against a good club— there'd be a check for you in the locker room for $200. He'd say, 'Go buy yourself a suit.' He was just always doing something for the athlete to make him perform better on the field. He was so appreciative. He understood your ups and downs. He'd stay with you. He took care of you salary-wise if you deserved it."

Veeck took care of Sievers in other ways, too. Two years after Roy had hit .306 to win that rookie award, he was back in the minors, playing for San Antonio of the Texas League. One night in Dallas, Sievers, playing left field, dove for a line drive and landed on his right shoulder. For the next year and a half, he would have a chronic shoulder dislocation.

"Veeck worked out with me in St. Louis after I first hurt the shoulder," he said, "He worked out every day in the wintertime, hitting me groundballs, showing me how to play first base. He really gave me a lot of my inspiration to come back and play after my shoulder problem. You know, he had the wooden leg, but you should've seen him play handball. And he could go up two flights of stairs faster than most people with good legs. He and Bill Norman, one of the Browns' coaches, worked out with me every day to get me back in shape to play ball again. Then he got me a job working construction to get my arm stronger. And the arm did get stronger."

But there were still problems ahead. "I built it up and I felt it was OK again by spring training of '52," he recalled. "That's when Rogers Hornsby, our new manager, hit me a grounder to my left—I was playing at third—and I threw off-balance. And the shoulder popped right out again. And that's when Veeck said I had to have the operation. He said 'We'll get the best man in the country to perform the operation.' And that was Dr. George Bennett at Johns Hopkins in Baltimore. Like Veeck says, Bennett was afraid to do it at first because he said there'd be no possible way I could play again. Then Veeck told him, 'The boy wants to play—whatever you do, just do something for him.' And that's when Bennett agreed to do the operation.

"Two years later, he saw me play and he couldn't believe how good my arm had gotten and what I could do with my arm. And he wrote it up in the Medical Journal, called it one of the best operations he ever performed on an athlete."

By that time, Sievers was with the Senators and under the influence of Cookie Lavagetto, a skilled hitting instructor. "When I first came up, I used to swirl the bat around while I waited for the pitch," Roy said. "It's hard to do, because you've got to be quick with your hands. Then I went to Washington and Lavagetto got hold of me. He got me to just lay the bat on my shoulder until the pitcher was set to deliver the ball. And then I'd just take the bat back."

He also came to Lavagetto with an open stance, something that Cookie showed him wasn't helping all that much. "He said, 'Take your bat and reach it out across the plate.' And I couldn't reach the outside part of the plate. He said, 'See what you're doing? Why not move up even with the plate and straddle it? Now look at your bat.' And I held it out and it covered the whole plate. Hell, I went over there and had some good years. Hit 24 home runs and drove in 102 runs the first year ('54). Didn't hit much (.232), but gradually I got better. I could see the ball better and I could hit the ball better."

By 1957, he was hitting the ball so much better that Sports Illustrated sent a reporter and a photographer down to Washington to spend a few days with Sievers and to develop a series on hitting. This, after all, wasn't just another power hitter. Roy was hitting better than .300 and, for a guy who was leading the league in homers and RBI, he sure wasn't striking out a whole lot. The record books show that Sievers struck out only 55 times that season. And he wouldn't strike out more than 69 times in any one season until he was a 35-year-old, playing in a new league—with a new strike zone—for the Phillies. The Sports Illustrated story was well-received, and Roy still has a copy of it at his suburban St. Louis home.

"Ted Williams said it was one of the best articles on hitting he'd ever read. What I tried to do, I tried to go from Little League on up. The things I stressed were getting a comfortable stance up at the plate, handling the pitching, the way the pitchers pitched you, learning their pattern as you got older.

"With photos, we then showed how Ford used to pitch me, how Early Wynn pitched me. I said that not everybody can hit like a Stan Musial, or a Ralph Kiner, or a Ted Williams. You have to learn your own style of hitting. I talked to Musial. He had a zone out in front of the plate. And when that ball come in that zone, he knew it was going to be a strike. The good hitters learn the strike zone. I used to follow the ball all the way into the catcher's glove. Gene Mauch would stand behind the screen during batting practice at Philadelphia and I'd take a pitch and he'd ask me, 'Where was it?' I'd say, 'A quarter of an inch outside.' He'd be amazed."

What amazes Sievers to this day is that the 1960 White Sox failed to win the pennant. He offered two possible explanations. "One thing that hurt us was that Lopez pitched (Herb) Score every five days. And Score never could win. But Lopez kept pitching him and pitching him. And then Klu's home run getting called back in Baltimore. After we lost that game, we just went the other way. Our whole season turned around right there. We couldn't do anything after that. We finished close, but we still should've won it."

Still, Sievers enjoyed his stay in Chicago. He was with a winning club and a fun group of guys. "Gene Freese was just a ball," he said, grinning. "Just his everyday activity was a ball. He was funny. He was wild. You went out with Freese and no matter what you did or where you went, you'd have a good time. He'd been part of what they called the Dalton Gang at Philadelphia, with Dick Farrell and Seth Morehead and a couple of other guys. They were wild. Freese and them were in this joint and were feeling good one night, and Freese said he wished the jukebox was closer to where they were sitting. And Farrell went over and unplugged it and picked the whole thing up and brought it over and set it down.

"Landis was kind of a funny guy, too. Minoso was funny. I'll say one thing about Minoso, though. Once he got on that field, boy, he was all business. Fox was the same way. Aparicio, too. I really found out the difference between the contending clubs and the bottom clubs. These guys really bore down. And they didn't make errors like the Senators always did. But I was really happy. I always wanted to find out how I would play on a first-division club. I wanted to prove to myself I could play well with a contender."

He proved it to himself and he proved it to the fans in the only way he knew how: with his bat. A pennant would have been great. But today, Sievers, a supervisor for Yellow Freight, seems satisfied with having been an outstanding major league hitter. He doesn't even feel cheated by knowing that the $38,000 paid him with the White Sox pales in comparison with what he might be making had he been born 20 years later.

"People ask me what my value would be today. I don't know. For a period of eight years or so, I had an average of 30 homers, plus 100 RBIs, and I hit about .290. Hell, today, that'd be phenomenal. I could get $400,000 a year, maybe even $500,000. But I'm not against the players today. The owners are offering 'em that kind of money, they might as well take it.

"But I enjoyed the time I played in, the players I played with and against. I met four presidents—had lunch with all of them: Eisenhower, Nixon, Kennedy, and Johnson. I even got to meet Khruschev when he came over from Russia."

Nixon, he said, was one of his biggest fans. "He was always fine

231

with me. I still have a picture of his daughters sitting on my knees when they were just little kids. It's sad what happened. But like I tell my wife, the only mistake he made was making those tapes."

And the only mistake Roy Sievers made was not getting into a White Sox uniform about five years earlier than he did.

HERB SCORE:
The Comeback Attempt That Failed

No one rooted harder than I did for Herb Score to make a big comeback with the White Sox—except maybe Herb's wife and his manager, Al Lopez. When he was struggling, it was all I could do to keep from turning off Bob Elson on the radio: "High again, and ANOTHER full count," or "Another wide one will fill 'em up and bring up Big Bob Cerv."

When Score pitched well, I felt so good that even the next morning's soft-boiled egg tasted all right. When he did poorly, and the Sox fans on the block would begin questioning how in the world Lopez could keep pitching that guy, I would grow morose.

I spent much of the 1960 season feeling morose. Herb Score simply wasn't the Herb Score of old. Everyone knows the story. Herb, as a 22-year-old rookie fireballer for Cleveland in 1955, was 16-10 with a 2.85 earned run average and 245 strikeouts in 227 innings. The next year, the young lefty was 20-9 with a 2.53 ERA and 263 strikeouts in 249 innings. The next season would have been more of the same, except that, on the night of May 7, Gil McDougald of the Yankees hit a liner that struck Score above the right eye. The eye, not to mention Score's career, was in jeopardy.

233

Herb Score

Eventually, he recovered, though he missed the rest of the '57 season. But by the opening of the '58 campaign, Herb told me as we sat down for dinner in the Comiskey Park Bards Room, he was as good as new.

"Before the season started, I had the flu, but I still pitched Opening Day for the Indians," said Score, now a member of Cleveland's TV-radio team. "We lost—and I hadn't pitched well but I hadn't pitched badly, either. Then I beat the White Sox. Somebody just recently sent me the box score. I shut 'em out, gave 'em two hits, struck out 13 or 14, and threw the ball as well as I ever had in my life. People say, 'Well, after the eye injury, he never threw well again.' That's not true. See, my injury had very little to do with my being a lousy pitcher. I was a lousy pitcher after I hurt my arm."

I told him I hadn't realized he had hurt his arm. "A lot of people don't," he said. "My next start after the White Sox game, it rained—it came down in buckets, so the start got washed out. And then we had more off days. So it was about 10 days in between starts. I finally pitched in Washington—a cold, rainy night. About the third or fourth inning, I felt something in my elbow, but I figured, 'Well, I haven't pitched in a while—I'm not gonna say anything.' I think the seventh or eighth inning—it was a close game, 1-1 or 2-1—I threw a pitch that didn't even reach home plate. Wound up, threw the next one, and it never reached home plate, either. My arm was so sore, I couldn't even get it through the sleeve of my jacket.

"I tried to throw with it on the sidelines the next couple of days, and finally I went to the doctor and he said I'd better take it easy. So I laid off a couple days, tried it again. I was stubborn: 'Aw, it can't be that much—I'll keep going with it.' Well, it turned out it was more than I thought it was. They sent me to a specialist in Baltimore, who said I had torn a tendon in my elbow and that every time I worked out and tried to throw with it, I was just tearing more fibers in the tendon. So I did 30 days on the disabled list, then started throwing again in batting practice and on the sidelines, and it really felt good."

So, Score felt, it was time for a test.

"One day, it got near the end of the ballgame, and we were way out in front. The manager said, 'You want to pitch the last three innings?' I said, 'Sure.' I think I struck out five or six, got the last guy out on a

235

pop-up. And as I threw the last pitch, as soon as I threw the ball, ooh —it was just like somebody stuck a hot poker in my elbow. So the ball goes up in the air and the game's over. I came in, the manager says, 'Gee, that's great—you really threw well.' I said, 'Yeah, but I think I hurt my arm again.' 'Oh, you're kidding.' 'I wish I were.'

"If hindsight were any good—which it isn't—you'd say to yourself, after I first hurt my arm, I shouldn't have thrown for a month, I should've rested it. And then when I hurt it the second time, I should've really rested it. But having missed a whole year ('57), there's no way. And when you're young, you know, you're impatient. I am certain that if the same thing happened today, I'd go right out and do the same thing I did."

Score had a so-so season for Cleveland in '59, but White Sox manager Al Lopez—who had managed Herb in '55 and '56— thought that trading pitcher Barry Latman for the still-young left-hander was worth the gamble. The deal was announced the day before the '60 season began, and the trade made the front page of the Daily News.

"Al knew my motion," said Score. "He knew me better than anybody else and I think he felt he would know the key to getting me back in the groove. And we used to go out and throw on the sidelines and he'd say, 'You're just not throwing right.' They took pictures and everything. But I couldn't get my old motion back. Apparently, I must have started favoring the elbow, compensating—like someone with a bad ankle. Even after it stops hurting, you still limp for a while.

"But I just never felt right. It was frustrating, because you knew how you wanted to throw, but it was always just a different feeling. Something to do with the coordination, I guess. And it was frustrating to Al. I could throw on the sidelines for an hour—my arm didn't hurt anymore. But the ball was straight. Used to be, the ball would tail or rise. Al would say, 'You're slinging the ball.' They'd take pictures. I'd look at them and say, 'I can see it.' But I couldn't make myself flip it anymore 'cause I'd lost the motion somewhere. I could still throw fairly hard, but it wasn't a live fastball anymore."

Still, he pitched some decent games. In fact, he was one of the staff's hottest pitchers right after the all-star break in 1960, beating Boston and Baltimore and two-hitting Kansas City as the Sox moved to the top of the American League standings in late July. Then came a Thursday afternoon showdown in early August against the Yankees in Comiskey Park. Chicago and New York had split the first two games of the series and Score was dueling Art Ditmar in the rubber match before a Ladies' Day throng totalling 51,344—largest weekday crowd in Comiskey Park history. Bill Skowron homered in the second inning and the Yanks led 1-0 when the Sox loaded the bases with two out in the bottom of the seventh. The Yankees' lefthanded reliever, Bobby Shantz, came in to face lefty-hitting Joe Ginsberg—the only healthy Sox catcher—and threw three straight jug-handle curveballs. Three straight times, Ginsberg ducked. Three straight times, the umpire yelled, "Strike!" Next inning, the Yanks scored five times against Score and his relief. But he had yielded just one hit—Skowron's homer—and had walked no one for seven innings.

"There were flashes, and I'd think I'd found it again," he said. "But it didn't last. I'd throw a good game here and there, but I just didn't have the consistency and I didn't have that, you know, little extra. But I pitched until I was convinced it wasn't gonna come back."

He pitched at places like San Diego and Indianapolis in 1961 and '62, trying to regain his old form. By '63, both he and Lopez had agreed to end the search. "Al just felt that if my arm was healthy, it was just a matter of time before I'd get it back. That's basically why I stayed in baseball an extra year or two. Somebody said to me, 'Well, why did you go to the minor leagues?' Because I didn't want to get to be 45 years old and turn around and say, 'Well, I could've still pitched.' I had to convince myself that I COULDN'T pitch. I had to convince myself. That's who you live with.

"So I have no regrets. I was very fortunate to have the career I had. I had a degree of success, made it to the major leagues, and had some success there. And so I never look back."

We'd finished dinner, and now Score had to go back down to the field to tape a pregame interview with Cleveland pitcher Ricky Waits. As he got up to leave, he told me, with a grin, "My chapter should be pretty short. I wasn't here a very long time. And I didn't contribute much, either."

Maybe not. But the story of a manager and his one-time rookie sensation patiently working together in an attempt to recover lost brilliance is one I'll never forget.

237

DEACON JONES:
If there'd been a DH rule
in 1962 . . .

It was, quite likely, the most remarkable comeback the White Sox have ever made. People who were there that night in September 1962 —and there were 32,711 of them—still don't believe it happened. But it did.

The Yankees, on their way to another pennant, were leading the Sox 6-1 as Chicago came to bat in the last of the ninth. The crowd was sticking around only for the fireworks display. The game was over. But then Nellie Fox and Camilo Carreon opened the inning with singles. Bob Roselli, the bullpen catcher, was waved in to pinch-hit. Roselli, who batted in a grand total of nine runs in his two seasons with the White Sox, drove a double just past the bag at third to score Fox and make it a 6-2 game. Then Luis Aparicio walked to fill the bases. There was still nobody out.

Now Marshall Bridges, a lefthander, was called in by New York manager Ralph Houk to face Chicago's lefty-hitting Joe Cunningham. Smoky Joe sliced a double down the leftfield line to score two runs. Now it was 6-4. Floyd Robinson walked, filling the bases. Still, nobody out.

Houk then brought in righthander Jim Coates to pitch to Al Smith.

Deacon Jones

But Smitty doubled to tie the game at 6-6 and put runners at second and third. Jim Landis walked, filling the bases once again. Mike Hershberger was the scheduled hitter, but Al Lopez sent up in his place a 28-year-old rookie named Grover "Deacon" Jones, who had made his big league debut a week earlier against Washington by lining a base hit on the first pitch thrown to him. Now, with the infield and outfield both pulled in close for a play at the plate, Jones ripped a drive to the wall in right-center to give the Sox a 7-6 victory.

There was still nobody out.

"That was an exciting night for me," nodded Deacon, now the Houston Astros' batting coach, when I met him near the batting cage at Wrigley Field. "But I had already settled down a little bit by then."

By then, he had already been given a regular Sox uniform—with No. 50 sewn on the back with his name. When he'd first appeared against the Senators the week before, during Early Wynn's 299th career victory, he had just arrived at the ballpark and was given a 1959-60 vintage uniform—with a big No. 20 on the back but with no name on it. It caused quite a stir. No one knew who this new guy was —even though he'd just hit .319 with 26 homers and 101 RBI at Savannah in the Sally League.

"I was in Savannah in Double-A ball and they told me I was going up," Deacon remembered. "I said, 'Are you kidding?' I couldn't believe it. And I was sitting on the bench in Chicago, and I was just awed. And Lopez said, 'Timeout—Deacon, you're hitting.' And I froze. I just froze. Finally, I go up to the batrack and I'm searching for my bat. And the guy in the on-deck circle finally realizes he has my bat and he says, 'Hey Deac, I got your bat!'

"Now I stumble out of the dugout and get my bat. And then Fox and all of these guys are hollering at me, 'Deac, come back!' How come? I'd forgotten my helmet. You gotta realize, all this time, time is out. I'm taking all this time. So I get my helmet and finally go up to hit, and it's late in the game and the white lines of the batter's box have been wiped out. So now I'm ready to hit—no name on the uniform, they announce me, people are reacting. I'm standing deep in the box, like I always do, except there aren't any lines. And the umpire says, 'Jones, get in the box!'

"Boy, here it is, my first time up, I'm nervous as it is, and this deep voice says, 'Jones, get in the box!' I say, 'Where's the box?' He asks the catcher to get out of the way and makes a mark with his feet. So now I get back in and now my front leg is just shivering, just shaking. So I ask the umpire, 'Mr. Umpire, timeout please?' He gives me a funny look. I've already taken maybe five minutes to hit. I step out, say a quick prayer, take a deep breath, step back in, and sure enough, the leg starts wiggling again. I say, 'Well, I guess I'm gonna have to hit like this.' And I swung and lined a base hit to right.

"After the game, the writers came around and said, 'Hey Deacon, what was it like? Were you nervous?' I said, 'Nah, I wasn't nervous. But I sure was scared as hell.'"

The last time he had been in Comiskey Park had been seven years earlier, in June, 1955. He'd been scared that day, too. He had just graduated from Ithaca College in New York with a bachelor of science degree in physiotherapy and now he was on the road, trying out with various big league clubs. "The Yankees, Boston, Philadelphia, Milwaukee—I went to all those places," he recalled. "Then I went to Chicago and I hung around for a couple of days. Marty Marion was the manager and Frank Lane was the general manager.

"And finally they get me in the office. Lane says, 'OK, Jones, I want to sign you. What do you want?' Now you've got to appreciate the fact that here I am, a young, punk kid, scared . . . and Lane's a very tough guy. I told him, 'Well, I'd like to have a car.' And he said, 'What kind of a car do you want?' 'Well, one like Marty Marion's.' And Marty had this new black Ford convertible, and he'd only had it a week. And Lane says, 'Marty, give him your car.' And he did.

"I got the minimum—$4,000. If you got more than that in those days, you had to stay in the big leagues for two years. I signed as a second baseman (he was going to be groomed to eventually replace Fox) and they sent me to Waterloo, Iowa, in the Three-I League. Willard Marshall was the manager there, and we had a good club and I had a good year (.318 average, 7 triples, 9 homers, and 58 RBI in 78 games—he'd gotten a late start in Waterloo's 126-game season). Johnny Romano, Norm Cash, Barry Latman—we had a good club. The next spring, I went to spring training with the White Sox and I was probably the brightest prospect in the whole organization."

But then came the injury which was to rob him of an opportunity

241

for big league stardom.

"I hit a triple in Tampa, Fla., in a big league exhibition game, and I slid head-first into third base. And all the weight came down on my right arm. I heard something pop, like when you crack your knuckles. It was sore, but I finished the game. Next morning, when I got out of bed, I couldn't move my shoulder. And that's when all my problems started.

"I'd torn the long-headed biceps tendon in my right shoulder. It eventually healed, but scar tissue covered it and limited the range of motion. So when I started my arm up, the pain would be excruciating. I couldn't get my arm up, so I had to throw underhanded—little flip jobs. If they were as advanced medically in those days as they are now, I probably would've had a more successful career, in terms of staying longer in the big leagues."

As it was, he was destined to spend the rest of his career—except for 49 at-bats with the Sox—in the minor leagues. The injury didn't affect his hitting at all, as witness his averages at Dubuque in 1956 (.409), Lincoln in '59 (.299), San Diego in '60 (.299), at Indianapolis in '63 (.343), at Sarasota in '65 (.325), and at Fox Cities in '66 (.353). But he couldn't throw well enough to play second base any longer. He played at first base, but his underhand flips meant he wasn't much on the 3-6-3 doubleplay. And if there was a runner at third and a grounder was hit to Deacon at first, there was no way he was ever going to throw the runner out at the plate.

Taking note of that, the Sox managment realized, sadly enough, that there was no permanent place for Deacon on the big league roster. Here, then, was the perfect designated hitter. Unfortunately, the designated hitter rule wouldn't come along until 1973, a half-dozen years after Jones had retired as a player.

"I can't lie to you," he said. "I always wished they'd had the rule sooner. But I guess I'm very realistic about life. What's 'fer' ya is 'fer' ya and what's 'agin' ya is 'agin' ya. Life is timing. It just wasn't 'fer' me. Maybe getting my arm hurt was the same thing. I knew then I wouldn't be an everyday player.

"I was lucky enough, though, to get to the big leagues, and I remember so many people telling me when I injured my arm, 'Forget it—you'll never make it.' And when I wore that big league uniform that first day—you saw it, with no name on it—I thought about all those people. Again, an indication that people can't tell you what you can be or what you can do. Only you. What the heck, you're gonna have setbacks in life, but if you want something bad enough, no one can tell you that you can't have it."

Deacon proved that to himself once again in 1976, when he was hired by Houston manager Bill Virdon as the Astros' batting instructor. He had served the White Sox as their minor league hitting coach for nearly eight seasons but had never realized his dream—he had never been named to the club's big league staff. Oh, sure, if a Bill Melton or a Jorge Orta went into a prolonged slump, the call went out from Chuck Tanner's office to send for Doctor Jones. And within hours after Deacon's arrival, Melton or Orta or whoever would begin to hit line drives all over the park once again. But then, Tanner would grow tired of reading in the papers about how Deacon Jones had solved this hitter or that hitter's problems and Jones would be sent off again to work with the minor league clubs.

"That upset me more than anything else," he told me. "Most of these guys—the Ortas, the Bradfords, the Meltons, the Herrmanns— I'd had them before. I was the minor league hitting instructor. That was my job. But they asked me to go up to the big league club, to be around them. Naturally, I'm an organization man, I'm very faithful to them. However, they had their big league coaches. And I wasn't getting big league pay. It was like it was just tokenism. Can you dig it?

"Sure, I wanted to do it. But when I asked to be a big league coach, to be part of the staff, they said no. That's what I couldn't figure out. And that's why I eventually left the White Sox."

He was ready to give up the quest for the job he had trained himself for ever since he had realized he would never become a major league star. He had devoted all his energies toward the science of hitting. He had spent hours discussing the subject with people like Willie Mays, Stan Musial, Roberto Clemente, and Tony Oliva. He had supplemented their ideas with his own. He was ready, and had been ready for years, to be a major league batting instructor. Yet the organization he had given 20 years of his life to was not ready for him. The dream was about to die.

"After 20 years," he said, "it's kind of hard to walk away. But a

243

funny thing: I put in an application for public relations with Con Edison, and I got word to fly into New York to be interviewed. I'd sent in my resume. And in the interim, Bill Virdon called me and asked me to be one of his coaches.

"And my dreams came true. I was in the big leagues fulltime."

The twenty-year wait, at last, was over.

RON HANSEN:
Maintaining the Shortstop Tradition

When the White Sox traded Luis Aparicio and Al Smith to Baltimore after the 1962 season, two things happened. First, Aparicio delivered what will always be known as "The Looie Curse." The White Sox, he predicted, would not win another pennant for another 40 years.

The second thing was an outcry from the fandom: Who would play shortstop? Management explained that Ron Hansen—acquired in the Aparicio deal along with Hoyt Wilhelm, Dave Nicholson, and Pete Ward—would have no difficulty in replacing the departed Venezuelan. Hearing this, I scurried for the record book. Hansen, the book revealed, had hit a lusty .173 for the Orioles the season before. This new guy, I thought, couldn't even hit his weight. And everyone knew he couldn't be the sensational fielder Aparicio had been.

Who was management trying to kid?

"I'd spent most of '62 in the service," Hansen, now a Milwaukee Brewers coach, explained over breakfast at the Continental Plaza Hotel. "I got recalled during that Berlin crisis and I was stationed at Ft. Meade, in the suburbs of Baltimore. I didn't go to spring training with the club, I didn't work out with them. But I did play on weekends. I'd

Ron Hansen raps a single during 1965 game against Los Angeles'
Angels.

get weekend passes and play, and defensively I guess I did all right. But because of the inactivity, I didn't hit anything. That's not an excuse. It's just something that happened. It was just a wasted year for me. I don't know if it was because of that, but that winter I was traded to the White Sox."

And so the newcomer would assume the same position played so well for so long by Aparicio, Chico Carrasquel, and the legendary Luke Appling. But Hansen, who had been named American League Rookie of the Year in 1960 and wasn't a humpty-dumpty, was not about to be awed by the Chicago shortstop tradition. "I didn't think there was any pressure," he said. "I did realize that Looie was a favorite here. But I knew when I came over here that they had complete confidence in me. And it was not a question of the job being open. It was mine. I was the heir apparent, so to speak.

"I was aware I was coming to a club that had always had great shortstops. And I think it was probably a compliment to me that I would be considered in a trade for Aparicio. Because I really respected his ability. He was a great ballplayer. He could field with anybody."

But Hansen, though lacking Aparicio's flashiness, was no slouch, either. He tied Aparicio for the best fielding percentage in the league in '63 and led the league's shortstops in assists each of the four years he served as the Chicago regular at that position. In fact, he still holds the major league record for most assists in a doubleheader—28—set in late August, 1965. "We played Boston here in Chicago, and Tommy John was one of the pitchers. I had 18 assists in the first game and 10 in the other."

Hansen's bat wasn't anything to write home about, but he wasn't an all-American out, either—especially not when men were in scoring position in late innings of close ballgames. As early as his first season in a Sox uniform, when he batted in the winning run in seven of the team's first 26 victories, Ron became known as "Mr. Clutch." "I don't really know why that was," he said. "But I was fairly successful at driving in runs in the late innings and winning ballgames. I guess maybe, looking back, my concentration was better at that time than it would've been earlier in the game."

Had he hit as well when the bases were empty as he did when the bases were crowded, he might well have hit more than the .234

247

lifetime average he finished up with. "But when I played," he pointed out, "with no designated hitter, I hit seventh and sometimes eighth. And when you're hitting eighth, a lot of times they're just pitching around you. They're saying, 'I'm not gonna give him a good pitch to hit.' And they'd throw maybe six inches off the plate, or high or low or whatever. So a lot of times you never get too many good pitches to hit."

Ron wasn't too proud, though, to accept a base on balls. He walked 78 times his first year in Chicago, 73 the second. The pitchers knew, too, that Hansen, a 6-3, 200-pounder, could hit a baseball a long way. He hit 20 homers in '64, the year the Sox finished a game behind the champion Yankees. I remember a homer he missed, too, in 1965 against the Yankees. With the game scoreless and the bases loaded, Hansen drilled a long shot to center at Comiskey Park. The New York centerfielder, Roger Repoz—in and of himself a sure sign that the era of Yankee domination was at an end—turned and ran back toward the bullpen fence—415 feet away. The ball hit the fence on a fly and Hansen, one of the slowest Sox players of the era, rumbled into third with a bases-clearing triple.

The blow was good for one fewer RBI than he would garner the entire '66 season. That's when he was sidelined from mid-May till the end of the year, forcing Sox fans to spend the campaign watching new shortstop Lee Elia make a fool of himself. "We were having a workout," Hansen remembered, "and I was getting in my work at shortstop, taking groundballs. And the outfielders were throwing balls back into the screen back of second. And evidently one ball hit the screen and bounced away and rolled behind me. I backed up and stepped on it, and I pulled a disc out. I had to have another disc operation. My second one."

The first one was in 1957, when Hansen was a 19-year-old rookie in the Orioles' spring camp. He had just one year of pro ball, but the Baltimore manager, Paul Richards, had told him the starting shortstop job was his. "Then I had a collision sliding into home plate," Ron remembered, "and just shortly after that I started having pains in my leg and my back. They sent me to Baltimore and they had it X-rayed and they found it was a ruptured disc. So I was out that whole year.

"I came back in '58 and made the club again. I opened the season in

Washington and Tex Clevenger hit me on the back of my left hand with a pitch and it broke all the metacarpal bones. And I was out another seven weeks and when I came back from that I hadn't played, really, in a year and a half. They sent me to Knoxville in the Sally League to play a little bit. Then I opened in '59 with Baltimore again, but they sent all of us—Brooks Robinson, myself, Marv Breeding, Chuck Estrada, and Jerry Walker—out to Vancouver. The next year I went back up to Baltimore and was Rookie of the Year."

And 1967 would be another kind of rookie year. His range was cut somewhat because of the back injury, although he again topped league shortstops in assists. The injury had drained him of some of his power, too: He hit only eight homers in '67 and his RBI total fell to 51, which was 15 fewer than his lowest production to date in Chicago—excluding '66. Yet he was still the guy you liked to see up there in a clutch situation.

One such spot developed on a Friday night in early July, with Dean Chance and the Minnesota Twins leading the Sox 1-0 with two out and two men on in the last of the ninth. J. C. Martin was batting for himself, which gives you an idea of what kind of a bench manager Eddie Stanky was blessed with. The count on J.C. reached 3-2. We were sitting in the upper deck, along the leftfield foul line. A friend of mine shouted, "J.C., you better not swing, or I'll blow your head off!" Dozens of us yelled, "Take! Take! Take!" Martin indeed took. Chance's pitch was a quarter of an inch outside. The bases were loaded.

Up stepped Hansen. Ron hit the first pitch up the middle. Zoilo Versalles, the Twins' shortstop, moved quickly to his left. The ball glanced off his glove and rolled out into short center. Tommy McCraw scored easily from third and pinch-runner Buddy Bradford scored from second. The Sox had won 2-1. Hansen remembered it well.

"Sure I remember it," he smiled. "They gave Versalles an error."

Which didn't make Hansen, who needed all the hits he could get, too happy. Hits were hard enough to come by as it was at Comiskey Park—what with the tall grass in the infield and the almost-muddy texture of the area in front of home plate. "Yeah, I think it affected us psychologically," Ron said. "Especially a guy like me, who never did

249

run that well. I was a pull hitter and I hit a lot of balls between third and short, and the shortstop would backhand the ball and throw me out. Where, you know, I'd go on the road and those were base hits. And when you're talking about 80 games a year (at home), and maybe 10 of those a year, maybe instead of hitting .250 you're hitting .270. And I'm not saying that might have happened to me, but that's one of the reasons why guys who didn't hit for a lot of average here hit better at other places after they left here. Look at Donnie Buford. He hit .240 here and went to Baltimore and became a .290 hitter."

Cold-storage baseballs didn't do much for Hansen's psyche, either. The White Sox kept baseballs to be used in games carefully locked up in a damp storeroom somewhere in the bowels of Comiskey Park. The Sox pitchers, of course, loved them. "Frozen baseballs," Tommy John told me as he grinned slyly, "were a figment of the batters' imagination." Hansen wasn't imagining anything, though. "Those balls felt a little heavy," he smiled. "I grabbed a groundball once and almost got frostbite. But if you keep a ball in a damp place for a fairly long time, it gets like a wet ball. You've seen them. It gets heavy. Well, those kinds of balls aren't gonna carry or go anyplace.

"We didn't have much gripe, really. We were winning. And when you're winning, you accept things that you probably wouldn't accept if you were losing."

The losing began, however, with the Black Wednesday fiasco in Kansas City the final week of that '67 season. Then came another loss —Hansen lost his shortstop job when the Sox reacquired Aparicio from Baltimore that winter. Hansen would move over to second base and, perhaps, fill in at third on occasion. But before the spring exhibition games had run their course, the Sox sent Ron to Washington in one of the really odd trades ever consummated. To the Senators went Hansen and pitchers Dennis "Home Run" Higgins and Steve Jones. To Chicago came pitchers Bob Priddy and Buster Narum and second baseman Tim Cullen. The four pitchers were so generally inept that they cancelled each other out, making the deal essentially Hansen for Cullen. When the season was barely four months old, however, the Sox sent Cullen—and his .200 batting average—back to the Senators and received Hansen in return. Hansen had hit .185 for the Senators, so the Washington fans weren't exactly crying their eyes out when the deal was announced. "I still don't know what kind of deal that was," said Ron, shaking his head.

Before he left Washington, though, Hansen put his name in the record book for his unassisted triple play against Cleveland, July 30— three days before he was shipped to Chicago. It was the first such play since Detroit first baseman Johnny Neun pulled one 41 years earlier— also against Cleveland. "Joe Azcue was the hitter, Davey Nelson was on second base and Russ Snyder (who had started the year with the White Sox) was on first," Hansen recalled. "Azcue hit a low line drive up the middle. Both runners thought it was gonna be a base hit and so they started running.

"Really, my momentum was going toward second base when I caught the ball. I stepped on second (doubling off Nelson) and crossed the bag and by the time Snyder could get turned around, I had the momentum going and I just ran him down. It was just a bang-bang kind of thing, a 'right-place-at-the-right-time' kind of thing. But it's the only one made in the last 53 years. Of course, someone could do it again tomorrow. Then again, it might not be done for 100 years. But it happened, and it's part of my career that was pretty neat."

So was fielding the groundball off the bat of Dick McAuliffe for the final out of Joe Horlen's no-hitter in September 1967. "I always liked the ball hit to me," he said. "I always felt, 'This one's coming to me—here it comes.' Maybe mentally you're a little better prepared for it that way. You can't play this game at all scared."

You can play it. But you won't play it as well as Ron Hansen played it.

PETE WARD:
The Pistol from Portland

The Downtowner Motel in Springfield is about the furthest you can get from big league accommodations. So when Pete Ward told me over the phone that he was staying at the Downtowner—a squalid, dingy edifice that had all the trappings of a cockroach haven—it finally struck home that Pistol Pete sure enough was back in the bush leagues.

Pete, at the urging of longtime friend and former White Sox stockholder Nick Kladis, had been hired by Chicago to manage its Iowa farm club in the American Association. Ward's team was in town to play the Springfield Redbirds, the St. Louis Cardinals' Triple-A affiliate. He told me to meet him out by the motel pool.

Twenty minutes later, we were sitting at poolside, trying hard not to notice the black specks floating in the water. I asked him if it indeed hadn't been Kladis at the wheel of the car Ward was riding in when it was struck from behind early in the 1965 season—an accident that was to literally give Pete a permanent pain in the neck.

"Yeah, Nick was driving," he said. "The ballclub had been in Washington and we'd been rained out on a Sunday. And that enabled us to fly back to Chicago earlier so we could still go to the Black Hawk

Pete Ward as a White Sox instructor during spring training, 1980.

hockey game that night. And we were coming home from the hockey game and we really weren't hit that hard. Nick was driving, I was in the front seat on the right. Tommy John was in the back left and a guy named Tyke Gianapoulos was in the back right—and he was hurt pretty bad. But we weren't hit that hard. I've been hit a helluva lot harder than that and not been hurt.

"Tommy wasn't hurt at all, Nick neither, I guess because they were on the left and we were hit from the right rear. But I know the next day my neck really bothered me. And from that point on it had quite an effect on me. Like for example, if I go take batting practice a couple days in a row now—which is a long time since 1965—it'll still come back to me. It's just real sore. Back in those days, I used to try and go to various osteopaths and chiropractors on the road, just to see what they could do to help. I remember one day in New York I was riding in a cab and everything we hit a bump, there'd be real pain.

"It was one of those things where an athlete can't really say anything about it, because as soon as you say something about it, it sounds like an excuse. But looking back on it now, that definitely was the fact of the matter."

The neck problem—preceded by back troubles during the '64 season—goes a long way toward explaining the sudden decline of the good-hit, no-field third baseman who had batted .295 with 22 home runs and 84 RBI as a rookie in 1963 and who had then hit .282 with 23 homers and 94 RBI in '64. He wound up with 10 homers and a .247 average in '65, missed two months with a hernia operation in '66 and hit .219 with three homers, bounced back with 18 homers the next year despite hitting only .233, then fell to .216 in '68—but led the team in homers and RBI with incredibly low totals of 15 and 50.

So a career that had looked so promising way back on Opening Day, 1963 at Tiger Stadium in Detroit never did flourish as had been anticipated. But there were big moments, perhaps none bigger than that first game as a White Sox. "Jim Bunning was the pitcher," recalled Pete, who had been the key to the six-player deal with Baltimore that winter. "I hit a three-run homer in the top of the seventh to bring us from behind and put us ahead (the Sox won 7-5). I think that was the single most exciting thing to happen to me in my career. My first game, 40,000-plus people there, just having been traded to the White Sox."

But it wasn't as easy as it looked, Pete discovered soon enough. "I hit good the first couple of games, then I went into a little tailspin and was making a lot of errors. And we had Charlie Smith backing me up, and Charlie's an established big league player—and I was struggling. I think I got down to .211 and I had about 15 errors the first month of the season. Lopez called me into his office and I really thought maybe I was gonna get sent down to Indianapolis. He just told me, 'Pete, when you throw the ball to first, grip the ball across the seams, come up on top, and pop it over there. That's all I wanted to tell you.'

"I said, 'What about my hitting?' He said, 'Aw, hell, you'll hit. You've hit everywhere you've played. Sometimes it just takes a little longer up here.' He showed confidence in me. Finally I gained my confidence and I got that thing up there to .295 by the end of the season."

Lopez wasn't always so nice to the rookie from Portland, Ore. "One day I was on second with nobody out and we were getting beat 1-0, in the ninth inning," Ward remembered. "And J.C. Martin laid a bunt down toward third, and the pitcher got it and flipped it to the third baseman and he tagged me out. And the next guy hits a long flyball that would've brought the run in if I'd been safe. I thought I'd gotten a good jump away from second, and that everything had gone smoothly. The pitcher just made the play and I was out.

"Well, I was right behind Lopez as he was walking into his office after the game. He turned around and said, 'Pete, what kind of a jump did you get?' 'I got a good jump.' He said, 'Do you think you should've made it?' 'Yeah, I thought I got a good jump.' He said, 'God damn it, you should've made it!' So I took my glove and I threw it from Al Lopez's office door to my locker, which was a good 15 feet. And before it landed, he was all over me. "You no-good rookie S.O.B. —I don't care if you hit .500.' I mean he just really tore into me. And I felt like about two cents. And usually I was the last one to leave the clubhouse, but that day I was gone before anybody got into the shower. I was really crushed—and I was gone."

The next day was Memorial Day and a doubleheader with Cleveland at Comiskey Park. Early in the first game, Ward got jammed and hit a little pop fly back to the pitcher's mound. "And I didn't run, and only Pete Rose and maybe two other guys probably would've run. And I just took off half-ass to first base. The sun got in the pitcher's eyes and the ball dropped at his feet. Max Alvis (Cleveland's rookie third baseman) came in and picked the ball up and threw me out by about half a step when I should've beaten it out easily."

This time, Lopez didn't tear into Pete, although the crowd sure did. "He just told me I should've run. If he'd have gotten all over me after having gotten on me the day before, it might've had a psychological effect on me. But he knew it and I knew it and everybody in the park knew it, that I had a base hit there if I'd just hustled."

So Pete's relationship with Lopez was far from stormy. But if he wanted to, Ward could blame Lopez for never getting a real chance to show how good a hitter he really was. It was Al—although he still won't admit it—who was the man behind the frozen baseballs used at Comiskey Park in the mid-'60s. It was also Al, most people think, who had groundskeeper Gene Bossard water down the infield in front of home plate to slow down hard-hit groundballs. And cold, damp baseballs—coupled with a wet, slow infield—won't do much for anyone's batting average.

"The hitters on the club used to complain about that all the time, but nobody's gonna listen," said Pete. "Frozen baseballs were something everybody just accepted. The hitters didn't like it. Hell, if the hitters had a choice, they'd heat 'em up. And then Bossard, he was just doing what he was told. We could have an eight-month drought in Chicago and there'd be a swamp in front of home plate. The hitters used to get on the pitchers all the time about their low ERAs and our low batting averages.

"We would do things like, during batting practice with the writers all around the batting cage, guys would hit down on the ball and try to splatter the writers with mud—thinking there'd be a mention of it in the papers. And there'd never be any. It's something that maybe we exaggerated. But you talk to Joe Pepitone about hitting in Comiskey Park. He didn't even want to come near the place. (Pepitone was 6-for-60 against the Sox in 1965.) You hit a ball good there and it doesn't go. I saw Harmon Killebrew go into his patented home run trot on a ball that didn't even get to the warning track. And Willie Horton the same thing.

"All I know is, it sure as hell felt like something was wrong with those balls. In '63, somebody hit a little pop fly and I came into the dugout and said, 'Golly, something's wrong with them balls. It didn't go anywhere.' Al called me over and said, 'Pete, every time there's a storm outside Gary, Indiana, it affects the wind currents in Comiskey Park so the balls don't carry very well.' Now, you can believe that if you want to, but I remember once we had a four-game series in Detroit and there were 22 home runs hit. Less than a week later, the same two teams played a five-game series in our park and Don Demeter hit a double. That was the only extra-base hit in the whole series."

We both laughed, but then he added, "But face it—if we're not gonna hit too many home runs, well, why not make sure no one hits any? And that makes sense. That's the same with the muddy infield. If we don't have good hitting, then hell, let's take the hitting away from the other guys."

The plan worked so well that in 1967 the Sox, despite hitting .225 as a team, still were in contention all season. And even though Ward wasn't hitting close to .300 anymore, he was still the threat that the other clubs' pitchers—as well as umpires and even his own manager—had to worry about.

"Labor Day at Yankee Stadium," Ward said, "Emmett Ashford was the plate umpire. Steve Barber was pitching and I had two strikes on me. And he threw me a close pitch in and I didn't want to give up on it so I just waited on it and it hit my hand. And Emmett called it a foul ball, which you can't really fault an umpire for 'cause that's a tough call. But I said, 'Emmett, look at my hand.' And he stuck his head up and wouldn't look down. So then finally I just lost my cool. Then Emmett and I were goin' at it and Eddie Stanky jumped in between us, and I pushed him away. Then Eddie went back behind me and came up and pulled me down.

"The whole thing was pretty funny. In fact, Mickey Mantle, everytime I see him, he says that's the funniest thing he's ever seen in baseball. Here we're coming down the stretch drive, seeing who's gonna get into the World Series, and here's a manager fighting with one of his players up at home plate. But all Eddie was doing was trying to break it off. I wouldn't have gone after Emmett. Yeah, I was pretty hot, but what really got me hot was when Eddie jumped between us.

"But the highlights of that year were Horlen's no-hitter—and I think

257

he deserves extra credit for pitching that thing with me playing behind him—and the game we scored five in the bottom of the ninth to beat the Twins 5-4. I got the game-winning hit, but what you don't realize is that Dean Chance had struck me out my first three times up. Then they took him out and I got the hit off Al Worthington. And what was funny about that was that they had Jim Kaat (like Ward, a lefty) warming up in the bullpen. But for some reason, they left Worthington in there.

"And the first two pitches Worthington threw me, I pulled foul. So I'm sitting up there with two strikes on me again. And all I'm thinking up there is, 'Make contact.' And I hit the ball just over Harmon Killebrew's head (at first base) to win it."

That hit came six days after Horlen's no-hitter. The Sox won the next day for a sweep of the three-game series with Minnesota. A week later, the Sox—with five games to go—seemed poised to wrap up the pennant. "We really felt we would do it," said Pete. "Then we went into Kansas City, and we were rained out Tuesday night so we had to double up Wednesday night. And we walked out there onto the field, and the A's, when they were supposed to be taking batting practice, they were running football plays in the outfield."

It seemed like a setup. The Sox would sweep the 10th-place A's and then return home for the formality of wrapping up the title with a three-game series against ninth-place Washington. Some setup. The White Sox dropped a pair and gave up the ghost.

"Then," Ward sighed, "we went home Friday night and Phil Ortega beat us 1-0. But, by then, it was over."

Also over, he would discover soon enough, was the 17-year Chicago string of first-division finishes. The next season, the Sox lost 10 in a row to start the season and never recovered. Stanky was fired July 12, and Ward welcomed back his former boss, Lopez, who had returned in an attempt to save the sinking ship. But Pete, who had been moved from position to position by Stanky and had every right to be displeased with him, felt sadness rather than joy when Eddie was dismissed.

"When Eddie took over, I just wasn't the ballplayer I'd been when Al was there. It's not Eddie's fault that I didn't produce. So I really felt badly when he was fired, and I think most of the players did, too. I feel that anytime a manager gets fired, it's because the ballplayers that he chose didn't produce for him—whether you like a guy or not. And we were the ballplayers he had chosen. I know Eddie was counting heavily on guys like myself, and when we didn't respond, then the manager lost his job. So I feel like I let Eddie down."

But, I argued, hadn't Stanky let Pete down by moving him first to left field, then to right field, and then to first base? Why hadn't he kept Pete at third and moved Don Buford to the outfield—as Baltimore did when the Orioles picked him up in the second Aparicio deal?

"The only move that really affected me was playing right field—'cause I was terrible. When I played left field, I know I wasn't embarrassed. But my experiences in right field were really difficult. It's hard to screw up as badly as I did and then hold your head up high and walk around in public. But I tried to do the best I could. It helped having Ken Berry in center, but he couldn't catch those balls hit out to right."

There was, then, no ill feeling by Ward toward Stanky. "But," Pete said, "you know the thing that surprised me the most about Eddie getting fired? He didn't talk to the ballclub. He was fired and he left. And, knowing his style, I felt that he would've talked to us. But we came to the park and he was gone. There was no communication from Eddie, and that really surprised me."

It surprised a lot of people when Ward, in 1969, suddenly developed into a superb pinch-hitter, going 17-for-46—a .370 average. Only Ron Northey (15-for-39 for .385 in 1956) did better for the Sox in the last 30 years, and only Smoky Burgess (21-for-66 for .318 in '66) was even that close. And both Burgess and Northey were older— and fatter—than Ward when they compiled their admirable pinch-hitting records: Burgess was 39 and Northey was 36, while Pete was a mere 30 when he was becoming adept at a job reserved previously for men in the twilight of their careers. Too soon, Ward discovered that it was the twilight of HIS career, too. By 31, after a year of relative inactivity with the Yankees, Pete was out of baseball, left to ponder what might have happened had Nick Kladis' car never been struck from the rear that spring evening in 1965.

But Pete Ward refuses to brood. "You hate to look back on something that little and use it as an excuse," he told me. "Because, really, I

259

always considered myself pretty lucky to be in the majors in the first place."

DAVE NICHOLSON:
Over the Roof and into Oblivion

A friend and I were sitting in the lower deck in right field at Comiskey Park, watching the White Sox play the Kansas City A's in the first game of a twilight-night doubleheader. It was early May of 1964 and the White Sox were leading the league, as they were wont to do every May in those years.

This night, the Sox were facing veteran Moe Drabowsky, the ex-Cub who, most everyone agreed, was the greatest pitcher ever produced by Ozanna, Poland. Moe looked in to get his sign and then fired a fastball plateward. The White Sox batter, young Dave Nicholson, swung and the ball took off, on a rising line, toward the stands in left-center. It was still twilight, so it was hard to follow the ball from our vantage point in right, but the ball still seemed to be rising as it neared the upper-deck facade.

"I don't think it's come down yet," I said to my companion, who had lost sight of the ball entirely. Then a fan behind us, who had been listening to the game on the radio, shouted, "It cleared the roof! Elson says it cleared the roof!" A Sox publicity man, armed with a tape measure, was sent scurrying out to Armour Park, back of the leftfield grandstand, and there he found a group of youngsters who had re-

Dave Nicholson gets a homeplate welcome after hitting grand-slam homer against Minnesota in September 1963. On base at the time were Jim Landis, Floyd Robinson (3), and Gary Peters. Also ready with a handshake is the next hitter, Jim Lemon. [PHOTO COURTESY CHICAGO TRIBUNE. PHOTO BY PHIL MASCIONE]

262

trieved the baseball. They showed the Sox man where the ball had landed and immediately he went to work. Within an hour, he announced his findings: The ball had traveled 573 feet, eight feet farther than what had been generally accepted as the longest regular-season homer—Mickey Mantle's opening-day blast at Griffith Stadium in 1956. We had witnessed history in the making.

Fourteen years since that May evening had passed when I paid a visit to Nicholson's sporting goods store in the Chicago suburb of Bensenville. Dave, balding now but still big and powerful-looking, didn't seem impressed when I told him I had been on hand for his king-sized Comiskey Park wallop. He grinned and said, "I think at least 300,000 people have told me they were there." Only when I reminded him that he had hit two other home runs that night—both of them well into the upper deck in left—did he begin to suspect that I really had been there, after all.

We began tracing his career from the January morning in 1958 when he signed with the Baltimore Orioles for a bonus of $110,000— stupendous money in those days. "They'd been the St. Louis Browns five years before and they were building and that seemed like the place to go," said Dave. "Both Chicago clubs offered me more money. The Cubs offered me the most ($130,000) and the Sox were second (at $115,000).

"If I had it to do all over again, I'd have signed with the Cubs. Just because of the ballpark. But at age 18, I didn't know one ballpark from another—and didn't think it made any difference. What a mistake THAT was. There's a big difference. If I'd have had a chance to play in Wrigley Field a little bit . . . well, there are a lot of home runs that go out of Wrigley Field that aren't home runs anywhere else. Especially when that wind's blowing out. Maybe I'd have hit a few more homers, stayed around a little longer.

"You can hit the ball out of Wrigley Field in any direction. The only home run I hit in Wrigley Field was when I was with Houston (in '66) and I wasn't playing much, except against lefthanders. I hit it to center field, I hit it good, on the good part of the bat. A high flyball to center field. And it went right into the stands. And I KNEW when I hit it that it was just an out. It was a long flyball to center. That's all it was. There's a few good parks to hit in, and Wrigley Field is sure one of them."

263

Baltimore's Memorial Stadium wasn't one of them, however. Nor was Comiskey Park. But those were the locales in which Nick was destined to spend most of his big-league playing time. The Orioles, who had first fallen in love with the 6-2, 215-pounder when he hammered 18 home runs in 34 games for Collinsville of the Missouri-Illinois Ban Johnson League in 1957, gave him a couple of chances to stick in the majors. And though he totalled 14 home runs in 286 at-bats in '60 and '62, Nicholson annoyed the Baltimore hierarchy with his penchant for striking out: 131 K's in those 286 at-bats.

So when the Orioles made their big deal with the White Sox after the '62 season, acquiring Luis Aparicio and Al Smith, they weren't at all hesitant to send him to Chicago. For the White Sox, it was a good gamble: Dave was still only 23 and he had all that potential. Manager Al Lopez gave him the starting leftfield job and Nicholson actually led the league in the early going with six homers. He cooled off eventually but still he finished with 22 homers to tie Pete Ward for the club leadership. His batting average, however, was a modest .229 and he had established a major league record for strikeouts with 175.

The next year, the year of the over-the-roof blast, the blond bomber began seeing less action. Used in 97 games, Nick hit .204 with 13 homers and fanned 126 times in just 294 at-bats. In '65, Danny Cater took over as the fulltime leftfielder and Dave batted a mere 85 times, hitting .153 and striking out 40 times. At season's end, he was traded to Houston (where he rejoined his first big league manager, Paul Richards) for a pitcher named Jack Lamabe. Nicholson's three-year stay with the White Sox had not cured the righthanded slugger of his strikeout fever.

"Yeah, I struck out an awful lot," he said, "but a strikeout in the big leagues is a lot of times better than hitting the ball. You come up to bat in the big leagues with a runner on first base and you hit a groundball, you've just hit into a doubleplay. They're turning close to 200 a team every year. So there's no super big deal about striking out, as far as I'm concerned. In the big leagues, if you walk to the plate and hit 30 groundballs to the shortstop, you may as well have struck out 30 times, 'cause you're not gonna get on base. You know, these guys now are fielding .980, so how many times are you gonna get on base?"

Yet coaches in Baltimore and Chicago stressed to Dave the importance of making contact. They tried a myriad of ideas on Nick, who may have wound up a mite confused by all the instruction.

"I listened to more suggestions and everything in the 12 years I played than you could shake a stick at," he said. "And all the suggested are given to you by some guy who played minor league ball or was a .200 hitter in the big leagues. You know, you try to listen. I tried to listen. But it gets pretty confusing.

"And they always say, 'Well, you don't have to be a good hitter to teach.' I don't believe that. If you want to learn how to bowl, you don't ask a guy who bowls a 150 average. If you want golf lessons, you don't ask your neighbor—who's shooting 115—for golf lessons. I've never heard of any sport where you go to someone who never did it himself and ask him to teach you. The real successful hitters have made enough money that they've got other interests to go into by the time their careers are coming to an end."

So the top-notch, big-name teacher wasn't there when Nicholson could have used him. But that didn't mean Dave didn't enjoy his time in Chicago, a period in which the Sox averaged 96 victories a year. "Oh, it was fun," he said. "We were pretty close to winning the pennant every year. We had a good ballclub. Real good pitching, adequate hitting, a good defensive club. We didn't lose too many ballgames by throwing the ball around. We just didn't hit enough to win it."

Which is unfortunate, because Nicholson would gladly have traded that 573-foot shot for a pennant. "I wanted to get to the World Series and get a World Series ring," he said. "I don't even wear rings, but I wanted a World Series ring. When I played, it didn't seem much like the guys thought about the money. They wanted that World Series ring. Now, with all the money they're paying, I'd probably be thinking about the money."

It was money—or, more correctly, lack of same—that helped convince Nick to quit the game after the 1969 season. He had spent the year with the Royals' Omaha farm club in the American Association and had hit 18 homers before a hernia operation sidelined him the second half of the season.

"I was ready to get out when I got out," he shrugged. "I just got to the point where I wasn't making any money playing Triple-A ball. I had four kids, three of them in school, and you're dragging them all over the country. And the last year or so, we'd go to spring training in Florida and put the kids in school down there, then we went to Omaha and put the kids in school there, and when the season's over we came back to Chicago and put them in school here. Well, they start whining, 'We don't have any friends . . . ' "

So he quit baseball and opened up the sporting goods store, where from time to time people will drop in and talk a little baseball. They ask him if he has any regrets about his failure to develop into a solid major league ballplayer. And always, his answer is the same.

"I'm not that disappointed—not at all," he told me. "I never expected to burn up the world. Other people thought I would, though. That's why I got so much attention. Some other guys who don't get the big money, they don't pay much attention to. They say, 'Hey, here's a guy named Joe Schultz, hit .330 in Class A. Let's move him to Double-A.' Then they say, 'Hey, he hit .320 in Double-A. Hey, we have something here . . . ' But I got all the attention. No, I'm not at all disappointed."

Al Lopez was, however. "When we made that deal with Baltimore, we thought he was a guy who had a chance to be a real superstar," Al told me later. "He had tremendous power, a big strong kid, a nice boy. But it was disappointing to me—not to him—that he didn't develop the way I thought he would develop. I thought, 'Just be patient and let him go up to the plate.' "

But it turns out that Nick preferred going to the mound to going to the plate. "I always wanted to pitch," he said. "I pitched all through high school and amateur ball and I pitched some in the minor leagues. Every time I pitched, I always did a good job. But the never wanted me to pitch. I always had some power, so they had me play the out-field. But I always wanted to pitch."

I mentioned that to Lopez, and Al just shook his head.

"That was exactly the problem," he sighed. "He didn't know how good a hitter he could be. He wanted to be a pitcher. Nick probably thought he COULD pitch. But, of course, he wouldn't have gotten a nickel to sign as a pitcher."

KEN BERRY:
Who's Afraid of an Outfield Wall?

Like Jim Landis before him, Ken Berry—a Landis-type ballhawk who stole so many base hits out in center field that he quickly earned the nickname "The Bandit"—started out as a third baseman.

"That's what I was playing when the Sox signed me," said Ken when I reached him in Greensboro, N.C., where he was coaching for a Yankee farm club. "I was in Liberal, Kan., playing Ban Johnson ball. We were like 24-3 that year—1960. I hit about .425 and the Sox sent Ted Lyons out there to look at me. And I had just injured my ankle for the second time that summer and I could hardly walk, let alone run. But it was my only shot at finding out if I was ever going to get to sign, so I went ahead and played and I hit a home run and two singles. I went 3-for-3 and Lyons couldn't believe it. He said, 'If a guy can play on a bad leg and do that well, I'll take a chance on him.' "

So he reported next spring to the Sox' minor league training complex in Hollywood, Fla. "I still felt I was a pretty good third baseman even after two weeks of spring training," he recalled. "The fields down in Hollywood were real soft and sandy—that red, sandy soil. It doesn't take but 10 or 15 groundballs before people are fielding in self-defense. And it really confused me because I'd never played on

Ken Berry is called out at the plate for the final out of the Sox' 4-3 loss to Boston, Aug. 27, 1967. Making the tag is catcher Elston Howard. The umpire is Marty Springstead. Berry tried to score on Duane Josephson's fly to Jose Tartabull in short right field. [© FIELD ENTERPRISES, INC. 1967]

anything like that before.

"I was having a lot of trouble fielding balls and having balls bounce off my chest. And about halfway through spring training, they decided to move me to the outfield and they put me in center and that's where I stayed."

He made it to Chicago to stay in 1965 and soon began making a name for himself by diving for liners, crashing into walls for long drives, and even going over the bullpen fence in center for balls that ostensibly were home runs. Again, like Landis, Berry had no fear of outfield fences.

"It's the same way I teach my players down here," he told me. "I tell 'em to get out in the outfield and play like every pitch in batting practice is a game situation. Run into the walls, dive for balls in batting practice off of live hitting. Pretend it's the real thing."

By doing things that way, he got used to diving and running into walls. And as experience came, fear departed. "I used to practice catching home run balls every day," he said. "I mean, if I had a situation where a ball was hit out there in batting practice, I'd go ahead and crash into the fence and jump up and see if I could catch it. Because I practiced it, I had confidence I wasn't gonna hurt myself. That's what I try to tell these guys here: You're not gonna hurt yourself if you work on it. The time you're gonna hurt yourself is when you go out there and you come to a situation where you've got to feel for the wall, or you've got to know where your teammate is— when you should know that by practicing in batting practice every day.

"I figured it out the other day. With 140 games, if the guys will go out there and take balls off the bat, and if they only get 10 or 12 balls a day, that's 1,400 to 1,500 balls for 140 games. And if they work real hard in spring training they're gonna get 2,000 to 2,200 balls in one year. So in four years, they're gonna get 8,000 to 9,000 balls. OK, if they can't be a very adept outfielder by the time they get to the big leagues in four years, then they haven't worked at it.

"So that's just the way I looked at it. That was my warmup routine. Every day."

It didn't totally preclude mishaps, however. One afternoon during his rookie season, he raced back toward the centerfield barrier at

Comiskey Park in pursuit of a drive hit by the Angels' Bobby Knoop, later a Sox teammate. The ball went over the fence and Berry went into the fence—at full steam. "Yeah, I remember it," he said. "I ran into the bullpen gate and it wasn't padded. And right after it happened, they had it padded. That's the way the White Sox did things. I'm not knocking the Sox, but after you look back on some of these things, there are some things that were neglected. One of them was that bullpen gate not being padded until after I hit it. I had 29 pieces of glass that they took out of a cut right above my eye where my sunglasses broke. That could've ended my career right there."

There were other problems for Ken that first year, too. "I had a real bad back that gave me trouble. I spent a lot of time at the chiropractor in Chicago, I probably spent $300 to $400 every year. An old football injury was part of it. I remember, too, lifting a trunk in Chicago, lifting it the wrong way and hurting my lower back. And it really gave me problems after that. But you know, I went ahead and played with it.

"I played with a lot of pain. Also that first year, I had muscle spasms both sides of my neck—I couldn't turn my head either way. And that's why I struggled so much my rookie season. I hit about .180 the first half (he finished at .218). And I was having trouble with balls in the outfield, the whole bit. They—Ed Short and Al Lopez—wanted me to take novocaine shots in my back so I could play. I'm not talking cortisone, now. Novocaine. To deaden the pain so I could play.

"Well, that was my first year in the majors. I could've ruined my career. You can write that if you want to, because that's just the way things were. I was the type of player who gave 'em 100 per cent all the time. I was too young and too naive but they almost bluffed me into doing it. And I could hardly walk and I couldn't throw and I couldn't run. And I knew I was hurtin'. They didn't believe me. They wanted me to take novocaine. And I resented that. I ended up, after all that, with an ulcer by the time that season was over. And no one ever knew that, either. But I still gave 'em 100 per cent."

The effort began paying off in 1966. He'd lost his centerfield job to a brilliant rookie named Tommie Agee, but new manager Eddie Stanky

270

simply put him out in left field and Berry began leaping up against the foul pole to steal home runs. His hitting started to pick up, too. He flirted with .285 for a while before finally settling at .271—a figure which would have been higher, he believes, if it hadn't been for frozen baseballs and Bossard's swamp.

"If we'd had a regular field, the way I hit the ball that year—I hit the ball pretty hard that year on the ground—I could've been in the top 10 or 15 in the league in hitting and it would've given me a heckuva shot at making more money. It really hurt me. Our park helped us win but it sure took the starch out of my situation."

Yet he got off to a great start in '67—his 20-game hitting streak in June helped strengthen the team's hold on first place—and was batting over .300 when the Yankees came in for a Sunday doubleheader late in June. His streak was snapped that day and then began an incredible 9-for-90 tailspin.

"I was at .305 when they voted for the all-star team and I was at .255 when they played it," laughed Ken, who struck out as a pinch-hitter for the final out of the American League's 2-1, 17-inning loss in the '67 midsummer classic. "So you can see I was really struggling. I had the 20-game streak and Fritz Peterson broke it. And that was a good indication of what was gonna happen, because I used to get at least two hits off Fritz Peterson every time I faced him. But he broke it—I went 0-for-3—it was downhill from there on."

Not that there weren't occasional moments of glory. Like the two-run upper-deck homer he ripped in the 16th inning of Game Two of a late July twi-nighter to give the White Sox a sweep over the Cleveland Indians. "It was at 1:50 in the morning," he said, laughing again. "I have that in my scrapbook. It was off George Culver. And J.C. (Martin) had won the first game with a homer. See, we were really rolling then. But the Sox fans—I don't know why—they weren't coming out to support us. If that team had been in the race now, they'd have had 50,000 out there every night."

There were 35,000 out there for a Friday night twin bill with the Red Sox the last weekend of August that season, and "The Bandit" won the second game with a line single to right-center in the last of the ninth off John Wyatt. The hit helped him "achieve" a final batting average that year of .241—which tied him with Don Buford for the club's batting leadership, embarrassing though that honor may have been.

"I don't really feel I was that bad a hitter," said Ken, who needn't be embarrassed by his averages in '72 and '73 with California (.289 and .284). "But I didn't have a whole lot of knowledge and help along the way with hitting. I learned more about hitting after I left the game than when I was in it. When I got out of baseball (in 1975), I spent $10,000 of my own money and went out and bought some batting cages and pitching machines, and set 'em up and gave batting lessons for two summers. And I really didn't know exactly what I was gonna do or say when I started, but I was able to observe the kids from four or five different angles. And finally the fundamentals started to come to me and then I would apply what I was seeing to what I had to do myself and work the whole thing in.

"And it started to get pretty easy as far as the basics. I thought after I was done with the second year that I could teach people to hit. That's when I got really fired up about getting back into baseball. I'd go down to Royals Stadium (his home is in Topeka, Kan.) and I'd see Frank White swing at a pitch and do something and then the next night I'd be down there throwing batting practice and I'd remind him to do one little thing. And he'd go out and get two hits.

"Now whether I had anything to do with it or not, I had no idea. But at least he had someone to suggest something to him. We had no one in Chicago. There was nobody who ever came to me and explained to me what I was doing wrong and how I could get out of it. It was always, try this or try that or you're jumping or you're lunging or you're on your front foot or you're overswinging. There are a lot of things that go along with why you're overswinging or why you're lunging or jumping.

"You used to hear, 'Be quick—be quick with the bat.' Well, shoot, anybody can try to be quick with the bat, but it's how to be quick with the bat. By getting the hands back in a ready position and having a little body turn and then letting the hands go and throwing them at the ball. That's how you do it. You don't get to be quick by standing up there and saying, 'I'm gonna be quick.'

"But I never had anyone who took me aside and said, 'Look, this is what you're doing and this is the way you can come out of it. Now let's go out and work on it.' "

No, the Sox were always more concerned about pitching and defense. Hitting? Forget it. The Sox could always win 2-1 or 1-0, because they had the good pitching and because they had outstanding defensive players like Ken Berry. They had him, that is, until the winter meetings of 1970, when new manager Chuck Tanner and new G.M. Roland Hemond sent him to California in a six-player deal which brought to Chicago a fine young pitcher, Tom Bradley.

"They traded me for a pitcher who won 15 games for them every year," said Berry. "It was tough for me at the time to accept the trade because it was my first time, and I didn't look at it as 'Well, they traded to get a 15-20-game winner.' Because if you've already got a couple of those, you know, that makes your whole ballclub. You can always come up with somebody who doesn't hit that much but can still go get the ball."

Perhaps you can, although I sure haven't seen many of them in a White Sox uniform these last 10 years. Certainly none as good as Ken "The Bandit" Berry.

TOMMY MC CRAW:
The Batting Coach Who Hit .230

Tommy McCraw, for some strange reason, was always one of my favorites. When he came up from Indianapolis in June 1963—after Joe Cunningham had stumbled over first base in Anaheim and suffered a broken collarbone—everyone figured he'd be with the White Sox a long time. And everyone figured he'd be one of the league's leading hitters, just as he'd been in Indianapolis.

Well, he WAS with the White Sox a long time—from '63 through 1970. But he never hit much more than .240. Still, he was a favorite. Maybe because of his flashy style around first base. Or maybe it was that grand-slam homer he hit against the Kansas City A's the night I graduated from high school. Or those three home runs he hit in a 14-1 rout of the Minnesota Twins one afternoon in 1967.

"Dean Chance threw two of them and Jim Kaat threw the third one," remembered McCraw—now the Cleveland Indian hitting coach, of all things—as we sat in the visitors' clubhouse at Comiskey Park. "And I had a chance for a fourth one, but I was scared. I figured they were thinking, 'Hey, this guy's coming in here hitting three home runs—we're gonna knock him down.' And Kaat was the pitcher the fourth time up and he just laid it right in there. And I hit it to the

274

Tommy McCraw, showing his aggressive style of play, upends Boston second baseman Reggie Smith to break up a doubleplay early in the 1967 season. [PHOTO COURTESY CHICAGO TRIBUNE]

warning track, but I was bailing out when I hit it. If I'd stayed in there, I could've hit that fourth one."

Home runs, though, were never Tommy's specialty. Hitting .235 or .236 or .238 was. And it seemed strange, because McCraw had hit .286, .327, and a league-leading .326 (at Indianapolis) in his three seasons in the minors. If ever there was a bright young prospect, McCraw was it. The whole organization was excited about him. After all, here was a guy who in 1962 had led the American Association in hitting after jumping all the way from Class C ball at Idaho Falls.

"From what I heard, they wanted to send me to Class B or A. But Mr. Donie Bush said, 'If I don't take McCraw north with me, I don't take the Indianapolis ballclub north.' Which applied a little pressure, because he was the owner of the Indianapolis club—and a good friend of Al Lopez. So they went along with him, probably figured, 'Well, let's let him go up there and we'll watch him close—let him fall on his face the first month, and we'll get him out of there before he loses his confidence.'

"And for a while, it looked like that was gonna happen, because I started out 0-13. But I wasn't worried, because Ramon Conde was 0-for-15, Suitcase Simpson was 0-for-18, Jim Koranda was 0-for-16. There was a lot of 0-fers. So I wasn't particularly worried. Then we went into Dallas-Fort Worth. I got a jam shot over first base for a double, and I ended up getting five hits that ballgame. Two doubles, two triples, and a single. I was on my way."

But not to Chicago. That wouldn't happen until the next season, barely two months after McCraw had been on the verge of quitting the game. "I led the Sox in every offensive category that they had that spring," he said, thinking back to the Sox' '63 training camp at Sarasota. "I'm not a power hitter, but I led in home runs with six or seven, I led in triples, runs driven in, runs scored, and of course, stolen bases. And I figured I had the club made."

He presumed Lopez would use him as a backup for Cunningham, who had hit a solid .295 the season before, but he presumed wrongly.

"The last day of spring training, I walked into Al's office, and he said, 'Tom, you've done everything we've asked you to do. But we're not gonna take you north. You don't have enough experience.' That was the low point of my career. I figured if my own people don't give

276

me the chance to acquire experience at the big league level, I certainly can't expect another organization to give me a chance to get that experience. So I was just crushed. I really wanted to quit at that time.

"As a matter of fact, I went back to the hotel and packed my bags. I was gonna leave. You figure, what more can you prove? You've won the batting title in Triple-A, the team has won the championship. Anything I do less than winning the batting title again is a down year. So I really thought seriously about goin' home. But I talked to my wonderful mom on the phone and she said, 'I sent you away from here to be a big league ballplayer. When you come back, that's what I expect you to be.' "

McCraw paused, grinning.

"So, you see, I didn't have no place to go then. I had to play ball."

So back he went to Indianapolis, hoping the White Sox would someday be calling for him. "We were playing the Yankees' farm club (Richmond) and Rollie Sheldon was pitching and I kept fouling off pitches and fouling off pitches," Tommy remembered. "I think it was about 12 or 13 pitches. And it was kinda quiet and as he was getting ready to pitch again, some fan shouted, 'C'mon McCraw, get a base hit—Cunningham might break his leg.' Next pitch, I singled on a slider and we won that ballgame. And I went into the clubhouse and got in the shower and the manager told me, 'Pack your bags—you're goin' to LA. Cunningham just broke his collarbone.' I was really amazed. That's a strange way to get your break, but hey, I appreciated it. I never went back down."

Sadly, however, his batting average never went up. I told him many Sox fans had figured it had been his part-time role in '64 and '65—after the team had acquired Moose Skowron to play first base—that had caused him to pick up bad habits and had messed up his approach. Tommy, shaking his head, straightened me out.

"I'll accept a lot of blame for that, because I just didn't know how to hit. Everything I'd done was instinct and God-given ability. I had never had anyone deal with me on the mental aspects of hitting. And that was they key. It was not the physical. I had hitting instructors. They'd say, 'You're gonna have to hit more home runs so you gotta get your bat in closer so you can pull the ball—open your stance up a little more so you can be quicker'—and all this stuff. And I was doing all those things. But you have to learn to hit from the head first if you're gonna be a successful hitter. But I had no one to deal with.

"The good hitters on the club, like Floyd Robinson—when you asked him about hitting, he'd talk about hands and feet. And those things are important, but they're not half as important as having your head straight, knowing what you want to do, applying discipline to your hitting. I flash back now to days, man, when guys got me out on fastballs I should've killed, and I never knew why. Or like if you go back through the books, you'll find when I'd go maybe two weeks where I hit .600 and just smoked the ball. And then all of a sudden for a month, man, nothin'—absolutely nothin'. And that's because, mentally, I just didn't know what was going on. I was just reacting off everything."

It wasn't until McCraw was traded to Washington—managed by Ted Williams—for the '71 season that he found someone who could help him. "I asked Williams about my stroke. He told me, 'There's nothing wrong with your blankety-blank stroke—it's your blankety-blank head that's messed up.' I'd never heard that before. He said, 'You don't have any idea what you want to hit, you don't have any discipline. You're just trying to swing and react off a ball the pitcher's throwing you. You can't do that. You've got to have some idea or plan.'

"He told me, 'You have to hit the fastball to play in the big leagues.' I'd never heard that crap. But he said that I had been looking for breaking balls to hit. And I wasn't even aware of it. But after he mentioned it to me, I surely became aware of it. I was taking the pitch they throw 80 per cent of the time—the fastball—and looking for the curve. And if they threw you a good curve, you weren't gonna hit it, anyway. So it was only after '71 that I became a good hitter. And sometimes I sit and really regret not having been a good mental hitter earlier, because I could've really helped Chicago in those years we were one game out, two games out. If I'd known how to hit—with my speed and stuff—I could've made a tremendous difference. That I regret."

He doesn't regret having been a part of the '67 club that almost won the pennant. Tommy was one of the leaders, along with Pete Ward, Ron Hansen, Gary Peters, Joe Horlen, Don Buford, Ken Berry, and

Tommie Agee. At a time when blacks in Detroit and Newark were burning buildings, McCraw was building bridges. Feigning anger, he began calling white players on the ballclub "those blue-eyed devils," and once announced, "I'm so prejudiced I won't eat white bread." Because of people like McCraw, the Sox of '67 were a happy, unified team. It was not, however, a team that excited the fandom: Only 985,634 paid to watch them, even though the White Sox led the league from mid-June through mid-August and were in and out of first place all September. The problem was offense, or the lack thereof. The Sox simply could not hit. Still, they scored enough runs to win. It was Eddie Stanky's ballclub, and McCraw loved playing on it.

"The highest point I've had in this game was the entire '67 season. That was a beautiful year, even though we didn't win it. But I enjoyed playing that season more than any other year in my career. I still play that season back in my mind. We did so many little things that won ballgames—that's why we enjoyed '67 so much, why we enjoyed the success we had. We went out and played. And we had a togetherness on that ballclub that Stanky had generated. We had good pitching— Peters, Horlen, Tommy John, those guys. It was just a fantastic year.

"Stanky liked my speed, my aggressiveness. I was his type of ball-player, doing what I had to do to win. That was his attitude—whatever it took to win. We played totally aggressive baseball. We made mistakes, but we forced other people to make a lot more mistakes than we made. And that's why we were in the race."

The aggressiveness meant running the bases hard, sliding hard, breaking up doubleplays, and all the rest. "If you broke up a double-play to help win a ballgame, Stanky would buy you a pair of alligator shoes, things like that, to not only let you know he's aware of what you're doing, but that he appreciated it. He appreciated giving the next guy a chance to hit. I remember I did it once in Baltimore with the bases loaded. Andy Etchebarren was the catcher. Our hitter hit a groundball to first base. Boog (Powell) threw home to force me at home, and Andy just kinda casually walked out in front of the plate and was gonna throw to first base for the doubleplay. And I slid in and knocked him down. And he didn't throw the ball. And there was a big argument. (Baltimore manager Hank) Bauer came out and they looked at the slide marks and the umpire said, 'It's a clean play.' I

279

didn't spike him—I just knocked him down. And then Ken Berry got a base hit, drove in two runs, and we won the ballgame."

And Tommy got his pair of alligator shoes. And, as the season went on, so did many other Sox players. "That's the Stanky-type ballclub," said Tommy. "Aggressive, not afraid of getting hurt, taking it to the other ballclub, even though we may have been out-talented. Look at Boston with Yastrzemski, Smith, Scott, Foy, people like that. We come in with Buford, myself—our best threat was Agee. But we did little things. I remember beating Dean Chance in this ballpark—he's got practically a no-hitter for eight innings, no balls even hit out of the infield. We beat him 2-1 and he's walking off the mound wondering 'How'd they beat me?' Heck, we'd score five runs in a three-game series and sweep it. You know, 2-1, 2-1, 1-0, that's it, see ya later."

But by 1968—McCraw thinks it happened in late '67—the White Sox had changed—even though Stanky was still the manager. "We lost Agee and Buford, and that hurt," McCraw pointed out. "We didn't have the same type of camaraderie we'd had before they left. We didn't have the same type of talent. You have to be an unselfish ballplayer or you have to have enough unselfish ballplayers on your ballclub to be effective. A lot of super teams aren't effective because all their superstars are concerned about just their stats. Unless you have a little guy who's willing to give himself up, move guys over, walk, steal bases for you, you just have superstars hitting home runs and you're getting beat 12-10. It's like basketball. You put an offensive player out there and he'll score his 40 points, but the guy he's guarding scores 42.

"If you look at '67, the thing that made us tough was we had a lot of speed—we didn't hit home runs. (The Sox hit only 89 homers but stole 124 bases.) We went as far as we went with speed. OK, I'm sure the front office was thinking, 'Well, if we acquire a couple longball hitters, it's gonna make it that much easier.' But in order to put the longball hitters in there, you're gonna have to take out some of that speed. And that's a transition we had to make down the stretch run. We waited for (Ken) Boyer and (Rocky) Colavito to hit a home run.

"I know Rocky hit a home run here to beat the Yankees one night, but that was about the only game-winning home run that was hit between the two of them. Before, we had speed and we were winning 2-1, 3-2, 3-1 without the home run. Our style of ball was bunt, scratch, run, make guys make errors, steal a couple bases, broken-bat flyball, we got the run, now hold 'em with good pitching.

"But when you get two guys like Rocky and Ken—they were great ballplayers, don't get me wrong—you take out two guys with speed, and now you're waiting on one of them to hit a home run. So instead of a guy like Agee or Buford or me stealing a base in a tight situation, we're waiting for these guys to deliver the longball for us. If we didn't have that longball possibility there, we'd go ahead and take the stolen base, and maybe we get a single or maybe the catcher throws the ball into center field and now all we need is a flyball or a wild pitch. So it was a transition we had to make for the final two months of the season. I still say it was a great year but that transition hurt us."

It was time for the Indians to take batting practice. We walked out onto the field, and I watched McCraw, the unlikely batting instructor, as he observed the swings of Rick Manning, Mike Hargrove, Toby Harrah, Ron Hassey and others. I asked Tommy what he stressed to his pupils. "You watch the pitcher—you know what he has working for him that particular night. When you go up there, you have a plan. You just don't go up there blank. You have a plan of what you want to do, and up until two strikes, you should execute that plan—which means you'll probably get a chance to execute your plan 95 per cent of the time. And even with two strikes, you're gonna get some base hits."

The Comiskey Park public address announcer was beginning to call out the starting lineups as I was leaving the field. I listened to the names: Morrison, Lemon, Johnson, Nordhagen, Baines. And then it was '67, and the names were coming over the P.A. system again: Buford, Agee, Berry, McCraw. I thought of '67 and what might have been, had Tommy McCraw only known then what he knows now.

281

BILL SKOWRON:
The Moose Finally Came Home

The license plate read "BMS 14." Surely this car pulling into the lot at Rascals, a suburban Naperville eatery, had to belong to Bill "Moose" Skowron, who wore uniform number 14 throughout his 14-year major league career. I was right. Out of the car stepped the Moose, still athletic-looking at age 48, still wearing the crew-cut he had worn as a player.

He had been a Yankee for nine years, a Dodger for one, and a Washington Senator for half a season before Eddie Short, who had been trying for years, finally put Skowron—a Chicago boy from Weber High School—in a White Sox uniform in July of 1964. The Moose, at long last, had come home.

"When I was in high school at Weber," he began, after we'd ordered lunch, "I only competed in football and basketball because the Catholic schools at that time didn't have baseball. I played a lot of softball midweek—Windy City softball—and on Sundays I played hardball, sandlot ball. Then I went to Purdue on a football scholarship and the Cubs and Sox both thought I'd finish my college education—so they never offered me anything. And the Sox scout—Doug Minor—he didn't like my dad for some reason, so he blackballed me.

Bill Skowron

Said, 'Moose will never make it.'

"Then, the summer after my sophomore year, I went to play semipro baseball in 1950 at Austin, Minn. And a Cub scout by the name of Bill Prince saw me hit four homers off four different pitchers in a single game. And he STILL didn't offer me a contract. But, thank God, there were two scouts there from the Yankees, Joe McDermott and Burleigh Grimes. They offered me a contract and made me a bonus baby—gave me a bonus of $25,000. And I quit school and signed professionally."

Then began a brief tour of the Yankee minor league system. Even though Skowron tore the cover off the ball, he didn't seem to make much progress—that's how loaded Casey Stengel's Yankees were in those days.

"My first year in pro ball (1951) I hit .334 at Norfolk, Va.—I led the (Piedmont) league. I'm playing the outfield. I get promoted to Kansas City (then in the American Association), I hit .341, 31 homers, 134 RBIs. I was named Minor League Player of the Year. And I wasn't even invited to spring training the next year with the Yankees. They sent me back to Kansas City to learn how to play first base, 'cause Casey said, 'Moose, you'll make the major leagues quicker.' Because all they had at first base was Joe Collins, and they had Woodling, Bauer, Mantle, Bob Cerv, and Irv Noren in the outfield. I went down there and played first base and I hit .318. The following year I got a chance to go to spring training."

He batted .340 for the Yankees in that rookie year of 1954, but he only played in 87 games. The Yanks had traded for ex-Sox first baseman Eddie Robinson, so Moose had to split playing time not only with Collins but also with the newcomer. But in '55, his playing time increased, and he hit .319. He became a regular for good in '56, hitting .308 with 23 homers and 90 RBI, and began a career seemingly designed to terrorize White Sox pitching—not to mention White Sox fans.

The tormenting reached its peak on a July afternoon in 1957. The Sox, before 48,244, had won the first game of a Sunday doubleheader 3-1 behind Billy Pierce. And Dick Donovan had a 4-0 shutout going into the ninth inning of the second game. Three more outs and the Sox would have a sweep and would be only one game behind the first-place New Yorkers. In the radio booth, Bob Elson made a rare prediction: "And the White Sox," he proclaimed, "are going to win a doubleheader from the mighty New York Yankees."

But then, as they so often seemed to with the Yankees, things began to happen. Mickey Mantle, Yogi Berra, and Harry "Suitcase" Simpson singled to fill the bases with nobody out. Jim Wilson came in to relieve Donovan. Hank Bauer beat out an infield tap, scoring Mantle and leaving the bases filled. Stengel then called on Skowron, hitless in four tries against Pierce in the first game, to go up and bat for Gerry Coleman. Moose hit Wilson's first pitch into the upper deck in left for a grand slam. Tommy Byrne followed with another home run and an apparent Sox victory had been turned into a 6-4 loss, thanks to Chicago's own Moose.

"I hit good against the White Sox in my career because I wanted to prove to them that their scouts had made a mistake not offering me a contract," Skowron said. "As it turned out, though, I could never complain, because I got into seven World Series with the Yankees. I get traded to the Dodgers, we win the pennant, we win the World Series. So I was in eight World Series out of my 14 years in the big leagues."

It might have been nine (and three in three straight years with three different teams) had Skowron been acquired by the Sox earlier in the '64 season, the season the Yankees finished a game ahead of Chicago in the final standings. Without Skowron, the Sox rolled over and played dead against the Yanks, losing their first 10 meetings. With Skowron, they won six of the last eight—including a four-game sweep in Chicago in late August that put the White Sox 1½ games ahead.

"That's when Phil Linz got out the harmonica on the bus and started playing the thing," laughed the Moose. "And Yogi Berra (then the New York manager) and (coach) Frankie Crosetti almost went after him. There was almost a fight. And I think that motivated them, and they went on to beat us out by one game."

But not before the Sox made a battle of it. A Friday night game against Cleveland the first week in September remains vivid in my memory. Pete Ward homered into the old bullpen in center to tie the game in the bottom of the 10th. Skowron followed with a line drive into the lower deck in right to win the game. I remember telling my father, "That's it—they're gonna win the pennant." I was, of course, proven wrong. But Skowron had given everyone a thrill with that opposite-field blast, the kind he had long since become famous for.

"I led the Yankees in grounding into doubleplays one year," said Skowron, "and Casey told me, 'If you don't learn how to hit to right field, you're gonna go back to the minor leagues.' So I started hitting to right field in batting practice. I was hitting some balls to right field into the upper deck, and I couldn't believe it. And I said, 'My God, if I can hit a ball like that to right field, I shouldn't even try to pull the ball.' So I was a Nellie hitter—left-center and right-center. I was not a pull hitter. It helped me to wait on the ball. And anyway, it was a long way to left and left-center in Yankee Stadium. I still hit three balls into the leftfield bleachers out there, though. I had that record for a while. Joe DiMaggio hit two in there and I'd hit three. Then I got traded and Mickey Mantle tied me."

It was funny, Moose said, but that home run to right field to beat Cleveland in '64 was one of only four he hit for the White Sox that year—he had hit 13 for Washington. "If I'd been with the Sox earlier, I'd have helped them a lot more," he said. "Before I joined the Sox, when I was with Washington, Chuck Hinton hit a line drive into our dugout, and Eddie Brinkman—our shortstop—I protected him. I put my hand up so the ball wouldn't hit him in the face, and the ball hit my hand. And that afternoon I found out I was traded to the White Sox.

"I met the team in Boston, I got 3-for-5. But my hand wasn't feeling good. The next day we came home to Chicago and I hit a home run into the upper deck off Wes Stock my first time up in a Sox home uniform. It was great. I was goin' from a second-division ballclub to a contender."

He was soon to become a respected member of his new team. "Maybe it was because I was used to winning," said Moose, who never finished a season on a second-division club. "In New York, we played as a team. There was nobody jealous of one another. If a guy went 0-for-8 and we won a doubleheader, I'd expect this guy to be happy, right? And say we lost a doubleheader and he goes 7-for-8 and he's joking around the clubhouse—forget those guys. I don't want him to be laughing when we're losing and he gets his hits. To me, that's an individual-type ballplayer."

286

Skowron became a team player after a run-in with Casey Stengel early in his Yankee career. "I remember I got taken out of a game in the first inning with the bases loaded and no outs—and I was the cleanup man," he laughed. "I'll never forget this as long as I live. We're playing the Detroit Tigers and Billy Hoeft (a lefty) is pitching against us. We load the bases, Casey calls me back, says, 'Moose, I'm putting Eddie Robinson in to pinch-hit for you.' Because they'd changed to a righthanded pitcher. And I was so angry, I threw the bat, went into the clubhouse, didn't even shower, and went back to the hotel.

"Eddie Robinson hit a double with the bases loaded and we went on to win 3-0. Next day, I come to the park, Casey calls me into the office, locks the door, calls me a lot of names, and says, 'Don't you ever do that to me again. I'm out to win ballgames.' And from that day on, I never questioned Casey Stengel."

He didn't question Al Lopez much, either. "Al's pet peeve was if a guy hit a flyball and didn't hustle. That's when he would get out of his seat and be on the dugout steps waiting for you. Like Floyd Robinson. Boy, Floyd would hit a flyball and he wouldn't run and the guy would drop the ball—and Floyd would still be at first base. Lopez would fine him $400-$500 on the spot. That was Lopez. As long as you gave 100 per cent, you did your job. But when you loafed, he was on top of you."

Skowron put in just one full year under Lopez. That was 1965, when Moose tied John Romano for the club leadership in homers (18) and led in RBI (78). Despite the personal success, Skowron was disappointed when the Sox, who got within striking distance of eventual A.L. champ Minnesota in September, floundered the final three weeks and wound up second again.

"The last month of the season," he said, frowning, "the guys were checking the road maps, getting ready to go on a fishing and hunting trip to Colorado. That's when I got angry. Instead of worrying about winning the pennant, they were worrying about Oct. 1, who was gonna drive the cabin cruiser, who's gonna meet who where, who's gonna drive, and all that. I finally said, 'Why don't you guys quit worrying about that stuff and worry about winning the pennant?' I was angry because I still thought we had a chance to win it that year."

But they didn't, and Lopez called it quits. Along came Eddie Stanky, who put Tommy McCraw at first base in '66 and relegated Skowron to reserve status—something Moose put up with for one season but wasn't about to for a second. In May of '67, he went into Stanky's office and indicated he had had enough.

"I wanted to get traded," he said. "Stanky comes in and he's going with the youth movement, he's got a four-five-year contract, and I wasn't used to Stanky. I said, 'McCraw hits .230 or .240. I want to play. If I can't play, I want to get out of here.'

"Stanky said, 'Where do you want to go?' I said, 'Anyplace.' He said, 'Cleveland's after you, so are the Angels.' I said, 'I'll go to California.' "

It was that simple. The Sox sold Moose to the Angels and ended up losing a pennant they should have won—maybe, just maybe, for want of a clutch hit that might well have been provided by Moose Skowron's bat, experienced as it was in this matter called a pennant race.

"But," said the crew-cut financial printing salesman as we rose to leave, "being home in Chicago—coming back here to play—it was a big thrill for me.

"And I'll never forget that year we lost the pennant by one game."

Nor, I thought as the car with the license plate "BMS 14" drove out of the parking lot, will any White Sox fan who lived—and died—through it.

JOE HORLEN:
A No-Hitter to Savor

The first thing I asked Joe Horlen was whether or not he had given up that awful habit of chewing Kleenex. I was relieved to learn that, indeed, he had.

"You know, I'd tried chewing tobacco before," said the Sox standout righthander of the '60s who these days builds homes in his native San Antonio. "I tried it 20 times and I think I threw up 20 times. That's why I started chewing Kleenex on days I was pitching.

"Then, about three years ago, I finally found some chewing tobacco I could chew—without throwing up. So now I chew it. I guess I've grown up."

Horlen was chewing the Kleenex hard that Sunday afternoon of Sept. 10, 1967. His opponents were the Detroit Tigers, tied for first place with the Minnesota Twins. Right behind those two teams were the Boston Red Sox, a half-game back. In fourth place was Chicago, two games out but on the verge of sinking slowly out of the race because of what had happened 24 hours earlier.

Gary Peters and the Sox had held a 3-0 lead going into the top of the ninth inning. With Peters on the mound and relievers like Hoyt Wilhelm, Don McMahon, Bob Locker, and Wilbur Wood poised in

Joe Horlen (right) tapes an interview with his good friend and roommate, Gary Peters.

the bullpen, the lead seemed safe—even against Detroit, which featured Al Kaline, Norm Cash, Jim Northrup, Willie Horton, Eddie Mathews, and Bill Freehan. Unaccountably, the lead vanished and Detroit didn't stop scoring until it had fashioned a 7-3 victory.

The Sox, everyone seemed convinced, were now dead. They had little, if any, offense. Everyone knew that. But now, in the loss to the Tigers, even the team's strength—the pitching—had collapsed. The confidence of even the manager, Eddie Stanky, had been shaken. An hour after the game, a Chicago sportswriter, finishing up his story in the Comiskey Park pressbox, looked down on the field and saw Stanky—still in uniform—walking head-down along the leftfield warning track with his new puppy, "Go-Go," trailing close behind. All of a sudden, Stanky's brave words of just a few days earlier, about how his team was going to be in the pennant fight up till the final day, seemed rather hollow.

But baseball, unlike football, is not a game of momentum. The next day, after reading in the Chicago papers that they were all but out of the race now, the White Sox scored five runs in the first inning of Game One of a doubleheader. That was enough of a cushion for Horlen—Detroit's lightning wasn't going to strike twice in two days, certainly—and now interest turned to Joe's mastery on the mound. The Tigers were still without a hit as the fifth inning opened. Sixth inning, same story. The seventh and eighth innings came and went and Detroit still was without a hit. Only two balls had been hit to the outfield and there had been only two baserunners: Freehan was hit by a pitched ball and Mathews reached on an error by first baseman Ken Boyer.

"There wasn't too much in that game, really." Joe recalled. "There was only one ball I remember being hit hard. Kaline lined out to short. But even that ball, he hit off his fists."

So it came down to the ninth inning. Three more outs and Horlen would have his no-hitter and the Sox would be given a genuine morale-booster. First man up was Jerry Lumpe. "He hit one just to my left," Horlen said. "Wayne Causey was playing second base and he went over and made a real nice stop. And if it had been anybody but Lumpe running, he'd have probably beaten it out."

The next batter was catcher Bill Heath, who had replaced Freehan.

Heath, once a Sox farmhand, smacked a low liner toward third. Don Buford moved to his left, grabbed the ball on one hop and fired to new first baseman Cotton Nash, whose 6-6 frame had already come in handy for a close call on Lumpe's ball.

Two outs. Now only Dick McAuliffe stood between Horlen and his no-hitter. "He always swung the bat good," Joe remembered. "He always hit the ball. I never could strike him out. I was throwing all fastballs by then. I hadn't thrown a curveball in three or four innings. I was determined that I was either gonna walk him or he was gonna have to hit one almost off the ground. He hit a sinking fastball. It was on the outside corner. He hit it to Hansen at short and Ronnie threw him out easily."

Horlen threw his glove up in the air in jubilation and was quickly mobbed by his equally jubilant teammates, who then went on to beat the Tigers in the second game 4-0 to move back into third place and right back into the race. Horlen had provided the spark.

"Jerry Holtzman (of the Sun-Times) was the official scorer that day," he recalled, "and he gave me the official box score of that game. And I had it framed and it's still hanging on my wall. It was a special game. But I always felt I was eventually gonna throw one. I'd come close before."

The closest was in 1963, Joe's second year in the majors. He had started the year with the Sox but had been sent to Indianapolis with instructions to work on his curveball. Instead, he developed a second fastball. "Warren Hacker was on that club then and he showed me the 'cut' fastball, which tailed away from righthanded hitters. My sinking fastball moved in on them. I started experimenting with the pitch Warren showed me and it helped get me back to the big leagues."

Four starts later, he was back with the Sox, pitching against the Senators in Washington. The Sox had a 1-0 lead and Horlen had a no-hitter going into the last of the ninth. With one out, Washington out-fielder Chuck Hinton stepped to the plate. Oddly, this ninth inning seemed clearer in Joe's memory than the Detroit game.

"Hinton hit about a 20-hopper—it dribbled by me and it dribbled by Ron Hansen out into center field. Guy by the name of Bobo Osborne was next up, and he fouled a bunch of pitches off. Got to 3-2 on him, and Hinton was a good baserunner, so he was running on 3-2.

And Osborne hit a perfect doubleplay ball to second, but we could only get one man (the batter, Osborne) because Hinton was running.

"Then came Don Lock, who'd struck out something like seven out of his last eight times up. I hung a curveball to him and he just about knocked down that back wall there at RFK Stadium. It sure wasn't a cheap one. He put a few cracks in that wall, he hit it so hard."

And so, as Jack Brickhouse told his TV audience back home in Chicago, "Young Joe Horlen loses his no-hitter AND the ballgame." As the years went on, it got so that Horlen sometimes almost had to throw a no-hitter to win games for the White Sox. His 1.88 earned run average in 1964 netted him only a 13-9 won-lost record. His ERA "skyrocketed" to 2.88 in '65 and Joe paid the price: His won-lost mark was just 13-13. The next year, he cut his ERA to 2.43, but he finished 10-13. In '68 he was down to 2.37 but his record was nonetheless an unimpressive 12-14. Only in '67, the year of the no-hitter, did his winning percentage approach what you'd expect: 19 wins and 7 losses with an ERA of 2.06. I asked him if he would have rather pitched for a ballclub that scored five runs a game than the Sox, who might score five in a week.

"I never thought about it," he said. "It never entered my mind—it never did. I thought I was very, very fortunate just to be able to play major league baseball. I think it helped me to pitch for a team that didn't score much. I had a tendency to lose concentration if I had a big lead. And anytime you pitched for Chicago, you had to really concentrate because you didn't get many runs."

He got fewer in '67 than in any other year, yet he still had the 19-7 record. But maybe that was because he had a little inspiration along the way. "That was the year my grandfather came up to see me pitch," Joe told me. "We'd always been close. I used to spend summers at his farm in Fredericksburg, just north of San Antonio. He had about 500 acres. I used to milk the cows. Can't stand milk to this day. Had to drink it warm, right out of the cow. Boy . . .

"But that August my grandfather came up to Chicago with my mom and dad. He'd never been out of the state of Texas, much less been in an airplane. He was 81 at the time. And he saw me pitch. They stayed seven or eight days and I won two games while he was there. He'd been an old farmer down in Texas and he just couldn't get over how

293

black the dirt was up there in Chicago.

"And he wasn't home but three weeks before he got a heart attack and died."

Horlen responded with a strong finish, but even he would have preferred the finish to have been stronger. He failed twice in his attempt at victory No. 20, and one of the failures was in Kansas City on Black Wednesday. He lost the second game of the twin calamity 4-0, after his roommate, Peters, had been beaten 5-2. The doubleheader defeat marked the beginning of the end for the Eddie Stanky era in Chicago and by next July, Joe was again pitching for the manager who had given him his first big league opportunity—Al Lopez. It had been Lopez who had predicted big things for the slim youngster from Oklahoma State University.

"I know Lopez was a lot quieter than Stanky," he laughed. "He wasn't perfect, though, just like Stanky wasn't perfect. I know he changed that lineup around an awful lot. I went out to dinner one night with Nellie Fox, Sammy Esposito, Jim Landis, Sherm Lollar and Don Larsen when I first came up in '61. We were in Boston. And they all put $5 into a pool to see who could guess closest to the starting lineup the next day. But Al got a lot out of his players. He managed well."

The same, alas, cannot be said for Don Gutteridge, who took over for Lopez in May 1969 and under whom Horlen had his worst year in the big leagues (6-16, 4.89 ERA in 1970). But it wasn't all the fault of the grandfatherly Gutteridge. A bad knee was preventing Joe from pushing off the rubber with full force.

"I had hurt my right knee playing football in high school, but it really hadn't bothered me since. But now it had deteriorated to the point where my right leg and thigh was an inch or so shorter around than my left leg. My whole leg was deteriorating."

An operation for removal of torn cartilage was performed during the season. "They expected I'd be out until the next spring. We weren't going anywhere anyway. I was back pitching 33 days after I was operated on."

A new manager, Chuck Tanner, was awaiting Horlen at spring training in 1971. Tanner saw Joe's knee was sound again and pronounced him ready for the regular rotation. But more trouble was ahead. Sliding into second base against the Cubs in Scottsdale, Ariz., on the final day of spring training, Horlen this time tore cartilage in his left knee. He flew back to Chicago that evening.

"In fact I flew back home with the Cubs that night," he said. "They were opening the season in Chicago, we were on our way to Oakland. They operated on me the next morning. There again, I was supposed to be out for six to eight weeks. I pitched a game 28 days later."

But he didn't gain his first victory of the season until he beat the Tigers June 15 in Detroit. He wound up with eight wins and nine losses, one of the defeats a 1-0 setback hung on him by Oakland's rookie sensation, Vida Blue. Outings like that one, however, were not coming with the frequency with which the Horlen of old used to deliver them. His ERA for '71 was a very un-Horlen-like 4.27, and that—plus the fact he was now 34 and he was the team's player representative to a union that was about to go on strike—helped the White Sox decide to give Joe his release just before the opening of the '72 season.

"I was the player rep that year, yeah, but that wasn't the only reason I got let go—but it probably didn't help matters any," he said. "But my spring training wasn't bad. It was better than usual. And they certainly needed starting pitchers. They had 'em going with two days' rest (Wilbur Wood, Stan Bahnsen, and Tom Bradley) and had Wilbur pitching doubleheaders and everything else. I don't know. They just felt that was it.

"But I went to the strike meeting in Dallas just to see what was going on. I had no official representation at all or anything 'cause the White Sox had let me go. And I ran into Reggie Jackson and Catfish Hunter there and they said, 'Finley's looking for pitchers—why don't you give him a call?' Reggie gave me Finley's private number and I called him up when I got back to San Antonio. He said, 'What's the matter with you? Your arm hurting you?' 'Nope.' 'Your leg OK?' 'It's fine.' He said, 'Well, damn, I tried to get you three weeks ago and they wouldn't let you go. Now they release you.' That made everybody kinda leery. But I said, 'Well, I'm ready to go.' 'Well, you come on out to Oakland when it looks like this thing's gonna get settled and you can work out with us.'

"So I went out there and pitched the first five innings of an

295

exhibition game against the University of California and they signed me on the spot."

Horlen appeared in 32 games for the A's, winning three and losing four. Nothing terrific, maybe. But he was pitching for a pennant-winning team that was on its way toward a World Championship. And Horlen was a part of it.

I was in a barber shop the afternoon of Game Six of the 1972 World Series. The A's were losing at Cincinnati when the radio announcer told his listeners that Manager Dick Williams was waving in Joe Horlen from the bullpen.

At last, I thought, Joe Horlen is pitching in a World Series.

Five years too late.

GARY PETERS:
The Joker Went Wild

Gary Peters was more than just a good pitcher all those years with the White Sox. He was a guy who liked to have fun. His specialty was the practical joke, and his ran from fairly pedestrian fare ("He used to get exploding cigarets and put 'em in Fisher's and Buzhardt's cigaret cases—stuff like that," said Gary's former roommate, Joe Horlen) to high-schoolish and all the way up to Big Time Craziness.

High-schoolish? Well, how about the time he threw that lifelike, black rubber snake at Tommy McCraw? "We were in Baltimore and Peters had bought this great big ol' black rubber snake," Horlen chuckled. "Looked just like the real thing. And we're on the bus waiting for it to take us from the hotel to the ballpark. And McCraw got on the bus, and as soon as he gets on, Peters threw that black snake at him. And McCraw was yelling and screaming—almost went through the window trying to get away from the thing.

"He finally got out of the bus and he was standing at the hotel entrance. We're yelling, 'C'mon, Mac—it's only a rubber snake.' He said, 'The hell with you guys, I'm taking a cab.' "

Then there was the really big-time stuff. "The first year I came to camp with the White Sox, Les Moss was still playing," said Gary when

I reached him at his Sarasota, Fla., home. "That's when they still were training in Tampa. Les and I went out one night and caught a baby shark and we snuck in and put it in Dave Philley's locker.

"Then another time I caught a bobcat down here in Sarasota and put it in Deacon Jones' locker. But Deacon was a lot more scared of that bobcat than Dave Philley was of that shark."

Sharks and bobcats weren't the only items to appear in the lockers of startled Sox players during the lefthander's stay with Chicago. Peters would go out and catch an occasional octopus as well. As a matter of fact, Peters, who's in the construction business in Sarasota, still catches octopus and other marine life. "Just about every Saturday," he said, "I go scuba diving or spear fishing. I'm usually out to get some black grouper—it's the best eating fish in Florida. I'll shoot a couple of them every Saturday just to have something to eat at home."

It's something that he counts on, just as the White Sox could always count on him to throw a low-hit, low-run ballgame just about every time out. He was the American League Rookie of the Year in 1963, when he was 19-8 with a league-leading 2.33 earned run average. The next year, he was 20-8 with a 2.50 ERA. After an off-year in '65 (10-12, 3.62) caused by some physical problems (during which one Chicago newspaper ran this memorable headline: "Sox Face Boston With Peters Out"), he rebounded to lead the league in ERA again (1.98) in '66 and then went 16-11 with a 2.28 ERA in '67. And yet, it was almost pure luck that the White Sox got such success from Peters, whom they were ready to cut loose in May, 1963. But an opportunity developed in Kansas City one night that month and Peters took advantage of it. With relief help from Jim Brosnan, he won his first big league start 5-1.

"It was almost cutdown date," Peters remembered. (In those years, teams were permitted to carry up to 28 players on their roster up until 30 days after the opening of the season, after which they were required to reduce the roster to 25.) "Juan Pizarro was supposed to pitch that game and he came down with the flu. So he was scratched and that's how I got to start, or I might've been traded or released, because I was out of options. But I remember that game pretty well. I hit a home run in that game, too.

298

"I hadn't pitched very much, and you could almost figure out that you weren't gonna stay around because you weren't being used. Nobody said anything to me before the game. At cutdown date, everybody kind of knew who was gonna go anyhow. But that was really a break for me. I got right in the rotation after that."

He went on to put together an 11-game winning streak, which tied John Rigney's club record that had stood for nearly 25 years. Included in the string was a one-hitter against Baltimore, a game Peters calls the best he ever pitched. "Robin Roberts (his mound opponent) got a hit off me in the sixth inning and he was the only guy to reach base. It was a fastball, he hit it on the hands. Just barely got over Nellie Fox's head. That's probably the best stuff I ever had. Real good stuff, real good control. One of those nights when everything was perfect."

And it was a night that might have never taken place had Gary not been granted that chance in Kansas City. "I was gonna go ahead and play out my option and if nobody picked me up, I would've probably gone ahead and taught school. I was close to my teaching degree and I would've probably finished—and then gone into coaching and teaching."

After all, he had had enough of pitching Triple-A baseball. He'd had four years of it: at Indianapolis in '59, at San Diego in '60 and '61, and again at Indy in '62. It was remarkable that he had stuck it out as long as he had. "But in those days," he explained, "the White Sox had a real good pitching staff to start with. And I was a starting pitcher. That's one reason why I figured I'd play out my option, because I felt there were probably some other clubs I could pitch for. The White Sox, I felt, was one of the hardest staffs to make, because they had so many veterans: Billy Pierce, Early Wynn, Bob Shaw, Ray Herbert, Pizarro. They had a pretty set rotation. I did find out later that if I'd been sent down again in '63, that Kansas City was gonna draft me anyhow."

But fortunately, the Sox had finally discovered Gary Peters. "We came real close to losing him there," Al Lopez admitted when I met him in Tampa. "In fact, we tried to peddle him once or twice and the other clubs would back off at the last minute. It's lucky they did. We were even talking about making an outfielder or first baseman out of him. He was a good hitter, a great athlete. (Peters had been signed as a outfielder-first baseman by the Sox in 1956, but had switched to the mound that same year. He hit .259 for the Sox his rookie year, hit 4 homers and had 19 RBI in '64, and hit .271 with 3 homers and 19 RBI for Boston in 1971. In his career, he hit 19 homers and his lifetime batting average was .222, excellent for a pitcher.)

"But that spring, I remember we split the squad up and went to Puerto Rico on an exhibition tour and I left Ray Berres in charge of the squad left behind in Sarasota. And that group played the Dodgers one day, and Ray pitched Gary for three innings.

"When I came back he said, 'Al, I wish you could've seen Peters pitch.' I said, 'What did he do?' He said, 'He made those guys look sick. He's come up with a quick slider and he's getting his delivery down. I've been after him all the time about staying in a certain position. If he keeps that quick slider, we're gonna have a good pitcher.' So by that impression he made on Ray Berres, that's how come he got more chances to pitch. Then we started him in Kansas City and he went 6 or 7 innings. I didn't want to get him in trouble. I wanted to build his confidence up, so I yanked him with us leading 4-1. And we won the ballgame.

"I started him again and he pitched seven good innings and I took him out. About the fourth or fifth time out he went nine innings and did a real good job. I always say, when you're using a young pitcher, get him out of there while he's still ahead. Don't let him lose a game like that, or you're tearing down what you've tried so hard to build up."

All Peters would build up was a well-earned reputation as an outstanding pitcher who could help his own cause with his bat. People weren't only talking about his sinking fastball, slider, and changeup. They were talking about the bat he swung, too. To this day, he claims that one of his biggest thrills in baseball was the grand-slam homer he hit on S & H Green Stamp Day one year off the Yankees' Al Downing at Comiskey Park. I asked him if he recalled another Comiskey Park blast he had hit—this one as a pinch-batter in '64 in the bottom of the 13th to beat Kansas City reliever Wes Stock.

"Yeah, I remember that one. I pinch-hit for Dave Nicholson. I remember it for two or three reasons. In the first place, Al sent me up there to bunt. We had a man on first and we were one run be-

300

hind. And I'd played with Wes Stock in Puerto Rico, and here he had a bunch of scoreless innings stacked up. Twenty-some innings.

"I fouled two pitches off trying to bunt, then Al took the bunt sign off and Wes threw me a hanging slider and I got it all. I hit a couple game-winning home runs in games I pitched, but I remember this one the most because I was pinch-hitting."

Lopez became so enthralled by Peters' bat that once, at Yankee Stadium, he penciled Gary's name into the No. 6 spot in the White Sox batting order—a noble experiment designed to give Peters an extra crack, perhaps, at that short porch in right. The Sox went three-up and three-down in the top of the first and then the Yankees shelled Peters from the mound in their half of the inning. End of experiment.

More often than not, though, Peters wouldn't get shelled around by too many teams. Oh, sure, there were the Twins, who Gary was unable to beat until 1966. But Minnesota was the exception to the rule. With his effortless delivery, Peters set down one hitter after another, no matter how fearsome. Even the Yankees of '63 and '64—with Mantle, Maris, Howard, Pepitone, Tresh, etc.—were seldom able to score more than a run or two against the Sox' lefty. Unfortunately, a run or two was all they needed, because inevitably Peters was paired up against New York's Whitey Ford. Ford could've pitched under-handed and the White Sox still would not have been able to hit him. They were that mesmerized by the guy.

"I got to talking to Whitey the last year he played," Gary remembered. "And I'd never beaten him. And he beat me five times, and four of them were by one run—either 1-0, 2-1, or 3-2. All during those two years, '63 and '64. I was trying to get him to go one more year so I could get another shot at him. But he retired."

That was in 1967. A year later, Peters must have been giving some thought to retirement himself. He won only four games for the Sox, who were in their slide from contender to loser. His victory total increased to 10 in 1969 but his earned run average climbed to 4.53, which meant he was giving up twice as many runs as he had in 1967. But then again, so was everyone else on the staff.

"When you're on a team like that and it goes bad, you don't reflect much on it because there are no pleasant memories," Gary said of the '68 and '69 seasons. "Especially after you play on a team that is a contender, like we were all those years. It makes it a lot harder to play when you're 20 games out than when you're two or three games out. It really makes it a job, and it's more tiring. When you have your team failures, you can't do much about it. I just try to forget it."

He doesn't forget the day he was traded by Ed Short to the Red Sox during the winter of '69-'70. In return the Sox received an infielder, Sydney O'Brien, who lasted only one year, and a pitcher, Bill Farmer, who didn't even last a week. Farmer showed up at spring training with a sore arm and the Sox demanded a replacement. The Red Sox gladly surrendered righthander Jerry Janeski, who immediately became a fixture in the Chicago rotation because the Sox were so short of pitching. Opposing hitters' eyes would light up at the mere mention of his name. The reasons were obvious: Jerry gave up the incredible amount of 247 base hits in the 206 innings he worked. In short, he spent the entire 1970 season in the stretch position.

Meanwhile, Peters was having a much better time of it. He won 16 games for Boston in 1970 (despite a 22-13 beating handed him on May 31 by the White Sox, of all people) and 14 more in '71 before closing out his career in '72 with 33 relief appearances. "I didn't like to leave Chicago," he said. "I always liked Chicago. But financially, I was better off being traded to the Red Sox. And at that time, I was going to a better ballclub.

"Fenway Park? They always say lefthanded pitchers hate Fenway Park. But I liked it."

I thought of Fenway's Green Monster, just 315 feet from home plate. Then I thought of Comiskey Park's distant walls, the heavy night air, the soggy infield, and frozen baseballs. Gary Peters may have liked Fenway Park. But he must have loved Comiskey Park.

TOMMY JOHN:
The Shutouts Just Keep Coming

I was sitting alongside Tommy John in the visitors' dugout at Comiskey Park. The night before, the ace of the New York Yankee pitching staff had made the White Sox look foolish. He had shut out the team with which he had spent seven years for the third time in the 1980 season—which was barely half over.

It had seemed odd to see Tommy in a visitors' uniform, pitching in Comiskey Park. He was still wearing that familiar No. 25 on his back, still throwing as effortlessly as ever, and still involved in another of his trademarks: a 1-0 ballgame. Only this time the tables were turned. The visitors had the run. The Sox were being shut out.

I asked him what was coming back to him as he sat and looked across the vast ball field he used to call home. "The teams that I remember here are the teams of '65, '66, '67, and '68," said the left-hander who had come to Chicago from Cleveland along with Tommy Agee and Johnny Romano before the '65 season began. "After that, I try to forget what happened. We had a changeover. They traded Peters, and Horlen was on his way out. Hansen was gone and McCraw was traded. All the guys started to filter out.

"Then they put the astroturf in (in '69) and my earned run average

303

Tommy John

went from 1.98 to 3.25. I'd just give up groundball base hits. See, when you have astroturf, it's imperative that you've got to have speed. We had zero speed. We had nobody to cover the infield like you have to have. A lot of groundballs were going through for base hits."

They were the same groundballs that, in previous years, had been slowed down by the soft Comiskey Park infield and its tall grass and thus turned into easy outs by Chicago infielders. By now, the astroturf had long since been torn out—a victim of Bill Veeck's overhaul in 1976—and natural turf was back in vogue. But the ground was nowhere near as soft nor the grass as tall as when Tommy had been pitching shutouts for the Sox. So when Roger Bossard, whose father Gene had been keeper of "Bossard's Swamp" back in the '60s, poked his head into the Yankee dugout to congratulate John on his previous night's performance, Tommy grinned and told him, "The grass could've been a little higher. You should make it a little softer around home plate too."

Bossard walked away laughing, but John surely wasn't laughing in the days of the astroturf. After all, his whole style of pitching had been predicated on keeping the ball down, so the hitters would hit nothing but groundballs. "Eddie Stanky bought us suits of clothes," he said. "You had to have 20 groundballs, go nine innings, and win. Now, they didn't all have to be groundball outs. They could be groundball singles, they could be line drives that the infielders could catch. Anything from the head down.

"Eddie's thinking was, if you keep the ball down to a line drive or groundball, you're gonna have to give up two or three base hits to score a run. You were better off that way than throwing up a lot of home runs or doubles and triples."

John won more clothes from Stanky than any other Sox pitcher, mostly because he threw so many sinkers and because he had long since mastered the mechanics of pitching as taught by Professor Ray Berres. "That's right—it was in the middle of a golf swing," Tommy said, remembering how Berres had gotten through to him back in Sarasota in 1965. "The things he was trying to tell me, I couldn't grasp. Then when he related it to golf, I said, 'Yeah—OK, now I see what you're talking about.' He just illustrated it to me in terms I could

305

understand. And, to me, that's a good instructor.

"I was rushing. I was really rushing with my body and I would get my body in front of my arm—tremendously in front of it. And he was just trying to get me to throw more like you would swing a golf club. Because almost everything in sports is timing. There are other factors involved, obviously. But that was one of the things that Ray and Al Lopez were really big on—timing, delivery, the mechanics of throwing a baseball.

"I know many a time I would hear Al Lopez's whistle when I would get to dropping down—not to where I'd be throwing sidearm, but where I'd be dropping my elbow. A lot of people say, 'Well, he's dropping down.' And they think that's throwing sidearm. But all it is is that your elbow drops down lower and it cuts the arc of your arm as you throw. And as a result you don't get as good a movement nor the speed on the ball."

Lopez and Berres brought John, then just 22, along slowly in '65. "The first game I pitched in was a relief appearance against Baltimore and I came in and struck out Boog Powell to save the ballgame," Tommy recalled. "And my first start was here in Sox Park against Baltimore and I beat 'em 3-1."

He wound up 14-7 that season, and then—under new manager Stanky—went 14-11 with a 2.62 ERA and a league-leading five shutouts in 1966. The next year, he led the league with six shutouts—yet won only 10 games while losing 13 times, despite a 2.47 ERA. That was the season Tommy missed almost six weeks because of an ailment that he acquired while serving two weeks of summer duty with the Indiana Air National Guard in his hometown of Terre Haute.

"I got some sort of stomach virus of undetermined origin," he said. "I lost 25 pounds in 10 days. I couldn't eat, and I had diarrhea, I was vomiting—really sick. They ran all sorts of tests for me, on me, through me, around me. And they came up with nothing. I just had some mysterious bug. I got sick in July (when he was 8-5) and I didn't come back till mid-August. When I came back, I was still weak. I'd go five-six innings and be pooped. My best game after that, I shut out Boston at Fenway Park and threw one of the best games I've ever pitched."

John's protracted absence is just another of the many excuses summoned forth by Sox fans when they try to explain why their team failed to win the '67 pennant. At least the next year, there was no pennant race to worry about. "I thought we made some bad trades after the '67 season," Tommy declared. "We got rid of Agee, Buford, Al Weis, and we just got a lot slower. We gave away our strength—speed. And that didn't help. Then we lost 10 in a row at the start of the season and I broke the string with a 3-2 win over the Twins in Minnesota."

Actually, '68 was one of John's finest years (10-5, 1.98 ERA) and it could've been much better had not his season ended earlier than expected. One August afternoon at Tiger Stadium, Tommy let a 3-2 pitch get away from him and Dick McAuliffe was flattened. Instead of walking to first, the Tiger second baseman made a beeline for the mound. "I wanted to go on pitching," said John. "So I figured a tackle and a roll on the ground would be the best way to avoid any trouble. I was worried about Willie Horton coming out and pinching my head off like a pimple."

So Tommy went down to one knee and got set to tackle McAuliffe. But McAuliffe's knee jarred Tommy's left shoulder, tearing ligaments and forcing John to leave the game. "That was the 22nd of August," he remembered. "And I missed the rest of the season. I never knew Dick before then and I don't know him now. I just never knew the guy. It was one of those things that happens in the heat of battle."

Sox pitching took a lot of heat during the '69 and '70 seasons, but John was by far the most successful of the Chicago hurlers. He was 9-11 in '69 (when the team was 68-94) and he was 12-17 in '70 (when the team was 56-106). Those were the years the Sox wore blue sanitary hose under white stirrups, and players complained that their toenails were turning blue. "No, my toenails didn't turn blue," said John. "My feet did, though."

The whole team turned blue—and died. "We just had a horrible team. It was like, you pitched until you lost. If you pitched a good game, you had a chance to tie. If you pitched a mediocre game, you had a sure loss. It was disheartening. You would go out to the ballpark and you knew you had very little chance to win. Everybody felt the same way. The best thing the Sox did then was to bring Chuck (Tanner) in here, get some new thinking, and trade some of the guys.

307

"And then, of course, to get me out of here and over to the Dodgers," he added, grinning.

I told him that, for a year or two anyway, the trade which sent him to the Dodgers and had brought Richie Allen to the White Sox had all the appearance of a holdup. "I tell you," he said, "the White Sox made an outstanding trade. Anytime you can trade a pitcher for a ballplayer like Dick Allen, you've got to make the trade. He was an outstanding ballplayer and he was exactly what this franchise needed at that time.

"I hated to leave. Well, I didn't mind going to the Dodgers because I was going to a championship-caliber ballclub. But I hated to leave Chicago because Chicago's one of my favorite places. My wife and I love Chicago. We have dear friends here and this is one of our favorite spots, because we're midwestern people and Chicago is a typically midwestern city."

Yankee coaches, having nothing better to do, were starting to chase writers out of the dugout by now. The game would start in less than 10 minutes, and Steve Trout was finishing his warmups down in the Sox bullpen along the leftfield line. I got up to leave, thanking Tommy for his time and wishing him continued success.

When I got home, I checked some figures. Going into the 1980 season, Tommy had won 108 games since leaving the White Sox—and that figure would be higher had he not missed a season and a half because of the elbow injury that led to the now-celebrated tendon transplant operation which provided him with what he calls "my bionic arm." He pitched for pennant-winning Dodger teams in '74, '77, and '78 and was a hero in the National League playoffs those last two years. The shutout of the White Sox the night before we'd met was his 13th victory of the 1980 season. He was going to be a 20-game winner again for the third time in the last four years. Tommy John was still going strong at age 37.

Richie Allen, the record books show, hit .240 in 54 games for the Oakland A's in 1977, was released before the season was half over and retired to his Pennsylvania farm at age 35.

Maybe it wasn't such an outstanding deal after all.

WILBUR WOOD:
Knuckling Down to Business

It seems strange these days to stop and realize that the White Sox don't have any knuckleballers anymore. The Sox, it seemed, always had a guy who threw the knuckleball.

Gerry Staley threw the pitch on occasion when he worked for Chicago in the late '50s and early '60s. Then came the knuckleball king, Hoyt Wilhelm. "Dr. Wilhelm and His Dancing Medicine Show," Bob Elson used to say. The Good Doctor was the most effective relief pitcher the team has ever had. His statistics, looking back, are simply incredible: 68 saves his first three years in Chicago, an ERA below 2.00 five straight years. Al Lopez would bring him in with a one-run lead and the game was over. The other team never had a chance.

The Doctor was joined in the bullpen by Eddie Fisher, the Donald Duck impressionist whose knuckleball helped to make life all the more miserable for the White Sox' designated knuckleball catcher, J.C. Martin. Fisher appeared in a record (at that time) 82 games for the Sox in 1965, when he won 15 games and saved 24 more. But the next season, with the Sox badly needing infielders, Ed Short sent Fisher to Baltimore for Jerry Adair. That winter, realizing things weren't the same with only one knuckleballer around to cause Martin grief, Short

Wilbur Wood

traded Juan Pizarro to Pittsburgh, which in return gave up a chunky lefthanded pitcher by the name of Wilbur Wood—winner of 14 games for the Pirates' Columbus farm club in '66 and, reports indicated, possessor of a pretty fair knuckleball.

The rest, as they say, is history.

"I'd always thrown the knuckleball, even in high school," said Wilbur as we sipped coffee in a small cafe no more than 200 yards from the Minuteman statue in Wood's hometown of Lexington, Mass. "So it wasn't an entirely new pitch. It was just something where, in '67, it was, 'Either I'm gonna make it or I'm going home.' I'd played seven years of pro ball and I had to make a decision."

He decided, with Wilhelm's help, to go with the knuckler all the way. "I hadn't been that successful with my fastball and curveball at the major league level (a 1-8 won-lost record before '67), so Hoyt just kinda turned it around. He told me, 'If you're gonna throw the knuckleball, you've got to throw it 80-90 per cent of the time—this is your out pitch and this is what you're gonna get the hitters out with.' So it just happened that I decided right then and there, the second day of spring training, that I'm gonna do it and let's see what happens. It worked out very well for everyone."

It worked out so well that Woodie wound up pitching a dozen seasons for the White Sox, first as a standout reliever and then as a workhorse starter. He led the league in appearances in '68, '69, and '70 and then led it in games started in '72, '73, '74, and '75. He won 20 games four straight years for the Sox and was named to the American League all-star team three times. But Wood, in his first year in Chicago, didn't give any indication of coming greatness.

"That year," he remembered, "I started eight ballgames, all in a row—during June and July when the doubleheaders started piling up. Those starts were my whole record (4-2). I didn't win or lose a game in relief. Locker and Wilhelm (and later Don McMahon) were the short men. I was more or less the middle man. I ended up in 51 ballgames with a good earned run average (2.45). It was my first year in the big leagues with any amount of success."

It was also his first pennant race. "We went into Kansas City the last week of the season," said Woodie, beginning to frown. "It was an off-day. We had five games left. And we all took a vote to work out

311

on that off-day. Now you'd wonder why we'd want to work out on an off-day with only five games left. But we'd had such a terrible record that year in games after an off-day—1-10 or something like that. So we voted to work out. We had like an intrasquad game, just to keep the momentum going. And then it rained the next day and we couldn't play, had to play a doubleheader the next day and we lost both games."

The losing continued into the next season as well. "We just got off to a horrible start—and it didn't figure," Woodie said as we began on our second cup of coffee. "We came out of spring training with a good record. We had what everyone considered a little better defense and more punch—without hurting the pitching staff, which was just about intact. But it just fell through. We were something like 2-18 and we never got back into it."

But for Wood personally, 1968 was a rousing success. He was the league's Fireman of the Year, with 12 victories in relief and another 16 saves in 88 games. "I set the American League record that year," he recalled. "That was just being in the right spot at the right time. Hoyt's arm was bothering him at the beginning of the year. And Bob Locker's arm was bothering HIM at the beginning of the year. And so I got a chance and I got off to a pretty good start."

He continued the good work in relief for two more years (10 victories, 15 saves in 76 games in '69, nine victories, 21 saves in 77 games in '70). Then came the arrival of a new manager, Chuck Tanner, and a new pitching coach, Johnny Sain. The pair came to Chicago with new ideas. "In '71," Wilbur said, "they had Terry Forster there. Nineteen years old. Both Johnny Sain and Chuck would rather have the young fireballer—someone with real good velocity—as a relief pitcher. So at the beginning of the season, I was kinda forgotten. I wasn't pitching at all."

But then Joe Horlen, one of Tanner's starting pitchers, suffered a knee injury. Tanner and Sain came up to Wood and asked him if he'd like to give starting a try. "I was apprehensive about it, because if I didn't do the job as a starter, the job in the bullpen wasn't waiting for me. As it turned out, if I hadn't said yes, I wasn't gonna pitch that much. So I started a few ballgames and did well. After a few games, I really enjoyed it. I didn't want to go back to the pen."

He didn't have to worry. True, he didn't win his first game until May 2, when he beat Washington 3-1. And he didn't win again until he shut out the Angels 13-0 in Anaheim May 22. But then, in quick succession, he downed the Royals 7-2 May 26 and the Tigers 3-2 June 4. Woodie was rolling. By July, he was working on a Wednesday-Sunday schedule, which meant he was pitching with only two days' rest when he went to the mound each Wednesday.

"They asked me if I'd like to try starting with two days' rest— which Johnny Sain had done here in Boston with the Braves. And I'd been aware of it. I said, 'Sure, I'd love to try it.' We did it for a year and a half or so."

Actually, it was more than that. In fact, Tanner even had him start both ends of a doubleheader at Yankee Stadium one evening in 1973. Wood lost both games. Earlier that season, Wilbur had completed the final six innings of a 21-inning suspended game against Cleveland and got the victory and then, the same evening, returned to the mound to threw a four-hit shutout at the Indians. "That was funny," Wood said, "because when they went out with the lineup cards at the start of the suspended game, Cleveland wanted 20 minutes between games and Chuck wanted 10. He didn't want me sitting around too long between games. They finally compromised and it wound up 15 minutes between games. So it was just like sitting through a long inning."

He wouldn't have picked up those two victories that night had it not been for the bat of Richie Allen, who, after watching Eddie Leon make a run-costing error in the top of the 21st inning of Game One, settled things with a game-winning home run in the bottom half of the inning. "Dick was gonna hit fifth that inning and he came over to me on the bench and said, 'If we get a couple of guys on base this inning, I'll win this for you right now.' And sure enough, he got up there with two guys on and cranked one out of there to win the game. I'll never forget that one.

"Dick was a helluva guy, on and off the field. Those were the years when the club was really close. You'd go out after a ballgame for a beer or two and before you knew it, there were 12-13-14 guys sitting around a big table—half the ballclub. I think that that had a lot to do with our success. We talked baseball off the field as well as on the field. And I know the last few years I spent in Chicago, you didn't see

313

that as much. You had one group going this way, another group going that way."

Wood himself was going yet another way: downhill. Perhaps the two-days-rest routine was taking its toll. Wilbur still won't admit it, however. "I know I pitched more than 300 innings four straight years (291 the next year, too), but as far as wear and tear goes, I don't think it hurt my arm bad."

I asked him if he thought the hitters in the league had finally gotten a pattern on his knuckleball. "I don't think so," he said, shaking his head. "I think any pitcher, they're gonna try to figure out and try to get a pattern. But the knuckleball—there's just no pattern to it, if you're throwing the ball well. And if you're keeping the ball down. Once you get the ball up, it's death valley."

His knuckleball must have started coming in higher, then, by 1975. The figures don't lie. In '71, his first—and best—year as a starter, Woodie was 22-13 with a 1.91 earned run average plus 210 strikeouts and only 62 walks and 272 hits allowed in 334 innings. The stats grew steadily less impressive until, by '75, he was going 16-20 with a 4.11 ERA, and just 140 strikeouts—and 92 walks and 309 hits allowed—in 291 innings. And then, after getting off to a decent start in '76 (4-3, 2.25 ERA in his first seven starts), Wilbur took a line drive off the bat of Ron LeFlore—then with Detroit—flush on the kneecap. Newspapers across the country carried pictures the next day of Woodie writhing in agony. The kneecap was shattered. Wood's year was over, and though he returned to pitch the next season, and in '78, he wasn't even a shadow of the old Wilbur Wood. His ERA was hovering around 5.00 and he was walking about one man every two innings.

"I think I was trying to be a little cautious with the knee," he said. "Psychologically, it worked against me a little bit, because I think I was trying to put the ball in a given area—which you really can't do. I was trying to protect myself a little bit. I'm not saying I thought about it that much. But looking back at some of the ballgames I pitched, every now and then I could sense myself trying to make that perfect pitch—keep that ball in, keep it in, keep it in. I think that's probably what helped increase my walks."

The walks increased and the losses increased until, in August of 1978, Woodie was dropped from the rotation in favor of rookie Ross

Baumgarten. Wood angrily accused owner Bill Veeck of pulling the strings for manager Larry Doby. Veeck, in turn, didn't hurry to negotiate a new contract with his veteran pitcher, who vetoed September trades to both Milwaukee and Pittsburgh (where he would have been reunited with Tanner) when those clubs refused to guarantee a contract for 1979. So ended the big league career of one Wilbur Forrester Wood, who had debuted in 1961 with his hometown Boston Red Sox. ("They offered me the most money so, yeah, they were my favorite team," he laughed.) And with it ended the drudgery of 12 seasons spent with the White Sox—most of those seasons losing ones.

"The pride was still there, no question about it," he told me. "But when you lose and lose and lose, it hurts. You come down to the last week of August and the month of September, that's when it hurts. You know, 'Do I have to go to the ballpark today?' That starts. You know, 'Gee whiz, do we gotta go out there again today?' You get in the habit of losing day in and day out, it's tough to break. When you're winning, it's great. You can't wait to get to the ballpark. You know, '67, '72, '73—and '77, when we had an awesome ballclub— the season would go by so fast, you'd say, 'What happened?' You wanted to start right up again because things were going so well for everyone on the ballclub."

Now, even though Wood was through with baseball, things still seemed to be going well for him. He appeared to have lost a little weight and he seemed in good spirits. Retirement from baseball, I thought, was suiting Wilbur just fine.

"I'm enjoying myself," he said just as we were parting. "This is the first summer in almost 20 years I've been home all the time with my wife and kids. Last week, we drove up to Maine. I did some fishing. Next week, we'll probably head down to the Cape. I'm having a great time."

And he doesn't have to worry about line drives coming back at his kneecap anymore, either.

315

BILL MELTON:
A Home Run Title for Chicago

Bill Melton did a lot of things for the Chicago White Sox. I was at Comiskey Park the September night in 1970 when he did something I really believed I would never live to see a White Sox player do: His 29th homer of the year disappeared into the leftfield stands, tying Gus Zernial's and Eddie Robinson's all-time club record.

I thought the record would live forever. You can imagine my shock, a few days later, when Melton hit No. 30. It was a stunning message for the baseball world: There IS a Chicago White Sox player capable of hitting 30 home runs in a single season.

Melton, who was in his second full year in the big leagues at the time, would finish the year with 33 homers that season. He would equal that number the next year, only then it would be good for the American League home run title. That was something else Melton had accomplished. No Sox player had ever before won the league home run crown. Later, in 1974, he broke Minnie Minoso's club career home run record of 135. By the time he left—in 1975 in a deal for California Angel first baseman Jim Spencer—Bill had totalled 154 homers in a White Sox uniform.

So he achieved a great deal in his seven years in Chicago. And yet,

Bill Melton makes a diving, backhanded grab of a line drive.

even today, as a successful commercial real estate salesman in Orange County, Cal., he wishes a lot of things could have been different. "The people in Chicago, I knew what they wanted—and that was a winner," he told me from his Newport Beach home. "I met a lot of people there, had a lot of good friends there. And it was frustrating as a ballplayer not to be able to give them what they needed."

Not that he himself didn't try. Here was a fellow who hadn't even played high school baseball. Not 10 years later, he was leading the American League in home runs and developing into an above-average fielding third baseman. "I remember a lot of fear when I was younger," he told me. "I didn't know anything about baseball. I'd played mostly football. I always loved that sport.

"So I had a lot to learn. Then I found myself in Sarasota, Fla., (at the White Sox' minor league camp in 1964), a very confused individual lost among 65 other guys. I think the only time I really thought I could get to the big leagues was when Eddie Stanky first invited me to a big league camp."

That was in 1968. He made it to the majors later that same season. He hit his first major league homer that September in New York and with it came the assurance that he would be the team's third baseman of the future. And that he was. Bill came through with 23 homers and 87 RBI in '69, his first full season, and then established himself as the team's big power threat by clouting those 33 homers in '70 and again in '71. Never mind that a sportswriter came up to him at the all-star game in Detroit in '71 and asked him, "What is it like for you to be named to the all-star team in your rookie year?" The rest of the country may not have known who Bill Melton was, but folks on Chicago's South Side certainly did.

He was king of the South Side that October afternoon in '71 when he hit the home run off Milwaukee's Bill Parsons which gave him the A.L. homer crown. "That was something I HAD to do," he said. "I remember it very well because I did it within myself. I had to prove something to myself."

He had tied Detroit's Norm Cash and Oakland's Reggie Jackson for the lead with two homers the night before while batting in the leadoff spot. All three men were deadlocked with 32 homers, but Detroit and Oakland had finished their seasons. Melton would have one more game left—one more opportunity to break the tie. "If I was competing with Norm Cash and Reggie Jackson," Melton said, "I was as good as or better than them because I wasn't on the same type of team.

"They were contenders (Detroit was second in the East Division that year, Oakland was first in the West). If you're on a good ballclub, you can never do badly. Our ballclub was just on the rise, OK? So it was something I wanted to do for the city. I'll tell you where it came from: from the city, from the ballclub, and from myself. That was my mental attitude. I was so determined.

"It's something I really felt the city needed. Maybe this is egotistical or selfish or whatever, but I really thought if I put my mind to it and tried real hard, I could do it. You could say to yourself, 'Why couldn't he do that for lots and lots of years?' It's something that once you're cornered—all you have to do is be cornered once in your life, and you can produce. But you've got to be cornered.

"So I went out and I did it. Chuck Tanner had me leading off again. First time up, I broke the bat in about eight places, 'cause I was trying so hard. Second time I walked up there and said, 'If he gives me something I want . . .' And I didn't even know what the hell I wanted. But I was determined to do something. I don't think I was satisfied with a tie. If we'd have gone into 15 innings tied, I'd still have been there.

"But I got it clean—nothing cheap. But I was cornered. I wanted to do something for the city No. 1, for the ballclub No. 2, and myself No. 3. That's why I got out of there. Two hours after it was done, I was gone. I was on a plane back to Los Angeles. I never stuck around for the banquet circuit, I never stuck around for any of that stuff. Because I thought it was false. I really thought that sticking around, riding on your glory—that's false. So I got on that plane. I was so happy with myself at that moment because I had done something for that city, for that ballclub."

He does not believe he did enough, however. "See, that day, that week, I was so determined," he continued. "Maybe I should have stayed that determined all through my baseball career. But I let too many things get involved." The main thing, of course, was broadcaster Harry Caray. "You can print this, because I don't like the S.O.B. anyway. But Harry Caray ran the ballclub. People favored him over the ballclub. Had we had a winner, he'd have been forgotten. But seeing as they'd always had a loser, he was gonna stay on top. I didn't mind when he said a lot of things about me. I just can't see running a franchise and tearing it down. I'm saying this six years after leaving there. If you hire a man to build up and create fan enthusiasm —certainly he's done that, he's a helluva announcer—don't tear 'em down to make yourself look good. And that's what he did.

"When you lose, all right, you've got to talk about why you lose. But he foresaw—he's a good forecaster—he foresaw that we were gonna lose this year and the next year, so he figured, 'Let me take care of Harry Caray.' That's the way I felt. But I'll always have that resentment. I'll never hate the man. I don't hate anybody. But I'll always tell myself. 'He went for himself.' And I think of 3½ million people. Not him. I'll always feel that Harry Caray's gonna take care of himself. If he says this stuff, fine, but if that's what it takes to sell the lousy million-dollar contract for radio-TV rights, you're still taking away from the city. I really mean that. That city's more important. Let him be a celebrity. If that's what he needs, fine. But he's still taking away from that city. And that city's a lot more important than he is."

Melton's troubles with Caray began developing after Bill had recovered from back surgery to repair a herniated disc in '72 (the problem had kept him sidelined the entire second half of the year and likely kept the Sox from winning the West Division title—"Without a doubt," said Melton, "we'd have made it happen"). He rebounded to have the finest all-around season of his career in 1973. But Melton slumped to .242 with just 63 RBI in '74 and the White Sox, a preseason pick of many to win a division title, struggled just to finish at .500. Beltin' Bill was the main scapegoat. Others on the team had off-years, but he was a constant target of Harry's because the performances of the Bill Melton of old were still fresh in Caray's memory.

At the time, I believed much of the criticism was unfair, that Melton's back was still bothering him and that he had been drained of much of his former power. Melton, however, set the record straight. "I came back from that injury stronger than I was in my whole baseball career," he insisted. "My mental approach is what caused my bad years in '74 and '75. It wasn't physical. It was all mental. I got down on myself because I wasn't living up to my capabilities and because I was getting tired of listening to that idiot in the booth. That's what tore me down. He was in control of the city. I used to be the darling of the White Sox and all of a sudden I turned into a nothing. Well, that's fine. I could handle that. But I let this stupid guy bother me. It was a mental thing."

Finally, he had to get away, after a '75 season in which he batted only .240 with a mere 15 homers. "I only asked to be traded to California because it was to take care of my family. It was tearing me apart. I felt the best thing for my family—not just because I lived in California—was to get the hell out of Chicago. 'Cause I could take no more. So I left.

"OK, I get to California, and I really wanted to play for them bad. I run into Dick Williams, very successful manager at Oakland, where he had great ballplayers. Now he's with a loser. I played some at the beginning and then, all of a sudden, I found myself on the bench. I made up my mind that I wanted out of California. Here I go again, saying, 'Hey, I can't handle this anymore.' So I said to Williams that I wanted to be traded and the last place I wanted to go is Cleveland. So where does he trade me? To Cleveland."

He sat in Cleveland, too, in 1977. A shoulder injury suffered in a home-plate collision with Carlton Fisk put Bill on the bench and opened up an opportunity for newly acquired righthanded hitter Andre Thornton. Thornton started pounding the baseball all over Cleveland's Municipal Stadium and Melton never did get another chance. "Oh, he just flat did it and I just sat the rest of the year," Melton said. "But that's fine. I lost my chance."

He gained free agency, however, at season's end. But there was limited attention given to the 32-year-old designated hitter and part-time third baseman who had hit but six home runs over the previous two seasons. "I made a few calls in the offseason," he said. "Obviously, there was little interest. They all thought I wanted too much. I guess $100,000 was too much. They're all making half a million now. But anyway, my salary got in the way and finally I just told myself I wanted to be home with my family. So I just said, 'I've had it.' "

He remains, however, a White Sox fan. "I follow them in the papers and I go out and see 'em play when they come out here, even though I don't know anyone on the team anymore," he said. He was pleased to hear that the Sox had signed Carlton Fisk. "I'll tell you one thing: I think the city needs something like that. By God, I hope they win something. I really do. That city can really support and if they can win something, man, they will go nuts.

"In '59, I was in the eighth grade and my dad took me to the Coliseum to see the White Sox and the Dodgers in the World Series. I remember that so well. I'll never forget it. Aparicio and Fox and all those guys. By God, they've done nothing since.

"But if it happens, if they ever win something—if it really happens—I think I'm coming back. I don't care if it's only the playoffs. If they get into the playoffs, I'll be there. I won't know a soul, but I'll be there."

Most likely, though, he will not go over and shake hands with Harry Caray.

JORGE ORTA:
The Mexican Bat Dance

Deacon Jones shook his head in disbelief when I told him, in July 1979, that the White Sox were starting to platoon Jorge Orta, the Mexican master of line drives.

"Gee, that's amazing," said the Houston Astro batting coach who once had been the White Sox' minor league hitting instructor. "Jorge is a very quiet young man. I tried to take him under my wing—take him to the post office, the store. He'd come over to the house and sometimes he'd sit there not saying anything for hours. I could speak some Spanish from playing winter ball for four years, and we sort of struck up a good friendship.

"Orta had a quick bat. He has a lot of natural ability. The guy can hit. It was just a matter of encouraging him, then reminding him to do a couple of things at the plate. And he sort of believed in me. Here was a young guy, in a new country, new customs. And he was scared. After a while, he branched out, met new people. He's still shy, but that's his makeup. I always wanted him to be a little more aggressive, but you can't change that.

Jorge Orta rounds third and heads for home.

"I always said that he would lead the league in hitting, but I'm sort of disappointed. I don't know what happened. But they had him playing second base, then they moved him to third, then to left field, then back to second. And that could've been one of the problems, 'cause Jorge is a very sensitive young man . . . very sensitive. And this could've really gotten to him, unless you just go up to him and tell him the reasons. I think he needs to be told, 'Hey, you're my second baseman, come what may.' You'd get more out of him, 'cause the ability's there."

In 1980, Cleveland manager Dave Garcia took Jorge Orta aside and told him that he was going to be his rightfielder, come what may. Jorge responded by being the Indians' most consistent player all season long, hitting between .300 and .310 before winding up at .291. He had hit 30 points less than that in '79 with the Sox, who couldn't seem to understand that when a good hitter gets off to a slow start he usually winds up near his lifetime average anyway. After hitting .180 by the end of May, Jorge started ripping the ball again and was up to the .260s when management decided he would no longer play. The main reason? Impending free agency which was granted Nov. 1. Forty-nine days later, Cleveland signed him to a $1.5 million, five-year contract.

"We would've liked to have had him as a designated hitter against righthanded pitching," said Bill Veeck, who had forgotten how well Orta had hit lefties. "Unfortunately, what he had in mind was simply too much for our pocketbook. He wasn't worth quite that much to us."

When the Indians made their second trip to Chicago in 1980, I was out at the ballpark early to meet Orta. I found him very quiet and still shy, at times almost painfully so. But he was polite and quick to note that he had had no particular desire to leave Chicago in the first place.

"I still miss Chicago," he said in the quiet of the Cleveland clubhouse, empty now except for the two of us and that night's starting pitcher, Ross Grimsley. "A lot of times in Cleveland I just sit and think about friends I have here and guys I used to play with here. My agent did all the negotiating for me. I don't know if the White Sox were close to what Cleveland was going to pay me. I know they wanted me and they told me I was going to play every day. That's all I wanted. I wanted to play every day."

325

And of course, with the White Sox' "talent-laden" lineup, there was no such opportunity. The organization that had told him he was not good enough to play second base or third base or left field for them was now telling him he was not good enough even to be an everyday designated hitter for them. The Cleveland Indians, however, decided differently. Orta would be good enough to play right field for them.

"In spring training," he told me softly, "I asked them where I should go practice. They tell me, 'Go out to right field.' So I did. It was tough at the beginning, but now I'm getting used to it. It has been easier for me than left field. Somebody said it (right field) might be easier for me because I see the ball coming off the bat the same way I did when I played second base. Maybe that is why. But I know other players can play left field and then go to right field and they have no trouble. I have to keep working, keep working."

Jorge Orta always did have to work on his fielding. Paul Richards, who managed the Sox in 1976 and was the fellow who decided Orta couldn't play second base well enough (later he decided Orta couldn't play third base well enough, either), once said, "Jorge Orta never got acquainted with his glove, never met a groundball he liked." But it can also be stated that Jorge Orta never met a fastball he didn't like. He has always been a hitter, ever since he signed at age 17 to play baseball for Fresnillo in the Mexican Center League. In his first full season in pro ball (1971), he hit .423 in 59 games for San Luis Potosi in the Mexican Center League and then hit .362 with 16 home runs in 58 games for Mexicali of the Mexican Northern League.

Sox general manager Roland Hemond, through his friendship with Mexican baseball figure Jesus Carmona, learned of the talents of this compactly built (5-10, 170) young hitter and dispatched scout George Noga to watch him play. Noga returned with rave reviews and Hemond himself went to watch Jorge perform. All it took was one night of Orta in action to convince Hemond to go after him. The Sox signed him to a contract with their Appleton, Wis., farm club and invited him to spring training in Sarasota.

Orta arrived at Sarasota a frightened, homesick 21-year-old. He spoke no English. His wife had just given birth to Jorge, Jr., and he longed to be back with them in Mexico. But he wanted to be a successful ballplayer in America, something his father—Pedro, an out-

standing player for years in Cuba before moving to Mexico in 1947—
had never been. The White Sox were just the right team, too, for Orta.
Manager Chuck Tanner had just about given up on Bee Bee Richard as
a shortstop. This new kid, Orta, was really swinging the bat and
looked like a decent second baseman. Why not, thought Chuck, try
him at shortstop?

When Jorge received word that he would be tried at shortstop, a
position he had never played, he became an even more frightened and
homesick 21-year-old. "I had played second base—just second base—
ever since I had started playing ball," he said. "But the manager can do
whatever he wants. He's the manager and if you want to play you
have to go where they tell you to go. I knew at the time I wasn't a
shortstop. But I told myself I'd give it my best. It was tough. Nothing
is easy, you know."

He opened the '72 season in Kansas City as the Sox shortstop,
playing alongside second baseman Mike Andrews. In three games in
KC, he distinguished himself neither at bat nor in the field. But when
the team opened in Chicago against Texas, Orta—batting second,
behind Pat Kelly and just ahead of Richie Allen—tripled once and
doubled twice and people knew that the White Sox had found themselves a hitter. He would need a bit of seasoning in Knoxville later that
season, but he would return late in the year to deliver a 15th-inning
home run in Oakland to enable the Sox to beat the A's and stay alive
in the American League West race. But his career as a shortstop would
be over and the next year, everyone said, he would be replacing
Andrews at second base.

That, indeed, came to pass. After a slow start, Jorge finished the '73
season a .266 hitter, than shot up to .316 in '74, the season he tied a
league record by collecting five hits in a game on three separate oc-
casions. Still, some doubted. Critics said he was seeing good pitches to
hit because of the man hitting behind him—Allen. So, with Allen
departed from the Chicago scene in '75, Jorge responded by hitting
.304, augmenting that average with 10 triples, 83 runs-batted-in, and a
career-high .450 slugging percentage—plus a spot on the A.L. all-
star team. And his glovework had improved to the point where,
among league second basemen, only Bobby Grich and Jerry Remy
turned more doubleplays than did Orta.

But then came '76 and Richards' decision to make a third baseman—and, eventually, a leftfielder—out of Orta. I asked Jorge how that affected him, if it hadn't bothered him that people were still doubting his ability. His voice was again soft, almost inaudible now. "I'm just a worker, you know. I just go wherever they tell me to go. You know, I'm not a superstar or anything, who would say, 'No—I'm not gonna play over there.' "

So he moved wherever Richards told him to move, all the while struggling somewhat with his hitting and finishing at .274. The next year, Veeck and new manager Bob Lemon decided to move him back to second base and Orta drove in a personal best of 84 runs and batted .282. Don Kessinger took over as shortstop in '78 and Orta seemed better than ever at second base and was hitting well when a wrist injury began hampering him and ultimately sidelined him for the final six weeks of the season. Then came the troubled days of '79, the decision by the front office that Orta's offensive skills no longer made up for his deficiencies afield, and the final embarrassment of being lifted—in a game situation—for a pinch-hitter. And what made it all the more embarrassing for Orta was that the pinch-batter was the diminutive, weak-hitting Harry Chappas.

But now, all that was behind him. His average the night I spoke to him was .306 and the only worry he had was his right ankle, which was now being worked on by the Cleveland trainer. Jorge had complained of soreness in his Achilles tendon, injured on a play at third base a few days earlier. But, he said, it wasn't anything serious. He would be playing that evening.

His name was announced as he stepped into the batter's box in the first inning, and the crowd's reaction was what it had been when he had played for the White Sox: borderline ho-hum. I had never understood why Sox fans, historically strangers to consistent offense on the part of their heroes, had never taken to the quiet Mexican. After all, as Deacon Jones had said, "The guy can hit." I stayed long enough to watch Orta drive a liner into right for a single. I got up to leave, a bit saddened by the realization that, even after eight years of steady, solid performance, Jorge Orta had not left too much of an impression on Chicago's baseball fandom.

Cleveland, perhaps, would be different.

BUCKY DENT:
Thank you, Bill Veeck

To tell the truth, I never really thought Bucky Dent was that great a shortstop. He had a good arm, though, and although his range wasn't terrific, his glove was sure and he always made the routine plays—the plays a major league shortstop has to make.

I think what made him seem better than what he really was were his immediate predecessors. To refresh the memory, although it may be a painful task, Dent followed such forgettable fellows as Bee Bee Richard, Luis Alvarado, Rich Morales, and the immortal Eddie Leon. After a succession of superstars like that, you or I could've put on a uniform and trotted out to shortstop and be declared a sure bet for Cooperstown.

So when Bucky came up from Iowa in August of '73 and didn't botch the first groundball hit to him, Harry Caray began raving about the White Sox' handsome new 21-year-old shortstop. With Harry behind him, Bucky quickly became a South Side favorite, winning more raves by hitting .274 his first full year in the majors and then by driving in as many runs as alleged RBI man Carlos May in 1975. And he led the league's shortstops in fielding percentage, putouts, assists, and doubleplays in '75, the year he was named to the all-star team. It

Bucky Dent

is the memory of those first couple seasons that helps Dent to maintain a warm feeling toward Chicago and its baseball fans.

"I enjoyed playing in Chicago," Bucky said before stepping into the batting cage at the Yankees' training base in Ft. Lauderdale. "I have a lot of good memories of Chicago. I played my first major league game with the White Sox. Roland Hemond and Chuck Tanner were good to me as a young player. They gave me the opportunity to play in the major leagues.

"As far as the town and the people go, I love Chicago. They're good people. They're good sports fans. It's a shame they haven't had a winner yet."

Dent's desire to play for a winner helped prompt his departure from the town he loves. He had his doubts about new owner Bill Veeck from the day it was first splashed across the front pages that Barnum Bill was on his way back to Comiskey Park. Because of those doubts, perhaps, Dent's performance fell off in '76. Still, Veeck offered Bucky a $50,000-a-year raise to $100,000 per annum for three years. Dent, knowing his agent—former pro football star and fellow Floridian Nick Buoniconti—could get him a much more lucrative package from the Yankees, who were desperate for a shortstop, said no thanks and prepared to play out his option. That's when Veeck sent Dent to New York for Oscar Gamble, a pair of minor league pitchers, and $250,000. Chicago's teeny boppers let loose with a flood of tears, yet Bucky received plenty of boos from the Comiskey Park faithful when the Yankees made their first Chicago appearance of the '77 season.

"When Bill Veeck took over the ballclub," Bucky told me, "he made some trades, took out the astroturf, just did some things that made me feel there was no future for the younger players on the club. He said he was trying to build a ballclub, but the kind of people he was trading away—like Gossage, Forster—well, you know . . .

"I just felt being traded to New York was the best thing that ever happened to me. I felt it was gonna take him years to bring a winner there (to Chicago). I didn't feel that he had the money at the time he bought the club, and it's just one those things, you know. If you're gonna be sincere about winning, and you're gonna offer people a championship ballclub, then you're gonna have to go out and spend some money. Coming to New York was the biggest break of my career."

331

Bill Veeck is happy things worked out for Bucky. "I never regretted for a moment the Dent deal," he told me this January. "Bucky's a pretty good shortstop—sure-handed—with their (the Yankees') club. He didn't mean anything to ours. I would rather have (Todd) Cruz than Dent. Lots of others I'd rather have than Dent. But he's good for their kind of team. Just catch the routine balls and they're gonna score some runs.

"Besides, I wanted Gamble. And I got Lamarr Hoyt in that deal, who was 9-3 for us last year. And I got a couple dollars, too."

The trade to the Yankees enabled Bucky to get into a World Series in '77, and for a time that season it looked as if the Yankees' playoff opponent might be the very team Dent had left behind just a few months before. "In '77," Bucky said, "the White Sox had a good ballclub. They had Zisk and Gamble, they had some power. They didn't have any defense at all, and, in the long run, that's what beat them— the defense. But as far as enthusiasm and power and scoring runs, they were right at the top. I think a lot of people were expecting them to do that again in '78, but you can't lose people like Zisk and Gamble and some of the other people they lost and expect to contend."

The only contender Dent had played on in Chicago—the '74 team— had flopped far worse than that '78 team did. "In '74, I thought we had as good a ballclub on paper as anybody, really," Bucky said. "We'd gotten Santo. We had Melton at third, myself, Orta, and Allen on the infield. We had Carlos May, Ken Henderson, and Pat Kelly. That's a pretty good outfield. A pretty good ballclub. It's just that injuries caught up with the ballclub that year. And some of the guys didn't play the way they were supposed to play. It was just a disappointing year all the way around. But it was the best club I played on in my three years in Chicago."

I got the impression from Bucky that the people he remembers with the most fondness from his days in Chicago were not his teammates but Chuck Tanner and infield coach Al Monchak. "Chuck has an inspiring way," Dent said. "He's a very good teacher. He's an exceptional teacher. He gives you confidence. He never at one time in my career in Chicago downgraded me in any way. He's the kind of guy, if you're just breaking into the major leagues, everyone should play for.

"Tanner and Al Monchak were the people who really taught me

how to play the game. I've got to give a lot of credit, too, to my minor league manager, Joe Sparks. I played for him for three years and I felt he molded me into a good shortstop and Al Monchak kinda put the finishing touches on. Al taught me how to play the game, to be knowledgeable about the game. I owe a lot to all those guys."

Bucky excused himself and moved into the batting cage. I watched him take his swings against Whitey Ford, who was pitching batting practice. I thought of the TV movie Dent had starred in, of the posters he'd appeared on, of the pennant-clinching home run he had hit at Fenway Park in '78, and of the two World Series he had played in since leaving Chicago.

He may owe a lot to Al Monchak, Joe Sparks, and Chuck Tanner, I thought. But Bucky Dent owes a lot to Bill Veeck, too.

OSCAR GAMBLE:
Na Na, Hey Hey, Goodbye!

The players' strike was on, but the man at the Yankees' spring training headquarters in Ft. Lauderdale had said there would still be a workout and an intrasquad game the next day. So the next morning, I went out to the small, attractive ballpark the Yankees call their spring home, and, spotting Oscar Gamble and Graig Nettles admiring Reggie Jackson's batting practice swings, approached the batting cage.

Gamble, a fun-loving sort who had helped keep the clubhouse loose during the heyday of the South Side Hitmen in 1977, saw me coming. "Hey," he yelled, taking note of my tape recorder, "I bet you came out here to interview ME, right?"

I told him he had guessed correctly, that I was doing a book on the White Sox. "You sure came to the right place," he said, pointing out to the field. Working out at first was Jim Spencer. Fielding grounders at third was Eric Soderholm. Throwing along the rightfield foul line was Rich Gossage. And standing on the other side of the cage was Bucky Dent, the shortstop the Sox had traded to New York just before the '77 season opened for Gamble, minor league pitchers Lamarr Hoyt and Bob Polinsky, and $250,000.

"I hadn't signed a contract with the Yankees," Gamble remembered.

Oscar Gamble

"I figured I was a six-year player so I was gonna be a free agent. And I was looking to go someplace and get a chance to play. See, around the league, they save a lot of lefthanded pitchers for the Yankees. And that way, being a lefthanded hitter, I got a few more days off—more than I wanted."

Bill Veeck wanted Gamble playing for his White Sox rather than sitting for the Yankees. Veeck held out throughout spring training for a seldom-used Yankee lefty by the name of Ron Guidry, whom he wanted included in the deal instead of the two minor leaguers the Yanks were offering. Finally, New York owner George Steinbrenner and manager Billy Martin, growing impatient at the impasse and not wanting to lose Gamble to free agency with nothing to show for it, were all set to include Guidry. That's when Gabe Paul and scout Birdie Tebbetts stepped in and convinced George and Billy to hang on to Guidry. Veeck, himself growing impatient, then accepted the two minor leaguers instead. At least he had gotten Gamble.

"I went to Chicago and I got a lot more at-bats than I would have if I'd stayed in New York," said Oscar, who got 408 official at-bats with the Sox, plus a team-high 31 homers and a .297 batting average. "I platooned (as designated hitter with Lamar Johnson) most of the year anyway, but the White Sox were a different kind of team than the Yankees were. The White Sox had more righthanded hitters over there, so we saw more righthanded pitching than the Yankees, with all their lefthanded hitters, ever saw.

"So I was glad to go over to Chicago. I got a chance to play. I had a good year, and I got paid pretty good for it after that."

He got paid pretty good, all right. The day before Thanksgiving, 1977, he signed with Ray Kroc's San Diego Padres for a reported $2.8 million for five years. Veeck, when asked if he'd been worried that Gamble would sign with someone else, replied: "I was more worried he would accept our offer."

Veeck's offer wasn't a skimpy one by any means. "Veeck offered me something like $1.8 million for five years," Oscar recalled. "But that didn't come close to San Diego's offer. No way. Over a million dollars' difference. So, you know, it's easy to make a decision when there's that much money involved."

So Gamble left Chicago, but not before he had given the fans a few things to remember him by. There had been that 450-foot blast at Minnesota to pull out a game in the 14th inning. There had been the time he had pinch-hit for Chet Lemon—much to my dismay, and Chet's too, most likely and drilled a shot into the upper deck at Tiger Stadium to win the ballgame. There was the 500-foot smash into the farthest reaches of the uppermost tier of the Kingdome in Seattle. And the big ovation he got at Yankee Stadium when he came up to pinch-hit one night during a six-run rally in the ninth inning of a game the Sox would lose when Chris Chambliss ripped a two-run homer off a lefty named Randy Wiles—who, thankfully, hasn't been heard from since.

"The score was 10-9, and we were down a run," Gamble said. "I got the hit with the bases loaded; that made it 11-10. Then Chambliss hit the home run in the bottom half to win it 12-11. But we played those kinds of games most of the year. We didn't beat the Yankees too often that year (three out of 10), but we played them some tough games."

They played Boston's powerful Red Sox tough, too, beating them seven out of 10, and doing it with power. Chicago, led by Gamble's 31 homers, Richie Zisk's 30, and Soderholm's 25, totaled 192 home runs to set a club record and to wind up second in the league only to Boston in that department. "You go up and down that lineup," said Gamble, "and we had a solid lineup. Everybody was capable of hitting, and everybody came through. I'd gone over there, and we weren't picked to win it, so the guys were nice and loose. We just played good ball and by the first of August, we had a 5-game lead."

But the pitching simply wasn't good enough. The defense wasn't very good either. "But," Oscar pointed out, "we made up for our defense because the guys who couldn't play defense (Ralph Garr, Alan Bannister, Jorge Orta and Zisk) were such good hitters. We didn't have the pitching, but at that point in August, we all felt we had a good chance to win it, anyway. But the last month and a half, we just couldn't get no pitching—couldn't get no starting pitching. And the relievin'—Lerrin LaGrow had had a good year, but I think we just about threw him out that year. He had pitched a lot of games and he was tired. We couldn't get no one to save any games. We'd get a lead and just couldn't hold it."

So the Sox finished third, four games behind second-place Texas and a dozen back of the Kansas City Royals, who simply didn't cool off the final six weeks of the season. Neither, for that matter, did Gamble, who, though not hitting as many homers as he had earlier, nonetheless raised his batting average 40 points over that same period.

"I had about 30 homers with two or three weeks to go," he said. "I was trying to take over the league lead that year." But the pitchers, not wanting to cooperate with Oscar, started giving him more and more pitches away, pitches he couldn't pull. "So I started to go with them, hitting the ball all over, and I think I became a better hitter. And now I think I'm a better hitter than I was with the White Sox, because I can hit the ball all over.

"And last year (1979) I proved to myself, after the year in San Diego when I had a lot of pressure on me, that I am a good hitter. In San Diego, I hit the ball good but nothing happened. I hit for the average, but I didn't hit home runs (he hit .275 with seven homers). The walls out there are 35 feet high. But last year, I came back and I hit the ball the way I want to hit it."

With Texas and the Yankees in '79, Gamble, in 100 games and 247 official at-bats, hit 19 home runs, drove in 64 runs, hit .358, and had a slugging percentage of .604. No one in the Chicago Cub organization had envisioned Gamble as a .604 slugger when Oscar signed with the Cubs out of high school in 1968. "When I was playing sandlot ball, I'd been a home-run hitter," Oscar told me. "When I signed, that's when the Cubs changed me into a spray hitter. They used to have me off the plate with a big ol' 'U-One.' You know, slap the ball and run. 'Cause I used to get down the line in about 3.5. I hit that way with the Phillies for a few years (the Cubs had traded their prize prospect for aging, ex-Sox Johnny Callison—once the Sox' prize prospect), but then I started having trouble with my legs—muscle pulls—and I was jumping at the bag and hurting my ankle. So I couldn't get down there in 3.5.

"So one winter, I went to winter ball and decided to go back to my old way of hitting, and I hit 10 home runs down there. In the meantime, I was traded to Cleveland, and that year (1973) I hit 20 home runs in 390 at-bats. And I was hitting the ball hard all year, so I figured I might as well stay with that rather than go back to trying to slap the ball. I wouldn't be making what I'm making now hitting singles."

338

He surely wouldn't be making what he's making now had he decided to stay with the White Sox. "What Veeck did was, you know, he didn't want to pay out all those big bucks. And it hurts, 'cause I think we had the team there in '77 that, if we'd been together in '79 or the year before that, we might've won it. If he had signed the players, like me and Zisk and Soderholm and the other players that got out of there, and with Lemon and Lamar Johnson, the hitting would've been there.

"Add that to the pitching staff they got now—the young guys they've got coming up and the way they're throwing the ball—I think we'd have won the division in '78 and '79, if you want to know the truth, if we'd have kept the same team. And with the crowds they got out there—I mean they were psyched. If we'd have kept the same team, they'd be drawing 2.5 million. The crowd pumped us up. It was a loud crowd. It was great. Every time you'd come up there, you'd be getting a standing ovation. Every time you'd take the field, you'd get a standing ovation. It was exciting."

Oscar Gamble helped make it so.

LAMAR JOHNSON:
The Elder Statesman

Almost 13 years have passed since Lamar Johnson first signed with the White Sox out of Wenonah High School in Birmingham, Ala. That's a long time, especially when you consider that the White Sox, in that period, have gone through three ownership changes and eight managerial changes.

But Lamar himself hasn't changed a great deal. He still can swing a bat, he still has an easy smile, and he still has an ample paunch, which is made to look even more ample by those strange uniforms the Sox have been forced to wear ever since Mary Frances Veeck decided to delve into fashion designing five years ago. The biggest difference is that Lamar has become the club's elder statesman. At 31, he is the guy who has been around—the guy who has seen it all.

"It's been a lot of ups and downs," he told me just before leaving for another spring training at Sarasota. "I've seen a lot of people come and go. Like when I first signed with the Sox, Art Allyn owned the team. Then his brother, John, owned it. Then Bill (Veeck) came in and now we get somebody else. Everytime somebody new comes in I watch how the personnel changes and watch how the new owners' way of thinking changes the ballclub."

340

Lamar Johnson batting against the Angels during 1980 season. Catcher is Brian Downing, a former White Sox.

And generally, during the big first baseman's time in the organiza-tion, the arrival of new owners hasn't made a great deal of difference on the field. The Sox have plodded on down the path of defeat. They first set foot on that path in 1968—the same year, oddly enough, that Lamar signed with Chicago.

"Sam Hairston scouted me and signed me, along with Walt Widmayer," Johnson said, remembering the rather accidental way in which he was discovered. "Jerry Hairston, Sam's son, was playing high school baseball in Birmingham, also. And Sam just happened to come out to see Jerry play. We were playing Jerry's team that day and I had a real good game, and he started watching me after that.

"I had a really good season and finally Sam asked me if I wanted to sign to play professional baseball. And I had thought about it when I was younger but at that time I was really geared up for football, be-cause I really enjoyed it—I played defensive end and outside line-backer—and I had a lot of offers, mostly from the black colleges in the South. I had already signed a letter-of-intent to go to Tuskegee Institute. Baseball was really secondary at that time, and it took a long discussion between myself, my brother, and my dad.

"We sat and talked about it and the thing about it was, in football I had had some injuries. And my brother pointed out to me that a football player's career is not that long. Sooner or later you wind up getting hurt. So we decided on baseball. But we had to convince my mom that that was the best thing to do, because she wanted me to go to college and I already had that free scholarship to Tuskegee. So we had to compromise, and eventually I went to two years of junior college."

And the career in baseball was under way. Early on, there were stops in Sarasota, Duluth-Superior, and Appleton. At Appleton in 1971, he hit 18 homers and drove in 97 runs. The Sox front office wasn't especially enthusiastic: He was sent back to Appleton for the '72 season. Such odd decisions were to become commonplace. After hitting .313 at Appleton in '72 and .293 at Knoxville in '73 and after getting off to an excellent start in '74 with Iowa, he was summoned to the big leagues that June. "They needed a righthanded hitter," Johnson recalled, "because Buddy Bradford had just broken his collarbone. So they brought me up."

But all Lamar did was sit on the bench. Richie Allen was still in his heyday and Ron Santo was the righthanded designated hitter, so no one could ever figure out why Johnson had been called up in the first place—least of all Lamar. "Then they figured they needed an outfielder, so that's when they brought Bill Sharp up and sent me back down."

But Lamar had had his first contact with manager Chuck Tanner, who was not destined to become one of Johnson's all-time favorites. The relationship hit its nadir in April 1975, when Johnson—who had finished the '74 season at Iowa with a .301 average, 20 homers, and 96 RBI—read in the papers that the Sox had acquired ancient Deron Johnson to serve as a righthanded designated hitter and backup first baseman. Which meant that Lamar was being sent back down to Triple-A ball.

"It was a big letdown," he said, "because they had told me if I had a big spring that I could make the club. And I felt I had done everything that they asked me to do. I thought they shouldn't have built me up like that and tell me one thing and then do another. I told Chuck how I felt. I think as a manager you should be able to listen to what your players have to say even though what they're saying you don't like. So I just told him and Roland (Hemond) exactly how I felt. We really had it going there for a while, myself and Chuck.

"I felt like he was hurting me as a ballplayer. That's one thing we've discussed, as ballplayers, about Tanner. I see now that he don't like to bring up too many young guys. He brings up maybe one a year. He don't give all the guys in Triple-A a chance. And it hurt me and hurt a lot of other players. I guess that's just the way some managers run their ballclubs. They'd rather trade for an experienced player 'cause they know exactly what he can do. They want to win right now and they don't want to take a chance on a younger player."

But Bill Veeck bought the club after that '75 season (which Lamar spent at Denver hitting .336 with another 20 homers and 101 RBI) and immediately disposed of Tanner. "One thing that stands out in my mind was my first encounter with Bill Veeck," said Johnson. "When he first came over here, he told me I would get a chance to play. Which is the one thing I hadn't gotten before. I have to say that he stood by his word and gave me the chance to play."

343

Lamar responded by hitting .320 in 82 games in '76 with the Sox and followed up with 18 homers and a .302 average in 374 at-bats in '77, when he enjoyed perhaps his finest moment as a big leaguer. Before a Sunday doubleheader with Oakland that June, he stepped up to a public address microphone behind home plate and sang the National Anthem in stirring fashion. Then the doubleheader began. Mike Norris of the A's surrendered just three hits the entire first game. Two of those hits were homers by Johnson. The third hit was a double by Johnson. The Sox won 2-1.

"That's one game I'll probably remember the rest of my life," he said. "That was my most outstanding day in baseball."

Later that same season, Johnson came up as a pinch-hitter for lefty-hitting Oscar Gamble in the fourth inning of a Friday night game against visiting Boston. The Red Sox had just changed pitchers, bringing in southpaw Bill Lee to replace righthander Bob Stanley. Sox runners were at first, second, and third. Lee's second pitch was launched to deep center field. Boston's Fred Lynn kept running and running, but the ball kept carrying and carrying. It finally bounced on the warning track, 440 feet from home plate. By the time Lynn had gotten the ball back into the infield, three runs had scored and Johnson was perched on third. And 41,597 fans were going wild. It was a scene typical of that '77 season.

"I think they put a really good team together in 1977," said Lamar, "and all we needed was just to be patient. We had young pitchers in the minor leagues who were throwing real well. We had a great offensive attack. All we had to do was keep the team intact. If we'd have kept the same team—a lot of those guys are still doing real well— we could be right up among the top teams in the American League. But unfortunately, Bill didn't have the capital to do that—to keep all those players here.

"Really, I think the White Sox have done quite well, for all the things we've had to go through. We change personnel every year, we change managers. We've lost six or seven guys to free agency. You just can't expect to lose that type of ballplayer with that type of experience and replace him with a rookie and expect the same job to get done. And I just think we've done really well with what we've had to work with."

With the advent of new ownership, there promises to be more to work with than there has been in all the time Johnson has spent in the Sox organization. At the time we talked, Chicago newspapers were filled with stories of the White Sox' pursuit of free-agent catcher Carlton Fisk, the Boston all-star. Lamar was impressed.

"It makes me optimistic," he said. "At least they're trying to get the type of player we'll need in order to be competitive. I'm happy to see that now someone's here who's thinking that way, that if they just keep what they've got and get a player here and a player there, they can make our team that much stronger.

"It's a great feeling. You know you have those type of people here who aren't interested in just puttin' on a show. They want to put a winning team on the field. And I think that if you put a winning team on the field, the people will come, regardless of what promotion you give 'em or don't give 'em. They want to see you win, number one."

And Lamar Johnson, who has seen so much defeat during his career in Chicago, would like nothing better than to be a part of that winning team. "I've had some great moments in a White Sox uniform," he conceded, "but the team hasn't been a winner. And I just hope somebody can give the fans exactly what they deserve. They've been very faithful and loyal fans and I think they deserve a winner. And I hope and pray that the owners we've got now can give it to them.

"It should be our time. We've been down for a long time. I think it's time for the White Sox to come back."

Untold legions of Sox fans will loudly second that motion.

BOB ELSON:
"ANdover Three, Two-oh, Two-oh . . . "

I grew up in an era when the only White Sox games on television were home day games. And even then, there weren't many of those. So you had to tune to WCFL radio if you wanted to find out how the Sox were doing. And the late Bob Elson was always there, ready to assuage your money problems, in that deliberate style of his, with a commercial for General Finance Loan Co., the Sox' perennial sponsor.

Then, it was back to the game. Seldom would Bob become excited. Even a Sox home run, rare though it was, would elicit only: "There's a White Owl wallop, and a box of White Owl cigars for Walt Dropo." Once Gene Freese belted a Pedro Ramos fastball into the upper deck in left to win a ballgame in the last of the ninth. Bob's reaction was, as usual, devoid of excitement: "There's a drive to left . . . it might be out of here . . . gone . . . home run . . . the game is over."

In other words, Bob was the complete opposite of Harry Caray. When the Sox pulled one out, he wouldn't be dancing in the booth. When the Sox blew one, he wouldn't be going on and on after the game, recreating for the fifth time that night the bonehead play or dumb pitch that had meant defeat.

"If the Sox lost, I wasn't gonna jump off the roof," Bob said between

The late Bob Elson shown interviewing Walter Williams, who has somehow managed to obtain an Andy Frain usher's cap.

puffs on his ever-present cigar as we chatted in the lobby of the Drake Hotel. "I was pulling for them, naturally. I knew the players, travelled with them, wanted the team I was with to win. That's a natural thing. But I wasn't gonna commit suicide if they lost. If they got beat on a two-hitter, well, Newhouser deserved to win the game—that's it for tonight, we'll see you tomorrow. I mean, what's the use of yelling and screaming about it? It's not gonna change anything. I think that's the sane approach."

And also the safe approach. Unlike Caray, whose comments often infuriate the players, Elson often infuriated his listeners with his apologist-style broadcasting. But that never bothered him. "I never had trouble with anybody," he told me. "And I broadcast big league baseball for 40 years. And I never knocked anybody—a player, a manager, an umpire, nobody. In my own personal estimation of my career, that's the highlight: I never knocked anybody. I always used to say that errors, like hits and runs, are all part of this game. Anybody can make an error."

Elson saw plenty of errors in his long career. "I started in 1930. I did the Cubs and the Sox. We had five stations all doing the same game. It's the only time in history that's ever happened in any city. We'd do the Cubs when they were home; when they'd leave town, we'd all go out and do the Sox. When they'd leave town, we'd all go back over to Wrigley Field to do the Cubs.

"So we had five stations, including four 50,000-watters, all doing the same game. There were no soap operas in those days, so the women either had to listen to baseball or shut the radio off. So the women learned their baseball by listening to the radio. Didn't learn it by watching it on TV, because there was no TV."

But there was baseball and, because of it, Elson, inducted into the Hall of Fame two years before his death this spring, had plenty of memories. "But I don't think back to the times," said Bob. "I think back to the people. I liked Ted Lyons very much—he came out of Baylor University right into the big leagues and stayed. One of only four in history who did that—one was Mel Ott. And Lyons was a great pitcher, a wonderful pitcher. I was very fond of him. Oh, and guys you'll forget, like Willie Kamm. They had a great shortstop by the name of Bill Cissell in the Kamm years. Then Jackie Hayes, the second baseman, a marvelous guy. I had a lot of favorites. I loved Jungle Jim Rivera. He was a show in himself. I saw him make a number of great catches—he was unbelievable out there. Nellie Fox was a great competitor—great attitude, a great love for the game.

"Thornton Lee was a great lefthander and Bill Dietrich—I saw his no-hitter against the Browns. So I had a lot of favorites, and not all on the Sox. I was always a Sox fan, but I loved the game for the people that doing baseball enabled me to become very close to. One of my best friends was Joe DiMaggio. Another one of my friends was Ted Williams. Whitey Ford—those kinds of guys had great talent. Lou Gehrig. I introduced Lou Gehrig to the girl he married. She lived on the South Side. That movie, 'Pride of the Yankees'—that was kind of a fallacy the way they had him meeting his wife. He was a great ball-player. He was a great person. I was very, very fond of him. He was one of the greatest Yankees of them all."

I asked him if there weren't, among all those thousands of games he saw, some that stood out more than others. "I broadcast the first all-star game, at Sox Park, in 1933," he told me. "Babe Ruth hit the home run with Charlie Gehringer on board. I broadcast the game in 1938 when Gabby Hartnett hit the home run in the darkness. I broadcast 12 World Series and 10 all-star games, so I've had a lot of thrills. But certainly that September night in Cleveland in '59 was one of my greatest thrills."

And low points? "The last week of the season in '67, when we had Horlen and Peters, our two best pitchers, going at Kansas City in the doubleheader and we lost both games. That was a tragic affair. If we'd have won even one of those games, we'd still have been in great shape."

It wasn't long after that that Elson, who rose to the rank of commander in the Navy and was also a master gin rummy player, left the White Sox and spent a year on the broadcasting team of the Oakland A's. "I didn't enjoy that year very much," Bob said. "No, Charlie Finley is not one of my favorite people. The reason I went out there, the Sox had lost 106 games in 1970 and it was very depressing. So after all, I'd done it for so many years, so I decided to give Oakland a shot. Red Rush (his Sox sidekick) was going out there and he wanted me to go with him.

"I never enjoyed it. Finley won't let you enjoy anything. He's a very smart baseball man, and he put together a championship team, all by himself. But he missed the human equation. People don't mean anything to him. And that's a sad state of affairs."

So Elson came back to Chicago after the '71 season and became Northwest Federal Savings' radio spokesman, doing a weekly sports show from the bank's lobby. Occasionally, he would comment on Chuck Tanner's "25 sets of rules for 25 players" system of managing, which, Bob said, simply meant two sets of rules: one set for Richie Allen and one for the other 24 players on the Sox roster. Elson predicted that eventually such a setup would backfire. He didn't gloat when it did.

"I have nothing against Richie Allen—he was a great ballplayer," he said. "But baseball as a career never meant anything to him. Look at Pete Rose. He'd go through that brick wall over there to save a ball-game. Sure he's getting a lot of money, but he deserves it. Richie Allen was well-paid, but the game didn't mean that much to him. I felt sorry for him. And I bet he feels sorry for himself now. If he had it to do all over again, he'd be a different man.

"See, if God has given you the gift to play major league baseball, the least you can contribute, besides your talent, is a good attitude. Appreciate it. If you don't appreciate it, in any business, what good are you?"

Bob Elson appreciated baseball and what baseball did for him.

"I loved the game. I loved the game for what it meant to me and what it means to the fans. Baseball's a great game. Anybody who's privileged to spend, as I have, 40 years in big league ballparks, has got to be lucky."

I count myself lucky for having been privileged to grow up listening to Bob Elson.

JACK BRICKHOUSE:
"Capturing these baseball headlines as they're being made."

A generation ago, Jack Brickhouse was imploring his WGN-TV audiences to forget their troubles, their day-to-day worries, and come out to the ballpark and let Al Lopez and Casey Stengel do their worrying for them. A generation later, Jack Brickhouse was telling his audiences to forget their troubles, their day-to-day worries, and come out to the ballpark and let Preston Gomez and Tom LaSorda do their worrying for them.

Nearly thirty years ago, I heard Brick say, as the camera zoomed in on Sox manager Paul Richards, "There's the bossman." Last summer, I heard him say, as the camera zoomed in on Preston Gomez, "There's the bossman."

Twenty-five years ago, Yogi Berra, with two on and two out in the ninth inning and the White Sox protecting a one-run lead, drove a ball deep down the rightfield line. The ball sailed into the seats, only a few feet foul. Brickhouse: "Whoo, boy! Next time around, bring back my stomach!"

Twenty-five years later, Mike Schmidt, with two on and two out in the ninth inning and the Cubs protecting a one-run lead, drove a ball deep down the leftfield line. The ball sailed out onto Waveland

Jack Brickhouse in the booth at Wrigley Field. [PHOTO COURTESY WGN]

Avenue, only a few feet foul. Brickhouse: "Whoo boy! Next time around, bring back my stomach!"

One of the charming things about Jack Brickhouse is that, in all the years he's done baseball on television, only the names have changed. Or so it seems. Actually, the teams have changed too. Jack, from 1948 through 1967, did both the Cubs and White Sox games on WGN. Then, when Marshall Field's new UHF station, WFLD, offered the White Sox a staggering sum of money for the rights to televise practically all the South Siders' games, the Sox said goodbye to WGN and Jack Brickhouse. (Perhaps not coincidentally, the Sox also said goodbye to the rest of the American League, losing, in the next three years, 95, 94, and 106 games.)

So Jack found himself totally aligned with the Cubs. Most of us assumed that's the way he preferred it anyway. With the Cubs, he could say "Hey hey" much more often than he could with the White Sox, because home runs at Wrigley Field, due to wind conditions and the not-too-distant ivy-covered outfield walls, come with far greater frequency than they do at cavernous Comiskey Park. But Brickhouse claimed loyalty in equal amounts to the two Chicago teams as we sat down to talk in a quiet corner of the cafeteria at WGN.

"I missed doing the Sox games immensely," he said, "because we did both sides of town, don't forget, on radio before television came along. And when I first came to town in 1940, there were so many people on both sides of town who helped me. You can't forget the Comiskey family, Harry Grabiner, Jimmy Dykes, guys like that, who were your friends—who put their arm around you as a scared youngster when you needed that kind of friendship and encouragement. Plus up on the North Side—the Gallaghers, the Wrigley family, Jimmy Wilson, Grimm, Hartnett—you know, pals, real good guys. On the South Side, Bill Veeck has been a great friend of mine for many years. If anything ever happens to Veeck, who am I gonna argue with?

"So there's no way, even today, that anyone could get me to pick friendship-wise between those two ballclubs."

Too many great memories remain. Like being in the booth the day the Sox and Yankees staged their big brawl in June, 1957. The fight began when Art Ditmar threw a fastball at Larry Doby's head. The

353

Sox slugger, after Ditmar had used a racial slur to indicate his readiness to continue any activity Doby might have in mind, went out and decked the Yankee pitcher with a quick left. Other participants included Billy Martin, Walt Dropo, Enos Slaughter.

"Greatest baseball fight I ever saw," said Brickhouse, who has seen his share of them over the years. "Slaughter picked Dropo and Dropo almost killed him. But, like I said later, there's never ever been any questioning Slaughter's courage. After all, there's a guy who's been married five times."

Recollections of the fight bring back to Brickhouse memories of Minnie Minoso, who was sitting in the dugout the Yankees' first visit back to Chicago after the brawl when Berra, New York's catcher, passed by on his way out to the field. "I just happened to be there," said Brickhouse. "And Berra says to Minnie, 'Next time, I'm going after you. You're gonna belong to me. I'm really gonna handle you.' Minnie says, 'You no get Minnie. Minnie got too good-a wheels for you.' "

Minoso trusted his legs, but that was about it. "He didn't trust banks or anything else," Jack recalled. "I remember one time he slid into second base and they had to hold the game up because the slide had jarred his money belt loose. He was wearing a money belt. And he had about $3,000 on him.

"Did anyone ever tell you about the time Minnie cosigned the loan for Hector Rodriguez?" asked Brickhouse, already starting to laugh. "Minnie cosigned Hector's note for $800 to buy a car. Now, Rodriguez is sold to Toronto. He's out of the country. And now they come on Minoso to collect the money. All of a sudden, Minnie can't understand one word of English. They couldn't get him to understand anything.

"Finally, the Sox are in Tampa, and Eddie Short got Al Lopez to corner him in the clubhouse and explain this whole thing to him. And you can't con Lopez. He speaks every type of Spanish you could ask for. So Lopez pins him up against the wall and now Minnie has to listen to this story. All Minnie could think of to say was, 'Minnie sign paper saying Hector nice fellow. Minnie no sign saying Minnie pay.'

"I think the first six times I interviewed Minoso on television, I don't think I understood one complete sentence. I had to pretend I understood what he was saying. I was real worried, too. You know, you say to yourself: 'I hope he's not using any bad language—I hope he's not advocating the overthrow of the government by force . . . ' But whatever his answers were, he gave them so sincerely, with such a serious look on his face, and his eyes would light up—you just knew the sincerity was coming out of his ears. It took a while, but I finally got used to that accent and I was able to pick him up. He was another of those 120 percenters. I never saw him once complain about playing hurt. I never saw him once when he didn't give everything he had plus some more."

Minoso was brought to the White Sox by Frank Lane, another fellow of whom Brickhouse grew very fond. "We got to be very good friends. In fact, I got Frank an apartment in my building. Near Surf and Sheridan Road. Frank and I would drive home together many times. We'd even nightcap together. Frank wasn't much for a drink—he didn't drink a lot. He'd have one, maybe two in an entire evening after a tough ballgame. One time, we were in our favorite nightcap spot there on Diversey, where the fellows who owned the place were good friends. And they kind of protected us a little bit. After all, Frank was a public figure. They let us sit in the back there and wouldn't let too many people come back there and ask Frank a lot of questions. Sometimes it was unavoidable, but sometimes you enjoyed it, too. But once in a while, you'd like to have one by yourself.

"And anyway, once they lost three in a row to the Red Sox—all tough ballgames, all hairline-decision games. And Lane—you could've lit a cigaret on the back of his neck after that series. I gave him a ride to the place, we were having a nightcap, and some guy comes back to us and starts giving Lane a hard time—a real hard time. And Frank was in no mood for this one. We had to peel him off that guy."

Brickhouse was with Lane another time when Frank's temper was steaming. The White Sox had just blown a game to the light-hitting Washington Senators 8-7 after taking a 7-0 lead. This was in 1949, Lane's first season on the job, and the year of "Home Run Lane"—the low wire fence Lane had put up in left field to cut the home run distance from 352 feet down the line to 332. It had been designed to help slugging rookie Gus Zernial pound out a few extra homers and to create a little more fun at the old ballpark. But when the Senators dumped a couple of drives into the area between the new fence and the permanent wall, Brickhouse kind of figured the days of "Home Run Lane" were numbered.

"The game was broken up by Mark Christman (brother of football great Paul Christman), who was not exactly a Hall-of-Fame baseball player. (Mark belted all of 19 home runs in his nine years in the big leagues.) And Floyd Baker got his first and only major league home run in that ballgame. So the Sox lose the ballgame, and the Yankees are coming into town next, from St. Louis.

"I'm driving Lane home and he's boiling. He is just absolutely frying. We're driving up Lake Shore Drive past Oak Street Beach. I said, 'Frank, don't worry about it. Take your mind off it. Take a look at all those beautiful girls out there in their bathing suits. I'll do the driving, and you can do the looking.' But in order to see them, he had to look through another wire fence. He finally yelled, 'All I can see is that lousy fence! Can't even enjoy this!'

"And so now we get home, and about one o'clock in the morning, after he'd been stewing and fretting about it all night long, I guess you know he got poor Leo Dillon, the maintenance chief, out of bed and whipped that crew out there to that ballpark in the middle of the night and that fence was DOWN by the time the Yankees came out to the ballpark the next day. And Phil Rizzuto, who never hit any home runs, told me, 'Even I was licking my chops—we came out and saw that fence was gone, we were really burned up.' "

It was around that time that Billy Pierce, acquired from Detroit in the offseason, made his Comiskey Park debut. "It was a Sunday— I'll never forget it—we had a pretty good house there, about 30,000 people. And Pierce has not pitched yet. Now, in he comes from the bullpen, this slightly built little guy, the kid they've gotten from Detroit. And now he takes a couple of warmup pitches. And on the third one he lets loose with that fastball. And you could hear an audible gasp from the crowd. He threw that next fastball. Again, the gasp. You know, 'Am I seeing what I think I see?' And right then and there, boy, the chances for a star being born were there. And Billy, of course, turned out to be just that."

There were other stars, too, beginning with Luke Appling, the Hall-of-Fame shortstop who specialized in fouling off pitches until he got the one he liked. "I remember one day during the early part of the war, Grabiner was the general manager, and Luke wanted a dozen baseballs for a Red Cross raffle back home in Atlanta so they could raise some funds. And Grabiner turned him down. 'Not on this one, Luke.' Luke said, 'OK.' Now they pass the word to Grabiner: 'You'd better come out and watch batting practice.' Luke fouled off about 15 pitches into the stands, and finally, Grabiner yells to him, 'You got 'em, Luke—you win—you got the balls.' He got the message real fast."

Appling's successors at shortstop Venezuelans Chico Carrasquel and Luis Aparicio, moved Brickhouse to search for new adjectives to describe their play. "Chico was a fantastic first-year player. I don't recall too many players having as good a first year as he had. After that, he had a little tough luck, he discovered the knife and the fork, and he slowed down a little bit. But I remember (farm director) John Rigney saying, 'Don't worry too much about Chico—we've got a little guy down at Memphis who you're gonna fall in love with.' It was Aparicio. Boy, was he right.

"Looie, taken as a total ballplayer—considering his bat, his glove, his baserunning, his base stealing, his competitive spirit, the way he could take charge in a quiet way out there, the way he could handle the doubleplay ball, the way he and Fox fit each other like a glove on the doubleplay . . . it was poetry in motion. Let me just say this: I have never seen a BETTER shortstop than Looie. Now whether I've seen some as good, I'd have to think a long time. I'd be hard-pressed. Even considering all the great shortstops I've seen down through the years."

Of all the great managers Brickhouse has seen down through the years, many have been stationed in the home team dugout at Comiskey Park. "They've had some of the greatest managerial talent over there that I've ever seen in my life. And I don't like to misuse the word 'great' or 'greatest.' You look at Dykes, Paul Richards, and then Al Lopez, who will always be one of my favorites. Richards was one of the really fine baseball minds. You'd sit there and almost see the wheels go around. He had that look of the eagle—that tough Texan look about him. That wiry, leathery, muscular look. He was good. No one could reclaim pitchers better than Richards. He was another marvelous man for his time."

357

Lopez impressed Brickhouse with his endless supply of patience. "The greatest single example of that, to me, was with Bubba Phillips. You look at that '59 team that won it. That outfield's a pretty good outfield, especially with Landis out there. And when you've got an Aparicio and a Fox, you've got a pretty good doubleplay combination. You've got Kluszewski and Torgeson—that's a pretty good combined first baseman. Sherman Lollar, of course, was a very good catcher. The pitching staff Lopez assembled was excellent. But third base was always a problem. So Lopez made a third baseman out of Bubba Phillips.

"That spring, and the spring before it, down in Tampa where the White Sox were training, Lopez himself must have hit a thousand groundballs to Phillips. He would just stand there by the hour and hit grounders to Bubba. He moved him to his left, to his right, moved him back, made him come in—he just wore him out. He hit so many doggone groundballs to that guy that fielding anything became second nature to Bubba. That's how you make a third baseman. And, of course, Bubba swung a pretty good bat. He got his big hits that pennant year."

The pennant was clinched on Sept. 22 in Cleveland, and Jack did the telecast back to Chicago. The show included more than just the usual postgame hoopla in the locker room, too. "We did a telecast from the Sox plane coming back from Cleveland. I remember Early Wynn going up to the pilots, saying, 'If you fellows want to take a coffee break, I'll be glad to take over for a while.' Rivera doing his dance in the aisle. All those thousands of people at Midway when we got back. They did almost $20,000 worth of damage to the fences, you know. They found out where the plane was coming in, of course. Now that I think about it, I guess we told them . . . "

Brickhouse was chosen to join the Dodgers' Vin Scully for the national telecasts of the World Series games on NBC. "The fifth game at LA—that's the biggest memory. If you don't win it, it's all over. If you want to bring it back to Chicago, you've got to win this one. Played before the largest crowd ever to see a game in history (92,706) —it'll never be duplicated again. And Fox scored a run on a double-play ball by Lollar and, by golly, they made that run stand up."

Outside, snow was falling. Out in front of the WGN studios, home-ward-bound traffic was beginning to build up on Addison Street. It was getting late, wasn't it? "That's all right," Jack smiled. "I'm enjoying this."

He went on to describe how the self-imposed pressure to outdo Leo Durocher on the North Side had eaten away at Eddie Stanky while the latter was managing the Sox in the late '60s. He told of his admiration for fellows like Joe Horlen and Gary Peters. He admitted that Chicagoan Bill "Moose" Skowron, the Yankee first baseman who finally came home to the White Sox in the mid-'60s, was "absolutely, positively, unequivocally one of my favorites of all time." And then, in closing, it was time for another funny story.

"One of my favorite memories is about a Sox-Yankee game at Yankee Stadium in 1960. Eli Grba, a Chicagoan by the way, was pitching against the White Sox one night. All of a sudden, about the fourth inning, as soon as the third out was made, about 25 Cuban demonstrators, on cue, raced out with a great big banner about 60-70 feet long and about three feet wide, with some lettering on it. And I have never seen anything more abortive than this one turned out. Talk about a planned demonstration, where they think they're gonna get TV publicity. Talk about something really going haywire.

"First of all, they didn't figure the wind factor. Now the wind grabbed the sign and twisted it up like a hemp rope. Now, nobody can read the sign. You don't know whether they're for Castro or against Castro. Then, secondly, they get all messed up on where they're supposed to go once they get out there. And the next thing you know, they run into Grba. And now they start to circle him from two sides. Next thing, the whole sign's wrapped around him—he's like the middle of the maypole dance.

"And these guys are out there trying to get untangled, and the wind has loused up their sign. And I've got to say this about those New York cops: There was one cop per demonstrator out there in a matter of seconds. You never saw so many headlocks and armlocks in your life. And off they go. That was a real nothing demonstration, I'll tell you. The guy who set that one up could've messed up a two-car parade."

He was laughing again. An hour or so later, doing the six o'clock sports on WGN radio, he would retell the Hector Rodriguez-Minnie

Minoso loan story to Bill Berg. And he would be laughing some more. And I would be thinking to myself, "Wouldn't it be nice to have Brick back doing the Sox games again?"

HARRY CARAY:
Holy Cows

I had been turned on to Harry Caray long before the raspy-voiced broadcaster, much-beloved by fans and much-hated by ball-players, arrived on the Chicago scene in 1971. My brother had moved to the St. Louis suburbs during the '60s and kept telling me that Harry was so good he could make a 3-and-0 pitch sound exciting. I immediately tuned in to KMOX radio in St. Louis, trying to catch Harry's act.

Eventually, through breaks in the static, Caray's voice came through. "Cardinals (pronounced Cord-nals) trail 11-1. We're in the ninth. If we get to Brock we have a chance." A few nights later, Harry was describing Julian Javier's problems handling a righthanded pitcher's curveball. Finally, he said to sidekick Jack Buck, "Hoolie's never gonna hit this guy, Jack." Seconds later, Harry spoke again: "Curveball . . . base hit like a bullet!"

I started to think how great it would be to have Harry broadcasting White Sox games instead of Bob Elson and Red Rush. Bob and Red, past Sox players hinted to me, were two of the reasons why the Sox of the mid-'60s—though in contention almost continuously—weren't packing in the fans like they should have been. "Put Harry Caray in the booth in '67," said a former Chicago outfielder," and we'd have

361

Harry Caray, circa 1972—well before any run-ins with Chuck
Tanner, Bill Melton, etc.

been drawing 50,000 every night."

Finally, after the dreadful year of 1970, my wish came true. Harry Caray, who had been fired by Gussie Busch in 1969 after 25 years with the Cardinals and who had spent the last year in Oakland ("Siberia," he called it), was coming back to the Midwest as radio voice of the White Sox. It was too good to be true.

But few people knew, apparently, how good Harry was: The Sox couldn't even land a major radio outlet to handle their games in '71. But that would soon change. Harry made listening to the White Sox fun again. Within two years he would be working TV as well as radio, and there wouldn't be a soul in Chicago who didn't know who Harry Caray was.

His approach was a drastic change from what Chicago fans— familiar with the sugarcoating of Elson, Jack Brickhouse, and Jack Drees—had become accustomed to. Players were no longer incapable of wrongdoing. No one escaped Harry's barbs, not even the great Richie Allen. Once Allen, who refused to take batting practice, was mired in one of his rare slumps. He grounded weakly to the second baseman and jogged down to first base, annoyed with himself.

"Little tap, easy out," groaned Harry in a disgusted voice. "And it's none of my business, but it sure looks to me like Richie Allen could use a little batting practice. And he didn't set any speed records running down to first base either."

Rick Reichardt's failures bewildered Harry, too. Reichardt was a big guy—6-3, 215—who crouched over the plate, never seeming capable of taking the big cut one would expect from a man his size. One afternoon, Reichardt topped a slow roller to the mound—the result of a rather weak swing. "Come on, Reichardt!" Harry growled. "Swing the bat!"

When Allen, Reichardt, Carlos May, Bill Melton, and Ken Henderson—the meat of the Sox order in the early and mid-'70s—all slumped at the same time, Harry could always be counted on for one of these: "One, two, three—nothing across. And our better hitters aren't hitting a lick." Melton fanning on a bad pitch always elicited a "Struck him out and made him look HORR-ible." In later years, when Eric Soderholm insisted on pulling even outside pitches and wound up hitting grounder after grounder to the shortstop, Harry moaned,

"Soderholm REFUSES to hit the ball to right field."

White Sox defensive lapses—Harry has seen many—have always brought verbal jabs from Caray. Once, an outfielder named John Jeter misjudged two foul flyballs on successive plays. Harry was willing to dismiss the first one, thinking that Jeter perhaps had fallen victim to a tricky wind. But after the second mishap, Harry could take it no longer. "What in the WORLD! What's going ON?"

There was the easy pop fly that second baseman Jorge Orta circled under one afternoon in Detroit. Orta, after struggling, finally seemed ready to catch the ball. Instead, the ball popped out of his glove for an error. "I don't understand it," Caray fumed. "The last couple years, we've had Latin American infielders who've had trouble catching pop flies—Luis Alvarado, now Orta." Bob Waller, Caray's TV sidekick, broke in. "I think he lost the ball in the sun, Harry." "Aw, how could he lose the ball in the sun?" Harry wanted to know, reasoning, "He's FROM Mexico."

Pitchers, too, have drawn Harry's ire down through the years. Wilbur Wood, pitching in Oakland in a late September 1972, game the White Sox absolutely had to have in order to stay alive in the West Division race, was getting rocked around pretty well by the A's. Harry, forgetting for the moment the 24 games Woodie had already won that year, complained bitterly, "Biggest game of the year and our best pitcher doesn't have a THING out there."

Stan Bahnsen's wildness ("Ball-l-l-l-l three . . . boy oh boy") would annoy Harry. Then one spring, Stanley Struggle seemed to finally conquer the problem. His control was pinpoint all March down in Sarasota. But then the season started, and Bahnsen, pitching in Oakland, reverted to form. "Boy oh boy," Harry moaned. "Same old Bahnsen."

But Harry has always been good for a few laughs, too, even before he was joined in the booth by the uninhibited Jimmy Piersall four years ago. A Minnesota infielder called Mike Cubbage came to the plate one night. Caray studied the last name for a moment, then exclaimed: "Boy oh boy, if that was an 'A' instead of a 'U', he'd be a cabbage." Then, as an afterthought, he pointed out that "The White Sox already have a Lemon."

There was the year Quasar, a White Sox sponsor, was giving away free TV sets when Sox players hit home runs. A name would be drawn from a jar, and the name invariably would be next-to-impossible for Caray to pronounce. One evening that season, Detroit brought in a relief pitcher named Dave Lemanczyk—pronounced "la-MAN-chick." "The new pitcher," Harry began, "is Dave . . . lemon-sik . . . la-MAN-sik . . . spells it, L-E-M-A-N-C-Z-Y-K . . . la-MAN-chick. Boy oh boy, he sounds like one of our Quasar winners."

Then there were the nightly reports on that evening's Falstaff Hotline Van deliveries. Harry would quickly give the game totals on his postgame wrapup, then get down to the important matter of the evening. "Deliveries were made tonight to G & R Tap, Julie's Bar & Grill, Mario's Liquors . . ." There was the Big Payoff Inning on WMAQ Radio: "Ball THREE! Even a walk's worth twenty-five dollars . . ." There were the Chicken Unlimited commercials ("Crisp on the outside, moist on the inside, marinated with an old family recipe—need I tell you, it tastes delicious?"), the put-on notes from people who liked to fool Harry once in a while ("Leon Russell, Stephen Stills, and Jethro Tull are here drinking Falstaff"), and the occasional comments on the shade of the heavens. "The sky," Harry once observed, "seems pink."

One night, Harry seemed startled that the Yankees could have outfielders named Juan Bernhardt and Otto Velez. "Funny thing," he began, "Look at Juan Bernhardt. His first name sounds Latin, his last name sounds German. And Otto Velez—his first name sounds German, his last name sounds Latin. It should be Juan Velez and Otto Bernhardt." He enjoyed discovering what players' names were backwards and once began an interview with Kansas City outfielder Joe Zdeb by revealing this remarkable finding: "You know, Joe, funny thing: Your last name backwards is B-E-D-Z. Bedz." Zdeb, surprised, didn't know quite what to say.

Harry, on the other hand, always had something to say. Knowing this, I contacted him at his winter home in Palm Springs, Cal., one afternoon and asked him who his favorite players had been during the 10 years he had spent in the booth at Comiskey Park. "Well, the only one good ballplayer they've had in the last 10 years was Richie Allen," he quickly responded. "And Bucky Dent was a favorite of the fans. But other than that, who could you name in the last 10 years?"

Chet Lemon, I ventured.

"I think he's just a good player," Caray replied. "But would you pay to go out and see him?"

I answered that I usually went out simply to see the team play—not just one or two individuals.

"This has been the remarkable thing about the fans in Chicago," he said. "They keep drawing an average of a million-three a year. And when the season's over and they've won their usual 71 games, you feel that those fans deserve a medal.

"But I really wouldn't know who else was such a favorite that you couldn't wait to get to the ballpark to see him." Which was exactly his situation in St. Louis, where he looked forward to describing the performances of Stan Musial, Marty Marion, Enos Slaughter, and—in later years—Lou Brock, Curt Flood, Bob Gibson, and Orlando Cepeda. "They had STARS there," said Harry.

In Chicago lately, the stars have been few and far between—despite what the fans and front office have thought. "I think most of these guys have played up to their normal ability," Harry said. "It's just that somebody in the front office keeps trying to tell the people that they're much, much better than what they're playing. And hell, they're only .250 hitters and everybody's trying to talk about how, 'Well, he should be hitting .300' and 'What a great hitter he is.' Lamar Johnson. What the hell, Lamar Johnson's not gonna lead any league in hitting. They have oversold—and knowingly oversold—a package from the front office. Especially these last five years."

Caray, of course, has been busy trying to sell the product himself. There have been times, too, when the selling became easy—when the Sox were so exciting and attractive that the crowds poured into Comiskey Park—Harry or no Harry. This was particularly true in '72 and in '77, years that provided Caray with moments he'll never forget.

"The second game of the doubleheader against the Yankees in '72," he recalled, "when Richie Allen was rested the second game. There's 50,000 fans in the stands and they're gonna rest the only star they have. And in the bottom of the ninth he comes out as a pinch-hitter against Sparky Lyle. In the dusk, as it were. And he steps up and hits a three-run homer to win the game.

"And then when the Sox were going so good in '77. That four-game series with the Kansas City Royals at Comiskey Park. The first game of the Sunday doubleheader, they go behind by two runs in the 10th. And Lemon hit a homer with a man on to tie it and then they won it on Garr's hit.

"The second game, Kansas City finally won. And the next day in the papers, instead of writing about the dramatic victory which gave the White Sox the first three games of the series, they were quoting Hal McRae and Amos Otis about how bush it was for the Sox to come out of the dugout to wave to the crowd.

"That's when Richie Zisk had a team meeting to talk the players into not coming back out onto the field to doff their cap to the fans. Next weekend, we're in Kansas City and everyone's doing the same thing— whenever a Kansas City player hits a homer, they give him a standing ovation and he comes out of the dugout and waves to the fans. Now, since then, it's spread all over baseball. So our fans started it all, but our players were too dumb to realize that this was the greatest appreciation and tribute the fans could pay a ballplayer."

The mention of Richie Zisk's name raised a question: Had Caray been angry with management for letting Zisk and Oscar Gamble get away via free agency at the close of the '77 season?

"I didn't have any quarrel about them losing Richie Zisk and Oscar Gamble," Harry said. "Except for the fact that when you trade the two best pitchers in your organization—Forster and Gossage—to get Richie Zisk, you would think that anybody with any kind of sense at all, the first thing they would do would be to sign the guy up for three years. But instead, Veeck was playing games, and he figured he could sign him any time he wanted to, I guess. And then here comes July and Zisk already has hit 20 homers and the price has really doubled.

"And the same thing happened with Gamble. So you know, you trade away your best shortstop, Bucky Dent—and they haven't had one as good since—to get Oscar Gamble, and you don't even sign Gamble to a two-year contract. So at the end of the year, you've given up your best shortstop and your two best pitchers for Zisk and Gamble, and when the year's over you don't even have them anymore.

"They've made so many terrible trades."

The talk turned from front-office management to on-the-field

367

management—and in particular, Chuck Tanner, with whom Harry had had more than one run-in. "I thought he was a good manager," Harry said. "Tanner in the right kind of an organization, with the right kind of a front office, would be as good a manager as there is. But with the White Sox, he was becoming the general manager and the public relations manager and the radio-TV manager and everything else. So he wasn't controlled and that was because Stu Holcomb had retired and they had made Roland Hemond the general manager.

"And (owner) John Allyn, instead of talking to the general manager, wouldn't discuss any player until he got Chuck Tanner's opinion first. Which really made Roland Hemond an errand boy."

An errand boy is one thing Harry has never needed. If he wants to get a message across, he'll get it done with a few well-spoken—though often hard-hitting—words. Often the words have been critical enough to turn fan opinion against a player, as in the case of Bill Melton, the league home run champion of 1971 turned .240 hitter (with only 15 homers) of 1975.

"But I was never down on him," Harry argued. "All I did was report. When the guy was hitting 33 home runs to become the first White Sox player to ever lead the American League in home runs, nobody ever said I was down on him. But when he's hitting .210, how the hell you gonna make him sound great?"

A difficult task, indeed. So Harry didn't—and doesn't—even try, which angers players' wives and girlfriends—who pass on the reports of Harry's evil words to the players, who in turn become angry with Caray. But not angry enough, Caray claimed, to cause an athlete to throw a punch his way.

"If they wanted me," he said, "I've been around for 37 years and I go to the same places they go, and they've had every opportunity. As a matter of fact, I don't know a ballplayer that I haven't gotten along with socially.

"But I've never discovered a way to say, 'So Joe Blow's error won the game,' or 'Joe Blow's striking out with the tying and winning runs on base in the bottom of the ninth scored a victory for the White Sox.' And that's the way some of these stupid wives and girlfriends are. If a guy's error lost a game, how are you gonna cover it up? 'So-and-so's error in the ninth inning allowed Boston to score the winning run.'

You can't get away from that."

JERRY REINSDORF:
Looking Ahead—New Uniforms and Superstars to Wear Them

It was the day after the White Sox had signed free-agent catcher Carlton Fisk, and new chairman of the board Jerry Reinsdorf was on the line, calling from the team's spring training camp in Sarasota. I could tell he was rather excited. That morning, after all, in the Chicago newspapers, the signing of Fisk had made the front pages— complete with pictures of the former Boston Red Sox catcher, Reinsdorf, and club president Eddie Einhorn, Jerry's old law school buddy.

"We're very excited," he admitted, "but really it's far more important that the fans be excited."

And Sox fans were excited. After years of penny-pinching, the Chicago White Sox would, from now on, be going first-class. The Fisk signing had earned the new ownership instant credibility and had given Sox fans and players alike new hope—hope that had been missing on the South Side for too many defeat-filled seasons, and hope further confirmed with the acquisition of slugger Greg Luzinski. It was the kind of event Reinsdorf, a 44-year-old real estate tycoon who lives in the North Shore suburb of Highland Park, had been looking forward to ever since he first grew interested in purchasing the Chicago American League franchise early last year.

Jerry Reinsdorf

Eddie Einhorn

"I'd been interested in baseball for several years," he said. "A friend of mine, John Alevizos, tried to buy several teams over the last five years and all of the deals aborted. I was gonna be an investor in each of his deals but they never got off the ground. At one time or another, he was talking about buying the Indians, the Giants, the Mets—he had tried for the Mets just before Doubleday bought them.

"And when that deal fell through, I got to thinking, 'Geez, rather than being an investor with somebody, why don't I see if the White Sox are for sale?' I knew the Cubs wouldn't be. So through a good friend of mine—a lawyer named Alan Muchin—I knew he had a client named Bill Farley who was a White Sox stockholder. Alan suggested I should contact Farley and see if the White Sox might be for sale. Farley talked to Bill Veeck and Veeck said, 'Yeah.' We set up a meeting and it went from there."

It did not, however, go smoothly. Reinsdorf and his group—which included television executive Einhorn from the very start—seemed to be running a distant second to Youngstown, O., multimillionaire Edward J. DeBartolo, Mr. Megabucks himself. No one seemed to care that DeBartolo's bid of $20 million hardly overwhelmed Reinsdorf's bid. All that mattered was that DeBartolo, with his vast personal fortune, was the man who could spend big money to make the White Sox a contender again.

"When he first entered the bidding," Reinsdorf recalled, "I figured he had so much money that he'd probably offer way more than it was worth and we just would never be able to match it. Because I would never go into a deal where I was paying more than I thought something was worth. But nevertheless, I didn't want to assume that. So we put in our bid and as it turned out, we were very close to his.

"At first, I really thought we were going to get the club. And I was very disappointed when the White Sox board voted for him. Because I thought we would be a better ownership, because even though he had a lot of money, he wouldn't personally be involved in it. We were a local group and I knew we'd be well-capitalized. And I don't think you need as much money as he has to operate a team.

"But almost within an hour after it was announced that the Sox were gonna sell to him, I was advised by somebody in baseball not to worry, that under the circumstances, he probably would not be an ac-

373

ceptable buyer."

I asked him who that somebody was.

"I'm not gonna tell you," he replied. "It wasn't (A.L. president Lee) MacPhail or anybody connected with the American League. It wasn't the commissioner. It was somebody else you'd never think of.

"So I figured, we'll just sit still. And within a week, all this started to become public. And we just kind of waited in the wings and let the White Sox know that we were there and we were available. And then, of course, well, you know what happened."

What happened was that the league owners twice voted down DeBartolo's application for membership, forcing the Sox board of directors to finally turn to Reinsdorf. The Brooklyn native, a fanatic Dodger follower as a youth, wrapped up the deal the final week of January, 10 months after the quest had first begun. Within two weeks, a pack of Sox players had signed their contracts—some of them long-term ones—the scouting staff had been expanded, dynamic Southern Methodist University athletic director Russ Potts had been brought in to head an energetic new marketing department, and the club had opened up new offices in the Hancock Center.

Not only that, Reinsdorf had discussed the possibility of a new stadium for his newly acquired team. Some reports claimed he was thinking of a dome for Comiskey Park. "My feeling," he told me, "is that Chicago is just about the only major city that doesn't have a new first-class sports facility for baseball and football. I think it's something that ought to be explored. But I have no plans to put a dome over Comiskey Park.

"We're gonna explore it and we're gonna have some people meet with the city and see to what extent the city has an interest in it. We have a background in real estate finance and we'll see what we can do. We have no concrete plans yet. But a sports facility can make money for a city and so I think the city ought to be willing to do something—you know, like tax-exempt bonds. We might be willing to throw in the existing ballpark and land as part of the price. I don't know. We're flexible."

But a new stadium is something way down the line. What is most important is the immediate future. "I don't see why we can't draw 2.5 million people," said Reinsdorf, who indicated that he needs about 1.3

million in attendance to break even in 1981. "I don't think we'll do that (draw 2.5 million) in 1981, but if we develop a competitive team—by that I mean one that contends for the division championship every year and wins it once in a while—I don't see why we can't draw 2.5 million. They do it in Philadelphia and that's a smaller market than this one. And they do it in Cincinnati and that's way smaller. I can't see why we can't have a very successful operation."

If he and his partners are able to attract more players of the caliber of Fisk, the seven-time all-star with the .284 lifetime average, the operation will indeed be very successful.

"I think our signing Carlton is a symbol of what we want to do with this franchise," Reinsdorf said. "He represents a lot of things. Not only is he an outstanding ballplayer, but he's a leader. He's family man. He represents a quality individual that we want to have with the White Sox. And we're trying to establish a real class image. Now when I say that, I don't mean to rap Bill Veeck or what went before. But our styles are different.

"And the style of this ownership is gonna be to try to create a New York Yankee-type of organization. Not necessarily a George Steinbrenner New York Yankee-type organization, but maybe a New York Yankee-type organization out of the George Weiss mold. Or a Los Angeles Dodger or Cincinnati Red-type organization. These are the organizations that we want to pattern ourselves after."

Anybody who has watched the White Sox the last two or three seasons will readily agree that Reinsdorf still has a long way to go before he reaches that goal. But Jerry is willing to give it some time.

"What you have to do is develop a team that contends every year," he said. "I want to contend every year. I don't want to have ups and downs if we can avoid them. Now, if you can contend every year, in some years you're gonna get the breaks and you're gonna win. Some years you're not gonna get 'em and you won't win, because I think, by and large, winning a division and a pennant and a World Series is to a large extent a function of luck. Like, if you don't have injuries and the other teams do."

The rise to contendership may come sooner than most people suspect. "I think we're gonna have a vastly improved team this year. Bill Veeck left us a better team than he had last year. And over the course of the next couple years, we'll be adding players. We're going to be significantly increasing our investment in the farm system. In the long run, my feeling is that to be a contender every year, you have to develop your own players. You can't do it in the free-agent market and you can't do it through trading. You can try to fill a gap that way. But a winning team takes 25 guys and most of them you have to develop. So we're gonna be spending our money on the farm system."

And he'll spend it on keeping the players that farm system has developed. And on that occasional, first-class, too-valuable-to-pass-up free agent like Carlton Fisk.

"It's gonna be different," promised Reinsdorf. "It's a new era."

Somehow, even though all the disappointment of the last 20 years has taught me to be a typically pessimistic White Sox fan, I get the feeling that Jerry Reinsdorf might be absolutely right.